73

News Clips & Ego Trips
The Best of *Next... Magazine*
1994–1998

℞

edited by G. Murray Thomas

Write Bloody Publishing
America's Independent Press

Long Beach, CA

WRITEBLOODY.COM

Thomas, G. Murray.
1st edition.
ISBN: 978-1-935904-45-8

Interior Layout by Lea C. Deschenes
Cover Designed by Jennifer Heuer
Additional Design by Bill Jonas
Edited by Zhanna Vaynberg, Derrick Brown, G. Murray Thomas, Victor D. Infante and Daniel Lisi
Type set in Bergamo from www.theleagueofmoveabletype.com
Printed in Tennessee, USA

Write Bloody Publishing
Long Beach, CA
Support Independent Presses
writebloody.com

To contact the author, send an email to writebloody@gmail.com

For Larry Schulz, because without him, none of this would have ever happened.

Kerry (Dudley)
Here's some letters
you may remember.
Thanks for being part of it
[signature]
5/3/18

NEWS CLIPS & EGO TRIPS

THE POETRY SCENE 1994 - 1998

ADVICE AND COMMENTARY

Cartoon by Charles Ellik

BEFORE...

By Victor D. Infante

The early '90s were a weird time to be a poet in America.

It was a strange lull in cultural forces – the Cold War had ended, bringing the nation into an odd gaze inward, and most of the previous decades' great artistic movements were largely absent: Beat was graying; punk was marginalized and largely co-opted by the record industry; hip-hop was waiting in the wings – ascendant as a musical form but not quite there yet as a cultural force.

Unlike today, when the Internet provides instant connection between poets, when the National Slams include poets from cities ranging from Normal, Illinois, to Paris, France, and poets tour regularly on a fairly established national circuit, the poetry world of the early '90s was a series of disparate archipelagos, its participants often only dimly aware of each others' activities. No e-mail lists, yet. No Facebook or MySpace. Everything traveled by word of mouth or by the printed word. The major poets – ones supported by publishers and universities – had their machines, of course. They dominated the major journals and magazines, their poets appeared at university readings around the country.

The rest stayed local in scope – community readings, coffee house open mics, mostly actual or spiritual descendants of the Beat movement, communicating by hand-made and photocopied zines inspired by the music zines of punk's heyday, and fueled by a desire to be heard that was reverberating through the growing hip-hop scene. The local poets around the country had learned the lessons of their antecedents well, and something was truly welling beneath the surface.

And truly, big things were starting to happen all around the country. Marc Smith was running poetry slams in Chicago, and Gary Glazner put on the first National Poetry Slam Finals in San Francisco. Bob Holman and Miguel Algarín were drawing crowds with shows at the Nuyorican Poets Café in New York City. Poetry was making its way onto stages at Lollapalooza, poetry videos were popping up on MTV, and poets across the country were beginning to link up and network through the poetry slam scene.

Amid the hullabaloo, three surf-bum poets from Orange County, California – G. Murray Thomas, Charles Ellik and the late Larry Schulz – decided it was time to launch a news magazine covering Southern California poetry. A Rolling Stone for poetry, if you will. Because this unlikely trio knew something that most hadn't really figured out yet: that the early '90s were a great time to be a poet in SoCal.

This was, you have to remember, SoCal in the shadow of Charles Bukowski, the definitive poet emerging outside of any proscribed system. And he was hardly alone – SoCal was rife with talented writers with unorthodox ideas. You had the legendary Bob Flanagan, running the regular poetry workshop at Beyond Baroque Literary Arts Center in Venice, where L.A. punk icons Exene Cervenka and John Doe famously first met prior to forming the band X. You had the veterans of the Watts Writers Workshop, including rap forefathers the Watts Prophets, Quincy Troupe, and Eric Priestley. You had the stalwart Allen J. Freedman, influencing a generation of writers in North Hollywood, and the gracious Laguna Poets founder Marta Mitrovich, bringing the living Beat giants to her sleepy Orange County beach town. (This was before the reality TV shows, naturally.) And that's just a handful.

Although these disparate players primarily existed in their own isolated circles, they were linked by a steadfast belief that poets' voices should be unique and vibrant, and that they could and should be enjoyed by everybody. That poetry was something alive, and that needed to be expressed in public, not just in the hallowed halls of universities.

Consequently, SoCal was alight with poetry – the Carma Bums taking to the road, the Ringling Sisters conquering Hollywood, Olin Tezcatlipoca bringing slam to Midnight Special in Santa Monica, Ellyn Maybe shining at the Iguana Café in North Hollywood, Lob bringing his anarchic punk-infused ethos to Huntington Beach's Jam's Coffeehouse and adventurous poets such as Roland Poet X, Merilene Murphy, Liz Belile and Mud Baron venturing out into the national poetry slam scene … it all seemed to spring from the ground like wildflowers.

What Thomas, Ellik and Schulz saw in this wildness was a need to link these disparate groups and poets, to inform poets what their counterparts were up to. But the act of observing changed things even more – groups braved the 405 to find new audiences, producers looked afield for new poets to put in front of their audiences. Kids who wouldn't have known where to begin looking for a poetry reading would find it sitting in coffeehouses, and suddenly, the germ of an idea was planted … that this was something they could do, too.

Never mind that the rest of the country, with its slams and festivals, was knocking on SoCal's door, telling its poets to come out and play. Everything was in motion, and more importantly, everyone knew it was in motion. Readings and venues were born and died, institutions collapsed and changed. Poets collaborated and competed, were inspired, and feuded bitterly. It was, for maybe the first time, a real poetry community, the new slammers and the hidden treasures, the hyper-literate and the defiant punks, the poets emerging from the universities with different ideas than their predecessors, and the poets emerging from the hip-hop scenes offering a different view entirely.

For poetry, both in SoCal and the rest of America, it was the moment when the sky opened up – a heady, exciting time that launched a SoCal poetry that remains active, vibrant and influential to this very day. And arguably – for all of its weighty back story – the explosion of SoCal poetry in the '90s was a tale that began with those three surf-bum poets from OC.

This is what happened next ….

INTRODUCTION
By G. Murray Thomas

It was never my intention, or my desire, to publish a magazine. And certainly not a free, monthly magazine. But sometimes destiny grabs you, and you are powerless to resist.

In 1992 I started Orange Ocean Press, a poetry publishing company. My intention was to focus on themed anthologies which would, hopefully, attract a wider audience to poetry. I would also publish the occasional book by deserving new voices (ie: my friends). The first Orange Ocean Press book was *Paper Shredders*, an anthology of poetry and short stories about surfing. It was also our most successful book, selling a few hundred copies (yeah, that's the kind of success we were having). It is still available, in expanded form, from iUniverse.com. I published a few more books, including anthologies on pollution and (no joke) dead opossums. But our sales were almost exclusively at local readings; we needed something else to push the company forward.

Larry Schulz, my sort-of partner in the enterprise (one of the books I had published was his *American Streets*, and he was advising me on marketing), had an idea.

In the early '90s there had been a publication called *OutLoud*, which listed all the poetry readings in the greater L.A. area. It had recently folded, and the poets of L.A. missed it greatly. Larry thought we should do something like that, funded by advertising.

I was resistant. I had some idea of how much work it would be (although, in the end, I was off by a factor of about twenty), and correctly surmised that it would distract me from the book publishing, where my real interest lay.

But everyone I talked to thought it was a great idea. That is, it was a great idea for me to do it. Hardly anyone was offering any help.

Still, I started to warm to the idea. Once I did, my ambition kicked in. I didn't want to just put out a list of readings, I wanted to put out a full magazine covering the poetry scene, with news, interviews, reviews and commentary. I wanted to be the *Rolling Stone* of spoken word.

So that is what we set out to do. We, by now, included not just Larry and myself, but Charles Ellik, who we brought in as an artist, but who quickly established himself as a prime visionary influencing the direction of the magazine. We would be a calendar and newsmagazine for SoCal poetry (eventually covering everything from San Luis Obispo to San Bernardino to San Diego), providing information and much needed critical review. One thing we would not do, however, was publish poetry. We were there to cover poetry, not publish it.

We were an immediate hit with the poetry community. We printed 500 copies of the first issue, gave them all away. For the second issue we printed 1,000, and by the third issue we were up to 5,000 copies every month. Within a year we were printing and distributing 10,000 copies.

We chose the name *Next…* because we believed (a big egotistically) that poetry was the "next big thing" in American culture. It also reflected our practical side, as poets would use it to find the next reading they wanted to attend.

Our business model was simple (perhaps too simple): we would give the magazine away for free, and pay for it with advertising. We also sold subscriptions, but they were a minor part of the financial picture (although, as time went on, every penny coming in was critical).

Initial funding came from the remnants of an insurance settlement I had, which is a pretty interesting story in itself, but too long and not relevant enough to go into here.

The flaws in this plan should be obvious. Poets are notorious for their poverty (it is often pointed out that there is only one letter's difference between the words "poetry" and "poverty"). Poets themselves had little money to advertise (with a few very generous exceptions), and we had a hard time convincing other businesses that poets were a worthy customer base to pursue. (You will find several articles in here lamenting poets' unwillingness to support the scene financially.)

So finances were a constant problem for *Next…*

Meanwhile, there was a magazine to put out. That, in itself, was quite an adventure.

Initially I did much of the work myself. Covering, as we did, a community of writers, we never had any problem getting people to pen articles for us. Charles provided artwork, and Larry helped with the business side (finding us reasonably priced printers, for example). I did most of the rest – editing, layout, maintaining the calendar, distribution, and so on. And keeping the books.

Over time, more and more people joined in to help. A number of people tried to sell ads for us, including Caron Andregg and Lob, with varying degrees of success (but none of them making the magazine solvent). Numerous people helped with distribution, especially in the far-flung reaches of our empire (I.e.: Ventura, Santa Barbara, San Diego), but also closer to home. Eventually Carlye Archibeque came on as our reviews editor (a big responsibility, as we received more chapbooks for review than we could handle). Victor Infante served as

Illustration of G. Murray Thomas by Charles Ellik

Managing Editor for our final year, choosing topics to cover, and making sure we got the necessary articles.

Then there were our "proofreading parties." One constant complaint was the number of typos we let slip through. So a night or two before we went to press, anyone who wanted to help was invited to the *Next...* "offices" (actually my garage) to proofread the upcoming issue. Considering how much beer was consumed at these parties, it's amazing there was any improvement in the magazine, but they actually made a big difference.

There was a definite excitement to the whole process. The constant stream of flyers, promos and review items (plus the rare, occasional check) which flowed through my PO Box. The occasional press pass into some big event (Lollapalooza, Laurie Anderson, a promo party for *Il Postino*, at which Patrick Stewart, Jacqueline Bissett, and many others read Neruda). The late, late nights putting together the magazine as the deadline approached (in four and half years, we only came out late a couple of times, and then only by a day or two). The thrill of picking up the stacks (and stacks and stacks) of magazines from the printer.

Distributing the magazine was another challenge, but one that could be fun. As a free magazine, we were on our own. As I said, we gathered a handful of poets willing to help with this, but right up to the end I spent two or three days every month driving the magazine all over town. It seemed that I must have driven every inch of the L.A. freeway system doing this, and encountered, or, luckily, just missed, every bizarre phenomenon of said system, including car chases, oil tanker explosions, and one particularly spectacular suicide.

I timed my route to always end up at a poetry reading (or sometimes two or three). I well remember the way poets' eyes would light up as I walked in with a stack of *Next...*s. That was the key to the whole enterprise. We quickly became an essential and beloved part of the SoCal poetry scene. Poets relied on us to tell them where the readings were, as well as to keep them informed about the hot poets in their midst, and the hot readings to go to, and the other happenings in the scene. Sure, they argued with us plenty, but they loved us.

They also wanted to be written up in our pages. Although not all of them who did get ink were happy with the results. We supported the community, but we were also critical of it, and we were not always nice about it.

I don't want to exaggerate our impact, but we did help to unite the SoCal poetry scene. Localized groups of poets began to see themselves as part of a larger community. Poets started traveling long distances across town to attend readings they had read about in our pages. They met other poets, until it seemed that everybody knew everybody. We actually manage to create (or help create) a poetry community.

Yet, despite this deep love of the community, the magazine continued to lose money. As I said, a steady stream of ad salespeople failed to produce the ad revenue we needed. Many people suggested we should go nonprofit. I resisted this idea for two reasons, one practical, one philosophical. From what I had seen of nonprofits, it really wasn't any easier to raise money, especially on a long-term basis. Secondly, I wanted to prove that a poetry magazine could succeed as a commercial venture. Of course, it didn't, but I still think it should be possible.

We tried various strategies to keep the magazine afloat. Our most drastic move came in March 1997 (our third anniversary), when we started charging for the magazine. To do this, we dropped our press run from 10,000 to 500. We primarily sold it through subscriptions, although I carted a handful around with me, and sold them for $1.50 each at readings.

In a way, this was a success. For the first and only time in the history of the magazine, we broke even that year.

But the impact of the magazine just wasn't the same. It wasn't reaching the same number of people. Most important, it wasn't reaching new readers. The only people buying it were people who already knew about it. One of our greatest impacts occurred when someone, who might have no idea what *Next...* even was, picked up a copy. Closet scribblers suddenly discovered they were part of a huge community of poets. We wanted, we needed, to get that back.

So in the spring of 1998 we attempted to return to the big time. We resumed our free status, and again printed 10,000 copies every month. For the first time we got a designer (Phish Blackler) to do the layout. Our new ad manager, Lob, gave a full press to getting more ads. We started featuring more high-profile artists, like Henry Rollins and Patricia Smith. And we poured more money, money we didn't have, into the magazine, adding color, and upping the page count, all in an attempt to make the magazine more appealing to advertisers.

But it was too late. Our finances were too thin to maintain the new look and coverage. With ad revenue still weak, we had no choice, and folded the magazine in the fall of 1998.

(I should note that I continued to produce the calendar and post it online. It eventually became part of Poetix (www.poetix.net), a webzine started by Larry Jaffe (and currently maintained by Richard Modiano and Larry Colker), which attempted to continue what *Next...* had started. Poetix does do a great job of getting information out to poets, yet somehow an online resource just doesn't have the same impact a flimsy piece of newsprint did.)

The demise of *Next...* left a huge hole in the SoCal poetry community. But in those four and one half years. we had managed to accomplish much. We helped unite the SoCal poetry community.

We also created a record of a transitional time in American poetry. (For more on this, see Victor Infante's Foreword.) You hold part of that record in your hand right now. We hope you enjoy it, and appreciate the effort it took to create it.

SOME INTERVIEWS

Cover Illustration of Gerald Locklin by Michael Paul

PLEASANT GEHMAN
Interview by Charles Ellik

Pleasant's credits are too numerous to mention, but among others, she is a professional writer (*SPIN, LA Weekly, L.A. Reader*, etc.), poet, musician (The Ringling Sister's latest, the *After the Circus* EP, is on the Tres Hombres label), painter, and belly dancer. She has been an integral part of the LA punk/spoken word scene for over a decade and has many tours to her credit.

Her poetry tells stories, often parables of over-the-top experiences in Hollywood, though they could be from a bar down the street, or shared over a couple of margaritas. As stated in the dedication of her newest chapbook, her work is indebted to "…anything that twinkles, sparkles, shines, glitters, ignites, or explodes." Her writing often reads as cute or silly, but every one of those sparklers is ignited by underlying tensions of sex and decadence. Consider "Earthquake Denial" from her chapbook *Buena, Bonita, y Barata*: "You know you're suffering/ from a full-blown case of Earthquake Denial/ when four months after the 6.8 disaster/ your earthquake kit/ is lacking such essentials as/ bottled water, a can-opener, and blankets/ but it is well-stocked/ with things like/ black cake liner eye-liner, red matte lipstick/ and disposable contact lenses/ as well as a small baggie/ full of magic mushrooms/ wrapped in Christmas paper/ and your flashlight/ is easily accessible but inoperable:/ last week/ you took out its batteries/ and used them to replace the dead ones/ in your vibrator." As can be seen, however, these are no dry intellectual musings upon creation and destruction!

There is no high or low culture in her work, just a whirlwind of interesting things to see. It is as if by looking at the pretty things she can remain optimistic about the looming chaos they sprung from. If it is easy to lose the underlying themes, it is because she does not force them on anyone. These pieces are enjoyable for their flamboyant style alone. Yet further investigation reveals, as it does in the interview, that dive bars can serve as models of society, band tours as coming-of-age explorations, and belly dancing lessons in Egypt as perspective broadening journeys into human nature.

Pleasant is the perfect poet to talk about traveling. Her writing style itself is like glamour tour of wacky scenes narrated by a tart with tats who gives a wink and smile after every punchline. Needless to say, our conversation at the incredibly kitsch Tres Palmas restaurant in Hollywood was loud and fast paced, though the other patrons didn't seem to notice it over the blaring Mariachi music. It took three days to copy our recorded conversation, so only a short excerpt is presented here. Picture your crazy cousin's favorite booth complete with red vinyl, tiki salsa bowls, and the velvet wallpaper where our talk begins:

NEXT…: The velvet wallpaper here is classic, perfect with the black velvet paintings.

Photo of Pleasant Gehman by Charles Ellik

GEHMAN: The second house I lived in was a Giant Victorian, and my room in the steeple had yellow ochre flocked wallpaper. I love shit like that, velvet paintings and feely wallpaper, that taste; I love good taste too, but I strive for tackiness.

NEXT...: After living in Long Beach, I have a hard time differentiating good taste from bad. It's just… people. There are strange people there. Not just freaks, but…

GEHMAN: Time Warp People?

NEXT...: An internally twisted weirdness.

GEHMAN: That's one of the reasons why I like L.B. I used to spend a lot of time partying there. The whole Pike thing was really wild, that dying seaport feel which is kinda gone now.

NEXT...: The Pike [a defunct amusement park] may be gone physically, but not in spirit. Everyone says L.B. is so dangerous…

GEHMAN: Nah, it's great!

NEXT...: I have a habit of walking around there late at night.

GEHMAN: I used to do that a lot, sort of stand in people's bushes and look in their windows.

NEXT...: And cruising dive bars…

GEHMAN: Oh, yeah! We went to all those bars right on the water. San Pedro is like that too, really good longshoreman bars.

NEXT...: What gets me is they're seedy but not that dangerous.

GEHMAN: Until they're corrupted by hipsters.

NEXT...: Mostly the hipsters have been building their own bars.

GEHMAN: Oh, yeah, the 'trying to be old' new places.

NEXT...: I'd love to establish a historical dive bar district for the kind of places with no windows…

GEHMAN: Just the tiny diamond window in the door!

NEXT...: My favorite is run by a little old lady who doesn't open until 10 p.m. When she goes to the bathroom, the locals watch her register.

GEHMAN: Does she have one of those total cigarette voices? "Hey Kiddo…" [in raspy voice]. It's the sign of a good bar, regulars.

NEXT...: What an interview — Pleasant's views on dive bars! So, how was Egypt?

GEHMAN: Egypt was amazing! This was the second time I was there. It's such a different world, it makes you see life differently when you see people living the same way they have for the past few thousand years. The extremes of poverty and wealth that are there. You could say that it exists here in L.A., because it's true, it does.

NEXT...: But not right next to one another.

GEHMAN: Yeah. Some of the people there are so poor that a homeless person here would be rich to them. Everyone is really religious, so there is almost no crime. People say, "Aren't you scared of terrorists?" I think it's scarier here in Hollywood. Walking down my street I have more of a chance of being blown away than by a Moslem fundamentalist there. Everyone was really friendly and happy, even in total poverty. I asked to go to the City Of The Dead, but had to find a cab driver who spoke English. A lot of people do, because they are around tourists. The third cab driver I talked to lived there, so we went there and looked at all the beautiful old mausoleums from the 14th century with incredible Islamic art.

NEXT...: You didn't wonder about him asking?

GEHMAN: It's just different. We went to his house and had tea with his mother and son. He lives in one of the tombs and was so poor! Mother got out her best glasses. There was a bare light bulb hanging, flies all over the place, goats in the street, tombs right outside, and all these little girls hanging around.

NEXT...: It gives you perspective.

GEHMAN: It's so different. I just described that whole scene to you, but I can't describe what it was really like. People thought I was insane for going there because I was staying in 5-star hotels at night, then the next day I was in the street where you could tell no one else from the hotel had been. Kids were coming out to look at me and play with my bracelets.

NEXT...: Did you feel out of your element?

GEHMAN: No, I just wanted to stay there.

NEXT...: Absorbing culture is the only reason for going to another country.

GEHMAN: Exactly what I think. The other dancers didn't do anything off the beaten track. You have to see and talk to the people. Otherwise, you won't get a real feel for the country. The other people from the group were typical fat, old, white tourists, and they had NO CLUE. They didn't make any effort to learn 'please' or 'thank you' in Arabic. They never strayed off the main streets or prescribed tour routes.

NEXT…: I'd feel claustrophobic. Traveling is a learning experience!

GEHMAN: I've always traveled, with my family, and later with my first band, Screaming Sirens.

NEXT…: How do you find out where to play if you're touring on the road?

GEHMAN: There was, and there still is, like, a network of people. Now there's coffeehouses and poets to ask "Where is the cool place to go in town?" There is also magazine for promoters that lists venues [for musicians].

NEXT…: *Next…*is compiling its own list for poets.

GEHMAN: So you can call yourself, or just get it off friends. People outside of L.A. were starving for bands, and I'm sure they still are. We used to get thanked for going places and everyone asked, "Do you want to sleep at my house?" All the tours were, like, couch-and -loor tours with an occasional Motel 6 when we really needed a shower.

NEXT…: So, if people like you they'll give you places to stay and go to?

GEHMAN: It's true. It's a lot easier than most people think.

NEXT…: This salsa is making my nose run!

GEHMAN: It's a successful meal when, like, your eyeliner is all blurry!

NEXT…: Anyway, it's great this community is being created.

GEHMAN: You know, I think that spoken word is at the same stage now that punk rock was in the late '70s and early '80s. It is a viable and growing scene, but hasn't really caught on with the corporates, yet there's total underground networks and lots of corporate interest.

NEXT…: We've heard lots of rumblings here at the magazine.

GEHMAN: There's clueless stuff occurring, though. The Ringling Sisters were in the office of this music executive, and when a spoken word piece started, he just fast-forwarded past it. Finally he asks, "What's all this talking?" Oh, yeah. We just didn't edit the tape, sorry!

NEXT…: Well, the problem with poetry…

GEHMAN: Most people think it's boring.

NEXT…: The other problem is…

GEHMAN: Most of it is!

NEXT…: I was trying to say it in a nice way.

GEHMAN: Let's just cut the crap here!

NEXT…: It's because so many people believe they need to be "Poetic."

GEHMAN: I don't have a name for this syndrome, but there's this weird way some people think they have to recite…

NEXT…: LA-LAAAH, LA-LAAAH, LA-LAAH…

GEHMAN: You don't need to do that!

NEXT…: I think it's poets trying to prove themselves.

GEHMAN: Just get over yourself and do it.

NEXT…: Then there's brilliant people competing with espresso machines.

GEHMAN: I've seen such great poets who will just be standing earnestly reading off the paper while someone's forgotten to turn off the bar music. I'd ask myself, "What's the fucking point?" At Lollapalooza they wanted…

NEXT…: Ha, Ha, Ha..!

GEHMAN: Yeah, let's chuckle about that one! They wanted people to take this soapbox out into the midway and rant to the people who were walking by. Why should I? I don't have to drive to Arizona to do that, I can do that on Hollywood Boulevard! That makes me a bag lady, not an artist! I don't think they knew what they were doing. They may be claiming they went on the road, but traveling in a tour bus and being paid for coordinating is not like going on the road. They weren't organized or seasoned enough to pull it off.

NEXT...: You always struck me as very professional. You are the only one who sent me a complete press kit (photo, bio, sample work) when asked to do a feature reading.

GEHMAN: Anybody can do it, even if they've only been reading a year. Just let 'em know where you've read. Keep it short.

NEXT...: Where does someone learn how to be a performer?

GEHMAN: I learned how to command an audience by being in a band and being a stripper. If a band instrument broke down, a joke just wouldn't cut it, so that's how I started performing spoken word. I'd tell a story about, say, how we were pulled over and the girl driving was wearing a fur coat with feet pajamas underneath. No one complained or threw anything, so I kept doing it. Even ten years ago, I would not have told anybody I was doing poetry or they would have said, "Hunh?"

NEXT...: Just in the last five years it went from "hunh?" to "Oh, right on, can I see some?" Especially with kids in high school; maybe it's the 'zine thing. When you think where the entertainment industry aims its dollars…

GEHMAN: It doesn't have the stigmas anymore.

NEXT...: Did you ever start a tour with a goal?

GEHMAN: Well, back home in one piece! I would like to go to Europe, but I'm not sure if my CD is going there. The Ringling Sisters may go on a road trip this summer.

NEXT...: Is there anything else you'd like to add?

GEHMAN: What I would say to your readers is, "Go and Do!"

(6/95)

ROBERT PETERS
Interviewed by Barbara Hauk

Robert Peters is uniquely qualified to assess academic and performance poetry. He has written several full-length books of poetry designed to be staged, among them *Picnic in the Snow: Ludwig of Bavaria* (New Rivers, 1982); *The Gift to be Simple: A Garland for Ann Lee* (Liveright, 1975); *Hawker* (Unicorn Press, 1984); *Snapshots for a Serial Killer: A Fiction and a Play* (GLB Publishers, 1992); and a work currently in progress about J. Edgar Hoover. A trio of his plays were featured at a Robert Peters Festival in Madison, Wisconsin this past May.

Peters is also a prolific critic. As a regular reviewer for many journals, including the *American Book Review, the Los Angeles Times*, and the *Small Press Review*, he has been especially alert to new voices in poetry. Two of his critical works have become classics. They are the four-volume *Great American Poetry Bakeoff* (1979-1990) and *The Peters Black and Blue Guide to Literary Journals* (1983, 1985, 1988). Another book, *Hunting the Snark:*

Press photo of Robert Peters

28

A Compendium of New Poetic Terminology (1989) takes on such topics as "Academic Sleaze," "Nature," and "Sleeping Spouse" poems.

At the same time, as a thirty year veteran of academia, as professor of English at UCI, he is vitally familiar with Academic Poetry. Long considered a maverick by his colleagues, Peters has a reputation for hard-hitting criticism. He cannot resist puncturing the pretentious, the hide bound, and the dull. I interviewed Robert at his home in Huntington Beach, California.

NEXT...: Does academia stimulate or retard poetry?

PETERS: For years now I've scathingly denounced writing programs, including the ones at UCI and Iowa, as suppressing the vitality of creative work. A workshop poem does exist, and if you are a bright, even gifted student (if you are too far out, or gifted, they wouldn't let you in in the first place) you soon learn to conform. You write the piece that's going to please a common denominator of workshop tastes, *American Poetry Review* tastes, etc. The writing program journals are boring, boring, boring.

NEXT...: Do you think academia nurtures obfuscatory poetry?

PETERS: I shiver when you imply that somehow "obfuscatory" verse is *ipso facto* bad. One of the best younger poets writing today is Jesse Glass, Jr., who has been so ignored here that he now lives in Japan. This summer, I taught his fantastic new book *Peter Stubbe* in my class in contemporary American poetry. I had him supply a glossary of sources, references, etc., so that I could walk my students carefully and fully through this amazingly difficult, important and beautiful poem. Among his various sources are medieval European and English texts. I've always preferred poems that make deep imaginative and mental demands — the antithesis of what passes for "poetry" in most "standup" venues here in Southern California. Yes, there are terrific masters of the direct voice — few though approach Wilma Elizabeth McDaniel, the Tulare poet, or Greg Kuzma in Nebraska, or Charles Bukowski, who is now in heaven.

NEXT...: How do you feel about performance poetry?

PETERS: Alas, I've tried to figure out for years now what the crittur really is. On the one hand, minimally talented "poets" brassy enough to strip naked to the accompaniment of electronic music, light shows, banging on tabors, and lighting candles, regale lobotomized cafe and bar audiences. Look at the incredible badness of most rock lyrics — banal end-rhymed blatherings of teenybopper weltschmerz ("world sickness"). I'm appalled by the inept verse I've been subjected to even in calmer venues. I'd like to be more generous, but I can't. Then, some "performance" works, like those of Tim Miller, Allen Ginsberg, are thoroughly professional, without gimmickry.

NEXT...: What differences do you see between the true theater piece and poetry performances?

PETERS: There are many, I think, and what I myself have been doing over the past two decades with my raft of characters is, I think, old-fashioned theater, where an actor appears on stage, has a set script memorized and honed, and presents himself as a character. Sure, plays are "performances"— you can't get away from that — but in their purest forms, including those for a single actor, they differ much from what I think you mean by performance poetry. In the latter, the audience can be as much a participating factor as the performer; also there's plenty of room for improvisation. I'm not sure I'm making myself clear. I don't regard myself as a performance poet.

NEXT...: Is there such a thing as "Performance Sleaze?"

PETERS: Yes: go to any announced "performance" venue in So. California and you'll know almost immediately what I mean. Again, I'm making a distinction between a terrific public presenter of his work like Robert Bly and the carryings-on of lesser folk, usually much younger, and including many who wouldn't know how to begin to read Yeats, or Tennyson, or Hopkins, McGrath, Snyder, or Bly.

NEXT...: Where did you get your inspiration for the staged books?

PETERS: From many sources. I have always had a keen eye, I think, for characters larger than life, risk-takers, often excessive to the point of being self-destructive; and I'd like to think there are ties with many of them to my own psyche. The Shaker books, for example, came in a period when I was trying to simplify my life, almost in a Shaker manner, as a way of keeping sane. I've always been an esthete, loving art, music, painting, architecture; and so when I discovered Ludwig of Bavaria he was made to order — and then, too, that he was homosexual fascinated me. The Cornish vicar Hawker was another wonderful eccentric who was as much child as he was a vicar, one who loved animals in his church. Also, a couple of my characters, the Blood Countess and Randy Kraft, not only are extreme personages, but were writing challenges. I set them up in antithesis to the utterly pacifist, non-destructive Ludwig and Ann Lee — to see if I could, as old Robert Browning used to in his great monologues, enter the skins and cortices of monsters. My sources have been various. My friend Paul Trachtenberg found the Countess through encyclopedia readings, and we both attended sessions of Randy Kraft's trial here in Santa Ana.

NEXT...: Your poetry has been called "a poetry of extremes" — sexual, violent and emotional. Some find your poetry adventurous and shocking and feel that you're "rubbing their faces in it."

PETERS: I'm aware of this, and resent that description, and am puzzled by it. Why will people condemn my *Serial Killer* play, or my *Blood Countess*, or the Bavarian King, or my Hoover, and stay away from them, and yet flock to films like *Pulp Fiction* and *Silence of the Lambs* or any score of murder/violence flicks? Perhaps the theater pieces are too real, in that you seem to have the actual perpetrator of monstrous things in front of you. I guess Neil Simon and Stephen Sondheim have destroyed audiences for serious theater — audiences go to be amused, regaled, pap-fed, escaping from realities of their on-going public and private lives. Images on the screen are less "real," in the sense that no Lector is going to come down off the screen to torture you — and this might happen when my Randy Kraft threatens to go into the audience, or when my Countess might select a lissome maiden from the audience and stab her breast with a fork. I'm baffled. As a writer of such themes, I've aligned myself with D. H. Lawrence, James Joyce, Patrick White, Selby, Burroughs, Miller, et al., who were also controversial, some to the point of inviting obscenity charges.

NEXT...: What would you say to those who would censor your more outrageous, disturbing works, say those on serial killers, blatant and bizarre sexuality?

PETERS: UP YOURS! They forget I've also written, to me, important mainstream works, my elegy for my infant son Richard (*Songs for a Son*, W. W. Norton, 1967)

and the extensive volumes on Ann Lee, the founder of the Shakers. And, also, I hope my series of memoirs of my Wisconsin origins and on my experiences in World War II will be remembered as mainstream contributions. All three are published by the University of Wisconsin Press.

NEXT...: How has your academic career affected your poetry and criticism?

PETERS: Very positively, for I have been very well-treated at U.C. Irvine, enjoying the freedom of being a non-conformist who is often controversial. The salary's been terrific, the teaching schedules and vacations most generous, and I've enjoyed plenty of time for writing, teaching, and acting. You can — as my experience shows — nuzzle academic teats and come off fat, sassy, and productive. As a critic too, I've felt no censorship, silent or otherwise, ever. And although I was once asked not to teach any further MFA workshops, for fear of upsetting conservative students, I was delighted to find myself free to go even further along my own road.

NEXT...: Where do you get your information for criticism? Magazines, poetry readings, networking, etc.?

PETERS: From my insatiable reading, and the hours and hours spent acquainting myself with as much contemporary work as possible. I'm currently in a period of reaction, being 70½ — and my skin crawls when yet another glossy book of poems, or some new magazine appears craving a review. Which is not to say that I won't do more reviews — but my energies now are going into playing tournament Scrabble.

NEXT...: How do your poetry and criticism affect one another?

PETERS: Well, I purposely began critiquing as a way of calling attention to my poetry. Poetry came first. My feeling was (taking my model from James Dickey who was an awesome critic, one of the best, before he was well-known as a poet) that if I generated interest in and respect for my criticism those readers might say, "Oh, that dude writes poetry too," and they'd go get it and read it. I don't know that much of that happened. Perhaps I've written too much criticism. Time will tell.

NEXT...: Pretentious people irritate you. You are known to your UCI students as "The great bullshit detector." What do you like to see happen in poetry and what is your advice to young poets in order to make it happen?

PETERS: To say anything would seem pompous, and about all I can say (and I'm thrilled to be known as a "shit detector") is that the fledgling poet has to find his/her own voice, listen to it, and to dismiss the censoring force of anyone looking over his/her shoulder trying to get him/her to conform to society's norms. None of our terrific writers has ever done this. Nin? Joyce? Lawrence? McGrath? Bly? You can write your own list.

(9/95)

MINDY NETTIFEE
By Lawrence Schulz

Her style is intensive yet light at the same time. There is no teen angst in her work — it's been replaced with a clear, descriptive writing that carries the reader and listener on a journey with her.

Mindy Nettifee is a 16-year-old junior at Huntington Beach High School. She's been writing poetry since 11, giving her first reading at 13. Her performance style shows maturity and depth that would put many seasoned performance poets to shame.

Recently *Next...* interviewed her, asking her opinion of other teen writers as well as comments about her own writing. Like other teen writers, Mindy said she was influenced the most by the beatnik writers of the '50s as well as the works of Tom Robbins. "I've been influenced a lot by Tom Robbins. A lot of Kerouac. Robbins more than anything. His quality of style in making a point while not making a point."

It's tough being a good, young writer at a high school in Orange County where conformity seems to be the mode of operation. When asked about the reaction she receives from her school environment she commented, "A lot of them don't understand."

"They tend to label me artistic, young, poet. The people who like me are pretty cool, but some people don't know what to make of this. I'm one of the different ones. I don't look like I'm into the hippie stuff. Some of them think, 'Oh, it's just Mindy expressing her views.'"

And her views — what are they?

"It's young," Mindy said. "People expect that your stuff isn't good if you're young. Some people have problems with my age [as it relates to the poetry]. It seems that you have to prove yourself. So I take an extra step to stand out." Mindy believes that "extra step" is reflected in the performance of her poetry.

With the expression you could only expect from someone who enjoys reading poetry out loud she said, "You get the feeling. It comes when you repeat a line... don't go for the straight image. When you think a little bit [about what you write]."

Photo of Mindy Nettifee by Phish Blackler

She enjoys reading her work to an audience. Recently, she gave a dynamic performance at Living Planet in Long Beach with another teenage Orange County poet, Beth McIlvaine. She was accompanied by a bass player, finding that, with her work, "the rhythm comes out" to add another level of intensity. While Beth's work tended to be dark, Mindy's work tended to be "you can get through this bullshit." While not exactly upbeat, it is a different approach from what you would expect from a teenage poet. "People told me later it was like night and day," she said regarding the contrasting style of the two poets.

She seemed optimistic about where poetry is going with young writers, especially within her local area of Huntington Beach. "It's just beginning," she said. "A lot more writers are starting to come into the art and perform."

Mindy admits that her first public poetry readings were scary experiences, but sees that over the last three years she has gone from that spot to getting up to read and "not even shake."

Despite her maturity as a poet and performer, it's still the high school grind. Her English teachers are aware of her writing; but it's still turn in the homework assignment. So when it comes to turning in the required essay, Mindy admits, "I'll deviate from the norm."

One of her teachers even attended one of Mindy's readings, a fact that left a definite impression. "If more teachers would pay attention to what goes on with us outside the school," she said. "Maybe education would be different."

When a poet like Mindy speaks, it's strong advice and worth listening to.

(11/95)

BOB HOLMAN
By Jayleen Sun & Mud Baron

Bob Holman always sweats and always works. His upcoming video series, *The United States of Poetry (USOP)*, will be airing in February. You will be amazed what electronics can do for poetry. The sneak previews he aired for the 1995 Taos Poetry Circus were an unscheduled highlight of the event. *USOP* can be given the highest praise: I didn't know video could do that. As the producer, Bob somehow did know. He, and director Mark Pellington (winner of MTV Video of the Year for his work on Pearl Jam's "Jeremy"), somehow talked enough people into making the camera shoot and the poets, well, be poets in front of it. You won't, however, see Bob himself in this video anthology of contemporary poetry. He is off camera like mom hen, the perpetual poetry activist.

Bob has been writing since he was wetting his bed. He escaped from Ohio in the '70s and moved to NYC. From 1977 to 1984, he ran the St. Mark's Poetry Project reading series. In 1992, he won an International Public Television Award for producing *Words in Your Face*. He also won a few Emmys and a Bessie while producing more than fifty poetry spots for WNYC-TV. He was jumped by the Nuyorican Poets Cafe, where he is currently co-director and weekly slam host. In 1994 he could be blamed for: winning an American Book Award for *Aloud: Voices from the Nuyorican Poets Cafe*, which he co-edited with Miguel Algarin; getting poetry on MTV; and teaching Lollaploozers a thing or two about how to pop heads with broken bottle metaphors. It's 1996 and on top of being run by his new spoken word label, Mouth Almighty, creating the poetry web page for iGUIDE, hosting the Nuyorican Slam, and promoting his newest book, *The Collect Call of the Wild*, he finds time to re: "verb"-erate with us. We have seen him in his undies and sock garters — this view of him is almost as vivid.

The following exchange is via American Online accounts dated January 19, 1996:

NEXT...: Ohio boy to Ohio boy, I found out this past Xmas back "home" all my punk squat friends in Ohio from the '80s are now addicted to alcohol, smack or cable. What would you have done if you stayed in HELL?

HOLMAN: Opened a gas station on Rt. 52. Bathroom graffiti haiku slam.

NEXT...: Is there enough love in your world?

HOLMAN: There is enough love in my world. However, love does not know this. Love, however, would be surprised to find out it does not know. Therefore, one must surprise love with love, creating, which is to say, "making" love.

NEXT...: Your love-child, the *United States of Poetry*, must have taken a chunk of you. What bodily fluid you lose, you use, the most of to get it done?

HOLMAN: I oozed all, all over. Brain juice squirts, matted sperm, flung dooty of sacrifice, and not to mention (NEVER MENTION!) frustration bloooooooood.

NEXT...: And video makes poetry do what?

HOLMAN: Vid makes Po go.

NEXT...: What's the big touchdown team Holman is shooting for?

HOLMAN: *USOP.* The rest gravies the "extra point."

NEXT...: Where does the poetry mobile crash and burn and make its mark on this ever-increasing tele-universe?

HOLMAN: Tongue totality. Air Beanbags. The end of war. Racism dies. I marry a hologram.

NEXT...: If you were Ms. Poetry America, how would you make the world a better place?

HOLMAN: Write yr own goddamn passport photo er I mean pome!! Talk ye like meaning (falls down in a fit). Allowance of $____ for the "Impossible Rap." Think The Other Thought!

NEXT...: After (is there an ever never after?) *USOP* your next at bat?

HOLMAN: The World of Poetry airs 2000.

NEXT...: Jimmy Carter was great in *USOP* with all his "twinkle little star stuff," how does he smell up close working? Presidential?

HOLMAN: Jimmy's a good man. We were informed he was very punctual, but he was, in fact, thirty seconds late. He has a sweet smile. His first words, "I've never done this before. Tell me what to do." He trusted this gang of poets, us! He spoke admiringly of what poets can do in the world, wistfully. He wants to be a poet, I think, it would behoove him in his peace missions, I said, hey, you published a book (Random House no less!) — you are a poet! (Sweet smile.) He spoke of Dylan Thomas, he spoke of oral tradition in his own family. His best poems (like the one in the show) seem to be plunging into syrup vat, then at last possible second, fill up into beautiful human-doubt overdrive.

NEXT...: Favorite finger?

HOLMAN: Ringo

NEXT...: Worst thing you can remember writing?

HOLMAN: "Over the world a stillness lay/All silvery and white"

Illustration of Bob Holman by Charles Ellik

NEXT...: Heckle Schmeckle, points for heckling? Give us readers of *Next...* Bob Holman's 1-2-3 heckle instruction kit:

HOLMAN: 1. There is no poem without a heckle

2. Shut the fuck up is not censorship

3. Dis this, Cuss that

NEXT...: What every poet should do at least twice:

HOLMAN: 1. Step in the same river once

2. Take both of them

NEXT...: "Hey Rap meet P, Poetry meet Rap, now you be pals!" Henry Louis Gates in the New Jerker said something like "there could be no Bob Holman without poetry."

HOLMAN: I am poetry addict. Gates got it. He gets it. He is gate. His Signifying Monkey bore great fruit when I hung w/ super blues poet, RL Burnside in Holly Springs, Mississippi. RL ran down a ten-minute version of "The Monkey Who Crashed the Party" that must go back to the Mother Continent. Hilarious rhymed couplets, a G version for the ladies up here and muttered under the breath ribald X for the men in the circle. Among other Theory to Practice Reality Belts of Mr. HLG.

NEXT...: And what could there be no HLG without?

HOLMAN: Read his Colored People bio, Mud — his West VA is our Buckeye.

NEXT...: Very apropos po title for your newest book, *Collect Call of the Wild*. But what's wrong with Jack London, did you too in fact shovel coal and get oppressed to write your cellular call of the phone card wilds?

HOLMAN: Nothin's wrong with Jack. He just didn't have a quarter or a phone card.

NEXT...: Question No. 666: Rod McKuen is:

HOLMAN: The reverse is far clearer. Stanyan Street I avoid, or, A Void. Actually, interesting piece on the Rhino Beat Box Set.

NEXT...: Where is *Aloud* being used as a teaching manual? Do you think it odd that it is?

HOLMAN: "Have I done this to people with wee hearts and big heads?" NYC jails. Rutgers. Notre Dame. Bristol, England. On and on! The Book gives good lie to those who say "It doesn't work on the page."

NEXT...: Thank you for mentioning Doc Williams so many times in the video and in the backseat of the car; he's become one of my favorite reads. I love all that death shit he puts life into.

HOLMAN: Williams is the American Grain. He said, "If it ain't a pleasure, it ain't a poem," on December 4, 1951. I love the opening to the shows, where Trudell kicks in "Listen to the skies, listen to the sound/ Something on the land, Something going down" and then WCW ends w/ the above. These two guys bracket the moment — and they're not even ID'ed! You have to dig to find out Who, but the Resonance is clear enough. That's the poem.

(2/96)

WATTS PROPHETS

By D-Knowledge

In 1965, after a very public display of police brutality, an area of Los Angeles known as Watts experienced a serious uprising, rebellion, revolt, social disturbance… choose your politically correctable classification. In the aftermath of the "Watts Riot," the Watts Writers Workshop was created. It quickly became a reservoir for culturally centered creative/artistic expression. It was at the Watts Writers Workshop that Richard Dedeaux, Amde A. Hamilton (a/k/a Father made), and Otis O'Solomon began developing their poetry and — as they say — "developing their own souls." With the help of some other poets, they created an informal poetry collective called Watts Fire — where they started getting out of the workshop environment to share their poetry at each others' homes.

The three men do not remember exactly how they came to be a group, but Father Amde recalls that, "There were so many poets at the Watts Writers Workshop. We used to all do shows together at the workshop. Just all get up there and start reading. But folks started asking for us to perform in so many different places that groups started forming. Somehow we started being together — but I can't remember exactly how.

"When we first got together, we didn't think that Richard should be in the group. [Otis interrupts: "Well… I don't know if that's true."] Yes it is! I'm just being frank. I thought his poetry was too soft. But Harry Dolan, the director of the workshop told us, 'It's the variety in each of you that's going to make the Watts Prophets. Some is going to like Richard… some is going to like Otis… and some is going to like Amde.' And we came to appreciate and respect that."

They acquired the name Watts Prophets at a talent show at the Inner City Cultural Center. As Father Amde tells it, "We were about to go on stage, and they asked us 'what are you guys called?' We hadn't even thought about a name at that point. But this lady looked at us and said: 'You guys are like prophets… Watts Prophets.' And that became our name."

In 1968 or 1969 (the Watts Prophets constantly debated each other over exact dates), the group was performing all over Los Angeles and beyond. Otis says, "We didn't get locked in. So we were able to read all over. We worked with the Muslims, we worked with the Panthers, the Red Cross, the Boy's Club — everybody. And we could relate with everybody. Man, everybody would claim us… but they couldn't lock us in."

By the early seventies, the Watts Prophets were proficient, profound, prolific, and — oh yeah — *prophetic*. In 1971 they released an album entitled *Rappin' Black in a White World* — shocking listeners by poetically asking questions like "ask not what you can do for your country, 'cause what the fuck has it done for you?" They wrote, produced and starred in the Emmy-nominated documentary *Victory Will Be My Moan*; they published two books of poetry through the Watts Prophets Press; they worked with artists like Quincy Jones, Stevie Wonder, Don Cherry, Marvin Gaye, Gil Scott-Heron, and The Last Poets; they performed live all over the country and even in Europe; and they were always active in political struggles. Most people spend a career (or two) accumulating such achievements; but the Watts Prophets did all this in the early seventies.

As the mid-seventies approached, the group significantly slowed down. Although they stress emphatically that they never broke up, their performances together became less and less frequent. Says Otis, "We just started doing our own thang. But I think we all were still involved with poetry and the arts, man."

When I asked the Watts Prophets to characterize their lives during the eighties, they said it was a decade of pure struggle and survival. Divorce, gambling, death, financial difficulty… these were words they used. But, even during this painful decade, they each continued writing poetry to help them get through their manifold difficulties.

Fast forward to 1991. Roni Walter (from Roni'z Backstreet Poetry) and Brian Cross approached Father Amde for an interview for *Urb Magazine*. They informed Amde that the Watts Prophets had been sampled by rap artists such as 2nd ii None, DJ Quick, Eazy E, NWA, Poor Righteous Teachers, Tim Dog, and Too Short.

Upon hearing this, Father Amde says, "I was amazed. I didn't even know the young folks knew who we were. And not only did they know who we were, they had memorized our poems. Then we started to meet those rappers. And somehow the Watts Prophet started performing a lot again."

The Prophets express a great admiration for the current rap/hip hop movement.

Otis says, "I have a lot of respect for the hip hop artists — 'cause I think they are talented. And they did something we didn't do… they made a lot of money. But, you know, with that maybe they didn't spend the years developing their craft."

Richard Dedeaux chimes in, "But we opened the doors for them to do that. We made it possible for them to make their millions. [Turning to me.] And to answer your question about 'How do I feel about it?' I listen to the pain that's in their poetry, and a lotta people ain't listenin'. And sometimes they get caught up in the curse words. But we've always expressed ourselves with a little color — we've always put a little color in the language. So my thing is, they're kids. And I accept all of it and I take responsibility for most of it… because it shows my shortcomings."

Adds Father Amde, "I love the hip hop world myself; I love what they're doing. I think some of the rappers like Tupac (Shakur) — who I think is one of the greatest poets in America today, bar none — brilliant. And I'm like Richard, I think we need to start listening to them and start working with them. They have a lot of sense. Now a lot of folks think they don't have any sense. But, man, they got more sense than a lot of us. So, I understand it."

The Prophets are currently at work on a new album. Otis says, "We have a lot of the young brothers working with us on our new album. We want to bring the generations together."

He continues, "With this album you'll hear some vintage Watts Prophets with some new Watts Prophets. And the poetry is very mature; it shows our growth through years and years of writing. This is tried and true poetry."

Photo of Watts Prophets by Charles Ellik. Left to Right: Unknown, Father Amde, Richard Dedeaux (crouched down), Otis O'Solomon

Richard adds, "In this album we talk about family. We talk about the ecology. In a poem called "Hey World" we talk about how we're destroying everything. We got a poem called "When the Nineties Came" that talks about all the changes that are going on today and how things are just going to hell. It's all positive."

Father Amde joins in, "We also show how you, the poet, can technically do poetry with jazz, hip hop, reggae, R&B.. 'cause in this album you'll hear all of that."

The Watts Prophets are not quite finished with the album, but they are almost there. They expect the album to be released sometime in the summer on Polygram Records. Although they have not definitively decided upon the title, they think they will call it either *When the Nineties Came* or *Wake Up World!* Whatever the album is called, peep it — 'cause the tracks I've heard are straight funky, groovy, inspirational, informative and just plain slammin'. It's amazing that this will only be their second album. But, hey, y'all, when you hear it, you'll know it was worth the wait… as if they were marinating their lyrics for twenty-five years. *Watt Flavor to Savor.*

But you don't have to wait until the summer to hear the Watts Prophets. Just consult a local paper (like *Next…*) and you will inevitably find this group performing somewhere. If you haven't seen the Watts Prophets, go immediately (hurry up). If you've seen them, go again… and again… and absorb… and embellish (and you don't stop). If you've seen them several times, next time introduce yourself and electrocute yourself with their incredibly powerful positive energy. And if you have already met them and been shocked, feel blessed. But most of all, cherish these brothas — for they are a national treasure deserving our respect, admiration, appreciation, gratitude and *love*. Remember: Ask not what the Watts Prophets can do for this country… 'cause fuck, they've already done more for this country than this country has ever done for them.

As the interview came to a close, I asked each member of the group to give a brief statement telling how they want the Watts Prophets to be remembered.

Richard: "We were a group that never gave up. Never! And we were the guys who lived what we talked about."

Father Amde: "We are lovers of humanity. And we've been misunderstood, but we have always loved humankind. We love the progress of life, period."

Otis: "We came with all of our heart and soul. We never knew that this stuff would reach the level it has reached. But we just did what we felt was right. And we always believed in truth — 'cause we've always believed that truth doesn't spoil."

And, as I have learned, the Watts Prophets don't spoil either.

(5/96)

THE CARMA BUMS

By Raindog

The Carma Bums, being five fiercely independent, opinionated, eccentric, and cantankerous poetic persons, have logged thousands of miles since their most recent incarnation began in 1989. Since then, they have sought to bring the bittersweet word-jazz of the late 20th century riding in on a sine wave, swinging high/low, coming for to carry anyone, who wants to go, home. The Bums are: Mike Bruner, S.A. Griffin, Doug Knott, Mike Mollett and Scott Wannberg. (Bobbo Staron used to be one, once). They begin a week-long tour, in part, to promote *Twisted Cadillac*, published by Sacred Beverage Press, on August 16th at Luna Park in Hollywood. Ellyn Maybe (who's logged a few miles with them) will be along, as well. Mike Bruner was unable to participate in the interview. No one knows where Bobbo is.

NEXT...: How did the Carma Bums come into existence?

MOLLETT: There was no one else to connect with in the void of the time: the bullshit, the poverty, the precious holy poetry reading. People of great diversity, our differences complimented our common obsessions with words going in same and different directions. This was good. We were all iconoclasts in love with exploration. Embarrassment was no obstacle.

KNOTT: Well, the Carma Bums were actually a transformation of the Lost Tribe, they were an octave on the Lost Tribe. I was in the Lost Tribe. We had an act that tended to comedy, but it was a poetic act with routines that were rehearsed. But with the Carma Bums, because we kinda knew each others' stuff (for better or worse) and were pretty comfortable with that, and because of that the Carma Bums never rehearsed. The idea was based on being a spontaneous group but knowing what we were going to do.

GRIFFIN: The Lost Tribe existed and the characters were involved with that particular entity and then that fell apart. Then about a year or so later, the idea of the Carma Bums popped up and those happened to be the characters that were involved in the next thing. So, in a sense it was an evolution, but on the other side of it, one doesn't have anything to do with the other. The Lost Tribe was a performance poetry ensemble. It was like a drill-team poetry ensemble with a lot of stand-up comedy and satire involved, where everything was rehearsed and on the money. And the Carma Bums is the exact opposite of that. It's like empathy, deliberation, and everything comes out of the moment; we deal with the audience, there's a lot of spontaneity involved. Although there are pieces and we have that to fall back on, it's more like what's going on, you know what I mean? It's more of a happening routine as opposed to a practiced sort of event. So, it just so happened that the same characters were involved in it and it was a good reason to bring Scott Wannberg on board and do the obvious natural thing and progress in that direction.

WANNBERG: I was doing readings around L.A. (the westside and Hollywood) and I met S.A. Griffin one night — he came to a reading that I was doing and we hit it off. Then I met (Mike) Bruner and we did some things and it just kinda evolved from there. We took a trip to SanFran and did an impromptu thing in a parking garage (among other things) and it went really well and after we got back to L.A., S.A. said one day, well you know we might wanta go on the road and do something like that; and we were sitting around all jazzed up trying to come up with a name for the group — which was basically what had been the Lost Tribe and myself and Bobbo — although Bobbo, who had known these guys (Lost Tribe) for a long time, had never been a part because he was, um, just too deliberate to be a part of any group (he's unto himself)... but I know the Lost Tribe had been together for a long time and was pretty well-known. What S.A. wanted to do was have a little more freedom from the regimen of the Lost Tribe.

NEXT...: The Carma Bums, as a group, seem to draw on a very diverse background of theatrical, as well as poetic, experience. In terms of your contrasting personalities, how do you get "in tune" and stay there?

GRIFFIN: Usually when we go up there, we don't always know what we're doing. We don't have a clue because that's the point! The point is to listen, and through the act of empathy and deliberation... we go up there to be deliberate. So, hopefully, in the act of being deliberate, we become not just a part of the walls, but a part of the people that are there and they become a part of us.

WANNBERG: Actually, it goes back to that Grateful Dead combination of improv and set stuff, which is evolving (or devolving depending on your point of view). What we did in '89 was go out on the road and have a set order in which we had rounds like, Doug goes first, then me, etc. And each round was set up that way, and one person could do a rap, you know like improv something, but it was loosely scripted. But as that went on it got more boring. And, then what it got to be, which was influenced by the Scott Kelman workshops, was real scary because it got really free, you know, unstructured, and some of the group had a hard time with that transition, you see? The shows were a blend of improv and set pieces, and, depending on who you talk to, how successful a show was depended on how good the blend was. I know what I like in a show and that is if we're all willing to take the risk of not worrying about looking too stupid (of course not everyone is this loose).

KNOTT: It's creating an empathetic bond with each of us and the audience at that moment where you are always recovering from making a mistake in kind of an enlightened passivity, okay? Action out of non-action.

GRIFFIN: The point is, all of a sudden the pretense is missing. There are no longer any ideas, and in that particular form now the new ideas are possible, because everything is possible. So we take that with the audience, because they are the show. When the show really works, that's what happens! Everyone is the show! We're just finding the path for everyone and we just follow it together, which is really exciting, because it's no longer the energy of just five people, it's now everybody in the whole room! It's really, really exciting! We get there once in awhile, but you're dealing with really different personalities... and that's part of the experiment, which means we've got to find the form and listen to each other! Really be empathetic and pay attention to everything! That's not an easy thing to do because, fundamentally, what you're dealing with is fear. We are fragile, fearful human beings, so it's not easy getting to that state of free jazz where there are no mistakes.

MAYBE: Experience the Amazing Wow!... dysfunctional family of words... life off the page... free-ranging creativity encouraged by nurturing... kindred spirits of the lost highway... yeah!

GRIFFIN: We learned many techniques to move from the linear into the non-linear. Bobbo and Scott needed no help, they were there naturally. Bobbo was the most deliberate member of the group, the devil of deliberation! Scott is empathetic in capital letters, you know? The rest of us did need to find out through Kelman, even though we had it in us, we had to kind of find it.

MOLLETT: The process, it's always becoming... not always seen consciously... deliberation and discovery, being accessible, open, non-protective, wildable... a space to be filled with words and listening... a sponge

Photo of Carma Bums by G. Murray Thomas. Left to Right: Mike Mollett, Doug Knott, Amelie Frank, Scott Wannberg, S.A. Griffin, Ellyn Maybe thing, at best (in momentous hindsight) it all goes for me into and originates from silence, where we all come from and return to. The Carma Bums was, in fact, a dysfunctional family of performing poets. We were to create new worlds improvisationally and empathetically.

NEXT...: Since the Carma Bums is essentially a "road show," what's on the horizon?

KNOTT: Well, we're off on a week-long book signing tour in August starting at Luna Park on the 16th; on the 18th, we'll be in San Diego; then we're going to Sonora (NoCal); then to Big Sur (at the Henry Miller Library); and then up to a couple of gigs in San Francisco. After that, I guess you could say that we will be promoting and entertaining delusions of grandeur!

GRIFFIN: Well, it's a strange sort of thing, the Carma Bums, it's like the thing you can't kill (Laughter). We have tried to kill the Carma Bums, because theoretically, it was only supposed to exist on the road; it was never intended to be anything else! In theory, in essence, the Carma Bums can never die. We are really "Bad Brothers" — we're fated to always be together (even the lost Bobbo — see the book, *Twisted Cadillac*) for the rest of our fucking, miserable lives (Laughter)!

WANNBERG: Yeah. I mean people get pushy about the Carma Bums appearing in town, but they don't get that it was conceived of as an out-of-L.A. experience. It was designed (A) for the car; (B) that sort of origami connective tissue of away from the L.A. rhythm, out there. And then when we came back we were individuals, but when we were on the road, we were the Carma Bums. Problem is, now, we've been Carma Bums for a while (seven years) and it's time to move on, but some don't want to, um, let go, you know? I mean, it's not that important, it's just something we do for fun.

NEXT...: You have a website that was your last "tour." What's that about?

MOLLETT: The Net is a new territory establishing its scope, its powers, its borders and its life. Its first border was technology. And then the entrepreneurs...$$$. And the government, and the people wanting power....$$$. Now, also, the masses are chiming in, realizing a hell of a lot of possibilities. I don't know what the fuck it is; it's so boggling, like a friendly medusa, like a vast library with infinite aisles, the traps are set, even for the wary. We hoped our Superhighway Tour of Words ('94) would include an add-to word piece that would allow anyone in our site to restructure it. We were naive. Stupid with a purpose that wouldn't fly. This was two years ago. We had problems with our website programmer. He couldn't communicate with us, especially us as creative visionaries in the log-jam of technological dumbness. Our ideas didn't know the format or the language. Fortunately, Robert Telck, a graphic designer, wanted to sink in and surf the web for us to find workable programs for our Superhighway Tour. Our material was there and Robert popped in the living color and the visuals.

GRIFFIN: The Internet is cool, but I don't know that much about it. It would be nice to take advantage of it more because these road trips really take a lot! We very deliberately put ourselves into this small space, the car, and hit the road and live together for a couple of weeks! It's really a lot of psychic work! You're dealing with five radical, eccentric, intelligent, creative personalities that all have opinions and throwing them into a six-foot square space to live for a week or two, you're going to get the highest highs and the lowest lows possible. So, it takes a lot of fucking work; it's not a vacation!

NEXT...: Another roadside attraction on the information super highway!

(8/96)

ELLYN MAYBE

Interviewed by James "Boomer" Maverick

When one thinks of poetry, one conjures a vision of smoky basements, beret-laden beatniks under interrogation lamps, goatees groomed just so, spouting non sequiturs at a staccato rhythm that made you feel that if you didn't get what was being said, there was something wrong with you. Although the vision is forty years gone, the hipper-than-thou veneer is still de rigueur for many poets and poetry venues.

Not so with Ellyn Maybe. When one reads or listens to her work, you almost expect to see a woman worn with the ravages of time, disappointments, and broken hearts. Instead, the Ellyn Maybe of fact is a bubbly, bright-spirited angel with the wide-eyed excitement of an eight-year-old, often talking in run-on sentences, compressing as much information as possible into a single breath, infecting those around her with much the same sense of wonder and anticipation as we had when we were children.

The affection that Ellyn enjoys from the poetry community is so widespread it's almost unavoidable — in fact, there were several times throughout this interview that poets and other admirers stopped to pay compliments, chat, or just to say hello. Her book is entitled: *Mantra's Best Friend/Man's Best Friend.*

NEXT...: I wanna start with the obvious. You express a lot through poetry. When did you get started?

MAYBE: Reading or writing?

NEXT...: Writing.

MAYBE: Oh, well, let's see, when I was a little girl, I wrote a little bit of stories and stuff, and then I didn't have any confidence, so I didn't really continue to do that too much. I mean, it was just a self-esteem [thing]; I thought, "That's too fun — I enjoyed that too much." I started to write again when I moved to New York; in fact, the first time I started writing again I was an apprentice at the Actor's Studio. I was leaving there — I just walked home, I wasn't feeling that well, and there was this bookstore with this mannequin holding all these books, and these lines of poems just came — it's just inspiring — and I went back, I was living at the "Y"

and just the poems, the lines just came — that's sort of just how I write the poems, they just come. It's more of an inspired stream of consciousness.

NEXT...: Okay... reading...

MAYBE: I started reading in 1988... and I never thought I would read 'cause I was way too shy, so I never expected that, I mean, people were saying they wanted my work out there — they were gonna have someone else read it, or they were gonna just have a tape player of me reading... I didn't think I could do that. Midnight Special was my first reading. They had nineteen readers and they wanted twenty, people were going "Ellyn, hey, read..." you know, like, that kind of thing they do, and I ended up reading there. That was November of 1988. They would encourage people in the audience to read and my name came from that... I would sign it "Maybe I'll read," you know, 'cause I wasn't too committed on that...

NEXT...: You mentioned inspirations... any major ones come to mind?

MAYBE: Well, I'm self-taught, so, a lot of times I find kindreds... I listen a lot to public radio, and I go to a lot of events, and stuff like that — there's a lot of kindreds out there you can find... you gotta look around for them, you know, like, seeking it out, like, I've gone to the Pacifica Radio Archives, they have such amazing stuff. I'm always just wandering around looking...

NEXT...: So is it that sometimes you just listen and you hear somebody reading and something inside you says "Hey! That's me!" and kind of takes it in?

MAYBE: Yeah, I guess. You know, I hear a lot of political speakers that are trying to get at what's going on, really, people that are aware of things, trying to get to the meaning of [everything]... I'm very — I'm not used to being interviewed!! (Giggles.)

NEXT...: Well, this is my first interview, so...

MAYBE: Ohmigod... we're like the Bobbsey twins, here...

NEXT...: Boy oh, boy oh, boy... so, what is it that poetry does for you? I mean, if you didn't have this avenue of expression, would you kinda be socked away in the back of a post office with an automatic weapon, or...

MAYBE: Well, I was a lot more volatile before I was writing, at least around the home, 'cause I had, really, no outlet for all the stuff I went through, so I was more volatile. It's like finding one's niche, you know, I met a lot of kindreds… you know the people I wish I went to high school with… you know, meeting them years later. I feel very fortunate…

NEXT…: And whose support have you enjoyed over the last eight years? I guess you went to a couple of workshops?

MAYBE: The workshop stuff was kind of like a welcome wagon for me. I had a totally different experience, I think, than most people, because my work wasn't critiqued at all… it was just sorta, like, "Oh, there's Ellyn's poem, okay, go on…" I mean, it was most unusual. I've heard sometimes it can be a real nightmare in workshops… In general, the community has been really warm. I'm grateful to my mom, I live with her, and she has to deal with someone who's not the most functional person on earth, and when she sees me she's always really supportive… I got a letter from Howard Zinn, who wrote *People's History of the United States* and Michael Parenti who's a historian and has written stuff like *Land of Idols*… Exene Cervenkova has been a really strong supporter of my work… There's definitely a benevolence in the community — they're very caring — like, after the earthquake, my mom and I lost our apartment and there were a number of [fund raising] benefits that helped…

NEXT…: You mentioned the support of the community — you've seen a lot of the positive side of it — is there anything you're less than happy with?

MAYBE: Let's see… (Pause.) I think, I can't explain it… I mean, I know, two or three dollars isn't a lot, but it seems if there would be an effort to try to see that the poets are given even a little bit— 'cause sometimes it feels like it gets to be, year after year… (Pause.) Why aren't poets able to live with some self-sufficiency?? That part is hard… that seems to be a societal thing… a lot of people don't have a back-up way of making a living, it's hard, it's a tough thing… a tricky thing.

NEXT…: Yeah, like people will pay to see HBO, or a play or paintings on a wall, but to see a poet read… you get so much more stimulation… you'd figure people would be craving such stimulation…

MAYBE: Oh, yeah… there's such an urgency with poetry and a lot of people wanna numb out, so they're running to the numb machines looking for that… and here, it's like a whole it's so different thing, urgent. A poem can come so quickly and it's such a tumble. It's amazing, it's an incredible art.

(10/96)

Illustration of Ellyn Maybe by Brian Hagen

MARC SMITH

By Victor D. Infante

"When you get to the top of the mountain/ Pull the next one up."
—from the poem "Pull the Next One Up" by Marc Smith

For all the success and controversy that has surrounded the National Poetry Slam Finals, an annual performance poetry competition that draws poets from around the country, and now, with teams and individuals coming from Germany, Canada, Stockholm and the UK, the world, it's hard to believe that it all started as one man's idea — as just a way of livening up a poetry reading a little.

Marc Smith, a former construction worker from Chicago, is very unassuming about his poetry-world celebrity and his monolithic creation.

"I've been writing poetry since I was 19," says Smith, "and did the thing of sending off poems for years, and was as successful as a 'cold-call' submitter could be. When I was 35, I had been pretty successful with it. My dream was to become a writer, so I chucked my job and decided to give it a shot. Which meant getting things published."

At first, he explored chapbooks by local poets to get a feel for what he needed to do to pursue this path, but found it extremely frustrating. "Let's face it," he says with a mild chuckle. "There's a lot of bad poetry in those chapbooks."

At this point Smith decided to explore local poetry readings — he claims that it had always been the sound that interested him, anyway — but didn't find much there, either.

"They were stupid, pretentious, and weren't trying to be accessible to the audience, and me, being an outsider, asked questions… like "what were you trying to say?" Their style was monotone, affected. I watched for about a year, and figured out that they didn't know what they were doing. I worked up the nerve to read. One person clapped, and that was all I needed."

For some time, Smith and other poets worked as in-house performance poets at a club called the Get Me High, where Smith's brand of "dramatized poetry" developed. Later, when the troupe was doing three-

hour shows at the Green Mill, the slam was added to fill up the last hour. Attracting media attention, the slam caught on and was duplicated around the country, most notably in San Francisco and New York.

In 1989, Smith was contacted by S.F. poet Gary Glazner, who challenged him to a Chicago vs. San Francisco poetry slam during S.F.'s now defunct International Poetry Week festival. Paul Beattey, of New York, also competed in this event. Although not accepted by the audience at first, Smith and company eventually, in his own words, "turned the audience upside down."

It was here that the National Poetry Slam Finals was born, as the success of this reading so inspired the poets that they decided to try it again — this time in Chicago, with eight teams.

"It was the biggest thing in Chicago poetry in decades," he says nostalgically. "We filled up the Metro. 750 people on a Saturday night. It was a miracle. I didn't think it would happen. There were only ten presold tickets. I had spent $6,000 of my own money, and was afraid I'd lose it all — and then people began showing up at 5:30 p.m. Two and a half hours early. The whole four days was remarkable."

Since then, the Nationals have moved around the country, each area adding a local flavor. "I think the

Press photo of Marc Smith

Connecticut Slam is going to move things towards being a little more reserved and formal," says Smith, without any condescension in his voice. "And maybe that's needed… Then, when it gets to Austin, I think that those folks are so young and energetic, that it will completely throw everybody for a loop. It's like a jazz improvisation. You can play really well inside the chords, which is what I think Connecticut is going to do, or you can play real well outside the chords, which'll probably be Austin. In any case, it'll be interesting.

"That's the great thing about the slam — as soon as people try to peg it, it's something else. Eleven years at the Green Mill, and it's different every week, but it's always standing room only."

In recent days, the National Slam Organization, which had always run along pure democratic lines (sometimes bordering a bit on anarchic), has been forced to incorporate, in order to protect itself and the original concepts from major corporations who would use the name for personal gain. At one point, there was even a "Poetry Slam" board game, which had nothing to do with the actual slam. That situation was handled easily, out of court. The creator had honestly thought the name was a generic term, but it made Smith and others realize that others might not be so ready to cooperate.

Slam, Inc., the National Slam Organization, consists of an executive board of directors, an advisory council, and the "slam family," which consists of all those poets involved or affiliated with the slams.

"They made me lifetime president because I displayed an inability to be greedy for power," Smith laughs. "I tried to think of an organization that works horizontally, where the people at the top are doing all the work, and the people at the bottom get the benefits… that's the way a true political organization is supposed to run."

Despite expressed fears of a homogenized "slam poetry voice" emerging, Smith remains pleased with the progress. "Pay attention to the personal journey this takes you on," he says. "The competition is just a form to put yourself into… Don't get caught up in who's the best. Write honestly. The only bad artist is a dishonest one."

Now, with a few hundred poets following his footsteps and a recent book of poetry published (*Crowdpleaser*, 1996: Collage Press), Smith's impact on today's poetry cannot be ignored. A far cry from the days when he was slighted by pretentious poets in Chicago. When asked what he wants to do next, he replies, "I hope to sit in the back yard and look at the trees."

He chuckles. "Hope somebody remembers me."
(8/97)

JULIETTE TORREZ

Interviewed by William McLain

It's a hard life, but someone's got to do it, and Juliette Torrez does it because she likes it. She travels wherever they need her, by car with friends or acquaintances, by bus, by train and occasionally by plane, always promoting the poetry scene. She sleeps where she can, on sofas in friends' homes, in cars, in overcrowded hotel and motel rooms, any place she can crash.

Juliette organizes slams, readings, writes numerous chapbooks, newsletters and websites and does perform, but is generally too busy to read as much as she would like. She handles chapbooks for other poets when she travels and every where she goes everyone knows her and loves her. If there is a party at any of these events she is the first invitee.

If you meet her once you will always remember the occasion.

NEXT...: How long in the poetry scene?

TORREZ: Not long, maybe five years.

NEXT...: How many chapbooks have you written?

TORREZ: Seven or eight. I publish new chapbooks constantly, so I can have something fresh to trade for drinks with the bartenders in the Mission. These titles are distributed by Last Gasp: *Spirit of the Stairs, Orchestra of Harpies, Devil in a Black Wig, Springboard to Stardoom, Rock and Roll Summer Camp, The Thief was Kind.*

NEXT...: Who do you handle books for?

TORREZ: No one officially, but once in a while I get some work from small West Coast presses like Manic D or Feral House. Last Gasp usually has some work for me when I'm in town and writers hire me once in a while for special projects.

NEXT...: Why do you come to slams and extravaganzas of poetry?

TORREZ: The gathering of writers. It's a party with guaranteed good conversation and a smattering of wildness. Someone told being a writer is like being in a drinking club; these events let us get together.

NEXT...: How often do you actually perform?

TORREZ: Not much right now. I'm working on two books and a festival at the moment. Autumn is an introverted time for me, I write a lot, sleep, work. I tour in the summer. I've been working my way out of depression, that's been my priority the past few months. Survival.

NEXT...: Where all do you promote and actually work in slams?

TORREZ: I started the slam in Albuquerque and host the slam at Taos Poetry Circus. I incorporated a few slams at the Albuquerque Poetry Festival. I volunteered at the Nationals Poetry Slam Championship last year in Portland, and I'm one of the organizers for the upcoming Nationals in Austin. But I also promote other aspects of poetry and spoken word, the slam is only part of it. I would never say I live in the realm of slam, I just enjoy its form.

Ask me about my Firestorm reading series.

NEXT...: What's Firestorm?

TORREZ: It's an all-fem reading series I started a few years ago in Albuquerque. Since then it has spread to Santa Cruz, Portland, Seattle and cyberspace. Basically it's an evening of spoken word with female writers, the proceeds of which usually go to a local women's non-profit group. I want to have one in San Francisco, probably sometime after the Albuquerque Poetry Festival. My plate is full right now.

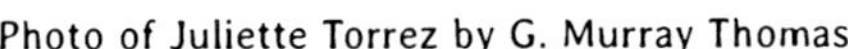

Photo of Juliette Torrez by G. Murray Thomas

NEXT...: What's the Poetry Channel?

TORREZ: Oh! That's my little e-zine. I talk about writers, readings, parties, and new books. Sometimes I get to mediate a little disagreement. Mostly, I try to have fun. It's a little controversial, people don't hold back. I have 400 subscribers across the country plus a couple of websites have picked it up. It's not the nicest zine, but definitely very entertaining.

NEXT...: Favorite venues and cities?

TORREZ: I can't answer that, I have too many friends that would grill me.

NEXT...: I think you know more poets than Bob Holman and Marc Smith put together.

TORREZ: Are you trying to get me in trouble?

NEXT...: Can you always find rides to other cities and find a place to crash?

TORREZ: No, not always, I've had to sleep in some strange places. Mostly though, there's a couch someplace. My new book, *Sofasurfing*, talks all about that. It's a modern nomadic's handbook that will be out next spring through Manic D Press.

NEXT...: Flying is expensive.

TORREZ: That's why I go Greyhound. The train is the best though, most comfortable way to travel.

NEXT...: You never seem to get drunk or hung over, but sometimes tired.

TORREZ: I behave on the road. In San Francisco, it's another story. People in L.A. always tell me I look tired; maybe I need to put some cucumbers on my eyes.

NEXT...: Do guys always try to take advantage of you?

TORREZ: No! Never! Once in a while, though, I get one of those 'charity ass grabs.' It doesn't happen often. I have a rich fantasy life. My boyfriend lives in Calgary, I don't see him as much as I'd like. Do I seem pent up? I probably am.

(12/97)

BUCKY SINISTER

By Charles Ellik

Bucky Sinister isn't just another MC, and the Chameleon, a reading he started, isn't just another reading. The Chameleon is the Mission district's most notorious open reading, and was a force on the scene before it became "the second hippest place to live in America" (*Utne Reader*). It is also host to many of S.F.'s best-known performance poets and slammers, like Beth Lisick, Justin Chin, and Tarin Towers (the new MC). True, this reading has been around long enough to be important by virtue of influence, but, more importantly to Angelenos, it was one of the few places an L.A. poet could get a feature in a city that loves to hate L.A. Sure, you might get heckled into oblivion, or a brawl might erupt at the bar mid-poem, but you got to read. Where most every other S.F. Host was a political broker, Bucky welcomed everyone to "suffer the fury of the open mic."

NEXT...: Where are you from?

SINISTER: I grew up in Arkansas, lived in Boston for two years, went back to Arkansas, to St. Louis, to Arkansas, back to St. Louis, then to Los Angeles. I ended up getting accepted to S.F. State and moved up to S.F. That was in '89.

NEXT...: What projects do you have in the works?

SINISTER: The scene is different now, with different needs to fill. I don't have the time to pick up the slack when I run a reading once a week. We need a new venue, with no open mike. It's time we graduated. There's plenty of places to read now, but there's no step up. Once you've featured somewhere, that's it. I'd like to get something better going. Check out the Kilowatt on Saturday to see what I mean.

NEXT...: How has your book, *King of the Roadkills*, done?

SINISTER: Heck if I know. Ask Jennifer Joseph (Manic D Press). She never gives me a straight answer on this one.

NEXT...: Books in the works?

SINISTER: I've got a manuscript called *Kill Em All* I'm shopping right now. I'm working on a novel called *The Church of Christ the Hygienic*, and a book of poems which I'm thinking should be called *Black Pearl*.

NEXT...: What pays the rent?

SINISTER: Right now, I'm working at Sony PlayStation writing strategy books for video games. It's pretty much my dream job.

NEXT...: Have you been performing your own work?

SINISTER: I don't get asked to feature all that much. People think I just read all the time, but, especially in the last two years, I haven't done a whole lot.

NEXT...: How did you start MC'ing?

SINISTER: I came to S.F. in 1989. I was barely 20. I went to a lot of poetry readings because they were all free and I didn't have anything else to do. One of the things I noticed was that the poets were all old. Like at least 30. That's how I thought about it, anyway. Jen Joseph had the Paradise running, and she was only around 26 at the time, but other than that, the scene was predominantly 35 and up. I couldn't get into the Paradise, because I had no fake ID. So I was left to the Cafe Babar and a few other places.

The Cafe Babar was an L-shaped bar at the time, and it was tiny. The back room's walls were corrugated tin covered and it got loud in there. The whole room filled

Press photo of Bucky Sinister

up with cigarette smoke in about ten minutes. There was some kind of vibe like, "we're going to be famous any day now, and you're not getting in this club."

I met some other young guys around town. We had all moved to town recently and were all upset by the Babar dominance and wanted our own spot. Rafael Carvajal was kind of the ringleader. He had the most energy and the biggest mouth, so he set up most of the events.

There were readings in North Beach run by Paul Landry at the Gallery Cine-Cal. That's where I met Raf and most of the others. Paul got so sick of us reading there that he quit hosting the readings. Raf took over and we quickly alienated the older set.

I mention this because it was the basis for starting the Chameleon. Cine-Cal shut down in '90 and the Chameleon started in March '91. I wanted a place for the younger crowd to go, for the good poets on the scene who were being ignored. We do have the rowdiest open mike in the free world, but sometimes it's just a little too much. Maybe I'm just tired of seeing it all over again. Old faces are gone, replaced by duplicates who think they're original. God damn it, the crowd used to shut up for the good stuff. Really they did. That doesn't happen anymore.

NEXT...: What's it like to be seen as a major player in the scene?

SINISTER: A lot of the newer poets keep asking me to help them in some way or another. They see my book out, see my Chameleon gig, and think everything is just rosy. Seriously, people have come up to me and asked me if poetry was my job. Can you imagine? There's a lot of people out there who think I'm a pro. Good god. A year ago my take-home pay was 200 dollars a week. They want me to get them gigs and book deals, when it's all I can do to get that myself. I've got a book of short stories that have kept editor's desks from floating up to the ceiling since June, and they want me to get them published? I usually just try to point them in the right direction, towards presses that would actually look at their stuff, but sometimes they still get mad like "all he has to do is make a call from the red phone in his bedroom and I'm in..."

NEXT...: Where do you think the scene is headed?

SINISTER: I'd like there to be a system much like the comedy scene has for touring and doing shows. They have money, though, and we don't. Not that we couldn't. It hasn't happened yet. It needs to.

Comedians go to clubs and stay there a week. Now, I'm not expecting that, but in S.F. we can put up a poet every night in a different place. So they come to S.F. for a week, do the town and it's close, but not the same. We need to have a step up. A better place. Reading first before an open mike isn't all that great. It would be nice to be able to put up a poet at the Fillmore, Slim's, or DNA, at least once a month, or early weekend shows.

The slams are interesting in that they can get some of the public interested. It shouldn't be limited to that. The Chameleon draws a lot of non-poets to watch the hate. I know if I had just a little quality control I could fill a room to see four good poets. That's one of the things I'm going to try at the Kilowatt.

I think touring is the next step for underground poets to conquer.

The next problem we would have would be money. Once we find the money to pay traveling poets, the whole shebang will get ugly. People and money, you know. A lot of poets will get even more pissy than they are now, and the majority of poets who make it will be the most generic writers you can imagine.

NEXT...: Favorite poetry journal?

SINISTER: Let's go down the list: University mags. Nobody reads these things. Not even the people who get published in them. A bunch of dry boring crap picked out by a bunch of students who are doing it for college credit. The work is picked by committee, almost guaranteeing that anything risky is going to be rejected.

Hoity Toity mags. *Paris Review, Granta*, etc. A few dozen people read these. Some of these will have good stuff in now and again, but the competition is so damn stiff jerks like us don't have a prayer. C'mon, do they really want to take one of my stories when they can publish Joyce Carol "Story Factory" Oates? Hell no! And I don't blame them one bit! They've got a hard enough time selling the mags without filling up the pages with writers that are going to keep the magazine on the shelf.

Fanzine Mags. *Chiron Review, Wormwood Review,* etc. These have a lot of good writing. Bukowski School poets. Where the heck are they? I used to buy them at Small Press Traffic, but now, there's nowhere good to get them. City Lights is dropping the ball on this one. Maybe I'm just too lazy to be sending off that many poems in the mail.

Local Mags, Freebie Mags. *Next…, Cups, Bull Horn,* etc. These magazines are money holes. Anyone who runs them better like what they're doing or they're going to go under. They turn out the best poems, because they don't care about sales. People actually read these because they're free. *Cups* is one of those things people pick up while fucking around in a cafe or a bar. Would you ever pay for the *Bay Guardian* if it was a quarter? Nope.

One thing we don't have is a national poetry mag that would do for the scene what *Maximum Rock and Roll* did for punk rock. *Next…* is a good example of what I'm talking about, but it's mostly Southern Cal. I'm not saying they should change at all, but I'm saying someone should do a *Next…* style mag for the whole country. An office in every poetry scene, and it all gets sent together and mailed in and mushed up into one mag every month. It could happen, but lord knows I don't have the organizational skills to make it work.

NEXT…: Fave reading?

SINISTER: The most entertaining open mike I've ever seen was the Klubstitute. It was run by Diet Popstitute. The scene was young, queer, and crazy. Anything was liable to happen. I remember the first Sick and Twisted players show. They did a stage version of Carrie, all in drag. I'm pretty sure I saw Elvis Herselvis there. Gwenfish and Bucket were there. Most of the people from then are gone doing something else now, and I never see them at open mike-type things. Diet showed me what it's all about. He proved to everyone that there was talent lying dormant inside them.

I wanted the Chameleon to have the same kind of flair, but it didn't work out that way. I like to think that I helped some people realize they had a few poems in them, convinced some people to express themselves.

NEXT…: Fave Poet?

SINISTER: In my opinion, Bukowski was the greatest American poet that ever was. Fuck Yeah.

An interesting phenomenon is the amount of people who started writing after reading this guy. I think it would outnumber the beats, definitely. As time goes on, it's only going to get bigger.

Who are we? Bukowski Nation? The Little Bukowskis? The Bukowski School? Team Bukowski? Definitely he's the first guy I think of when someone asks me about influences or what style I use. I'm not even close to the beat poets.

(2/98)

GERALD LOCKLIN

By Rita Mitzner

Dr. Gerald Locklin is well known and respected for his longstanding career as a professor of English Literature and Creative Writing at California State College, Long Beach, as well as his poetry. His own educational background stems primarily from Catholic Schools. He credits the Jesuits' highly verbal approach to education as a key factor in producing verbal ability, and notes what he sees as the decline of said ability as correlating to the decline in classical education.

He began his teaching career in 1964, at Los Angeles State College. The following year, he began his career at Cal State, Long Beach, where he has taught for thirty-three years. It was on the Cal State campus that I spent a delightful hour with Professor Locklin and the following conversation unfolded.

NEXT...: Dr. Locklin, in addition to your teaching career, you've managed to create an international reputation as a writer of both prose and poetry. How have you managed to blend the art of both achievements?

LOCKLIN: Teaching is what I love to do. Some writers seem ashamed of saying they teach, as if it's only what they do to support themselves so they can write. I could never understand their shame in teaching. For me, it has always been a privilege.

When I started teaching in 1964, I found a stimulating flow between life and the classroom; there was no radical wall between learning and living, and no compartmentalization of teaching and writing. I was in an atmosphere rich in literature where I shared the work of great writers with my students. Reading such works and writing went hand in hand for me, and I found my activities as an instructor stimulated my own creativity in writing. Thirty-three years later, teaching is still a source of creative inspiration for me. I love coming to the campus and being with the students. Ninety-nine percent of the time I come out of the classroom feeling good about the experience and interaction I've had with them. So many people have jobs where they go home and it's Miller time, but teaching has been great for me; it fuels me for writing. My teaching and writing have fed one another and I've been privileged.

NEXT...: I guess it's fair to say then that the blending of teaching and writing has been a natural one for you. Does one give you a greater feeling of accomplishment than the other?

LOCKLIN: My writing gives me a great feeling of accomplishment, but my teaching provides me with the ongoing enjoyment of my students' accomplishments. Again, both teaching and writing are very satisfying.

NEXT...: Let's switch from your duality as teacher/writer and focus on your writing, specifically your poetry. You've spoken of knowing you wanted to write while you were still a child. I know that Dylan Thomas, an early favorite of yours, also felt called to write early on in life. He stated that he fell in love with words. What created and nurtured the desire in you to write?

LOCKLIN: Maybe it's in the genes, but my mother was an elementary school teacher, and she and my aunt, a stenographer, encouraged me to write by recording any verse I would come up with. My aunt would stand me on the bed and have me look out the window, ask me what I saw, and write my answer down. My mother read to me a great deal. I would choose a story that I wanted, then she would choose one she thought I should hear. Consequently, I was reading before kindergarten. I was always encouraged to read and write and felt very confident that I could do so. I just grew up thinking of myself as a writer, and I was made to feel proud of any accomplishments along those lines from an early age.

NEXT...: That idea of fostering and nurturing talent must have been valuable to you. You've certainly carried its principle into the poetry community through your personal support of so many of its activities, and professionally, you, amongst others at Cal State, have been instrumental in establishing an MFA program. Can you tell me the purpose in establishing the program? What makes it distinctive?

LOCKLIN: Well, the largest justification for its establishment is the need for it in this area. There are so many fine writers in this immediate area, and why should they have to go elsewhere to seek a writing program? The program is fairly new, and its candidates have been primarily drawn from a local pool of talented individuals. Our first graduating class included many fine students such as T. Thrasher, who is known in the performance poetry arena. T is an excellent example of a poet whose work became richer and more mature by being in the program. No one worked harder than T. No one put more of themselves into it. I'm very proud of what T accomplished and that he was able to flourish in our program. He is an excellent example of what a poet can achieve in a program that admires accessible poets such as Edward Field and Allen Ginsberg, has a staff influenced by Bukowski, and at the same time offers an academic program that isn't anti-academic.

As word of our students' success becomes known, I'm certain that the area from which our program draws its applicants will increase. The distinctiveness of our program lies in the acceptance of the wide variety of writing styles and experiences of our students, coupled with academic quality. We expect to see fine writers and capable teachers graduate from our MFA program.

NEXT...: You mention performance poetry. Our readers should know that you are a favorite reader at many venues. I've been to some of your readings, and you seem to derive a great deal of enjoyment from sharing your words. What is your opinion concerning performance poetry and print poetry?

LOCKLIN: Performance, or stand up poetry, is part of poetry's oral tradition. It goes back to Homer. In general, I don't like to hear actors read poetry because they tend to impose self and try to add too much to the words. I prefer a writer to read his own work and let the words do their thing. In my own readings, I don't perform. Oh, I might finish off with a little song and dance, but I prefer not to perform my poetry. I want to let the words stand. That doesn't mean that others shouldn't use elements of performance in their reading, it just means I don't like to in mine.

The music of what the poet writes is of prime importance. Poetry is the music of language. There's music to the poetry of Pope, Dylan Thomas, and to Bukowski's poetry, in the organization of words, the rhythm of words. And it can occur in one or two lines or fifty. In my poem "Why I Don't Teach Kindergarten," there is only one line: "No night classes." I could have said, there aren't any classes at night, there are no evening classes, etc., but the alliteration in the one line is musical. The words fit together to form a nice sound. Music is the essence of poetry, and I like to read it on the page and hear it in my mind. I don't think poetry must be read out loud; it can be read in the silence of the mind. The value of poetry readings is the social aspect it adds to poetry, the focus it gives on a poet's work, and the fun to be had between poets and audience. In the old days, poetry readings were an excuse to party. They brought people together. Today there's a fascination with the non-print media and the stage. That may pass, but I don't believe print will disappear. There's too much social convenience involved.

NEXT...: I think it is fair to say that you are a beloved part of the local poetry community. Many poets and students you have taught call you "Uncle Jerry." They obviously hold great affection for you as well as respect for your teaching and writing accomplishments. It would be great if more poets could profit from your mentoring. So, to that end, what would you say are some of the important things a person must do to improve their writing?

LOCKLIN: Henry James said, "A great writer is one upon whom nothing is lost." So my advice to writers is to be open to learning and adding to resources by reading as widely as possible, learning as much as possible through books and personal experience, and journalizing all that occurs. A great reservoir of material and ideas can be created this way.

Most of all, practice writing. Don't view yourself as a genius: practice, work, learn new techniques. Oh, and pay attention to grammar and spelling!

NEXT...: Spoken like a true writer and teacher.

(3/98)

REGIE CABICO

Interview by Victor D. Infante

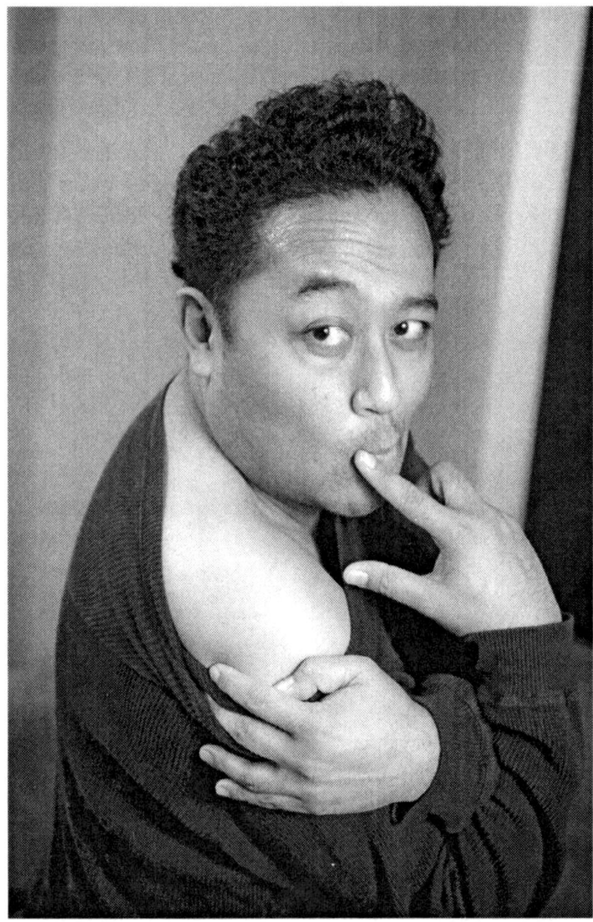

Regie Cabico, a 27 year-old actor turned poet from New York, has found himself in the middle of some the most controversial situations imaginable in today's poetry scene, and yet has managed to maintain a reputation for being one of the nicest guys in poetry. A strikingly unique voice, even in New York City, the young, gay Phillipino poet emerged in 1994 from the Nuyorican Poets Cafe, the much-venerated "star factory" of New York poetry.

Born in Baltimore, Cabico moved to Clinton, Maryland, when he was seven. "The big thing about Clinton is the liquor store," says Cabico, in a recent telephone interview. "The town is about half redneck and half black. Being between two cultures made me very observant — aware of differences between groups.

I moved around a lot, and it was very important to me to fit into groups. I learned early to fit into as many groups as possible — a lot of that was through humor.

"I graduated NYU in 1992, then took a year off" he continues. "After that year, I was ready to perform, to act. I worked Pan-Asian Repetoire, and I hated the experience. I was treated horribly... I did stand-up comedy — I'm very comfortable with stand up, but I hate comedians. They're really very bitter people. I was writing a lot of 'Asian-American' poetry and a lot of 'gay' poetry at the time. I decided to make fiction, but I also submitted for a poetry class, and got in! It was really intimidating, but I did well in the class.

"Then I started to read at every open mic in New York, including the slam at the Nuyorican. It looks like this deserted saloon from the wild west, and they were scoring my poems! I thought, 'This is a joke. This doesn't really mean any thing,' then I realized that I wanted that $5 prize. I decided I wanted to win! It took me four weeks to win. People gave me a standing ovation, and I started to cry. Here I was, an actor, not really appreciated for what I wanted to do, and here I was in this cafe. I think it was God saying, 'don't go to law school, don't listen to what they say, keep writing.'"

And he did. Shortly after winning the Slam, Cabico qualified for the New York National Slam Team. In addition, he had his first published poem appear in *In The Name Of Love: 100 Classic Gay Love Poems* — a major anthology. Riding a wave of uproarious critical approval, Cabico found himself with a short video on MTV (which he says was a miserable experience), and as a road poet for the 1994 Lollapalooza concert.

"I felt like, 'Yeah! I'm a poet.' I could be broke, I could bounce five checks. But if I write one poem, I'm so happy. But really, I feel that my genre is performing, if people call me a performance poet — that's the term I hate the most. I think it's a misconception, that it's an excuse for people who can't write. Call me a 'cabaret poet,' give me a jazz band and let me do Judy Garland impersonations and let me tell jokes. I write poems, but in some ways it's a ghetto. I think poetry was never meant to be commercial, unless you do something with it — music, dance, theater. The biggest battle has been for me to do my own solo show. I've been envious of a lot of poets who have crossed over. I think the problem with me is I don't know what it would be yet. It really hasn't dawned on me. I think I'd like it to be a lot like Denis Leary, only I'd be less abrasive."

Cabico is an engaging performer. While his poetry itself is whimsical and delicate, Cabico shakes up his set with everything from physical humor to the best Tina Turner impersonation that this writer has ever seen (and trust me, he's seen a few.) To top it off, his timing is impeccable. "I had a boyfriend who was scared I'd write about him," he recounts at a recent reading at Providence, Rhode Island's AS 220, "and I told him I wouldn't, so this poem is called, "I WANT TO MAKE OUT WITH MARK BIBBENS!" The audience erupted into laughter.

Cabico's recent accomplishments are numerous, including being published in several major anthologies, including *On a Bed of Rice: An anthology of Asian American Poets*, and *Aloud: Voices from the Nuyorican Poet's Cafe*, as well as appearing on Mouth Almighty Record's CD, *Grand Slam: Poetry from the 1994 National Poetry Slams*. Although a member of the champion 1997 National Slam Team, sponsored by Mouth Almighty records, Cabico believes that, for now at least, that might not be the avenue for him.

"I feel I don't know what the slam is — it's changed. I've been away for two years — I don't know what kind of place it has for me. I'm grateful to the slam, it gave me a built-in audience, but I'm sort of perplexed to how it's growing and what sort of place it has for me. The real slam is outside the slam — being able to write the next poem. That's the pain of art. When you do a play, it's not enough that the words are great, you have to do it each night. Each night it can fall apart in your hands. I'm so happy I've left the competition behind — emphasize 'competition' at all cost. It's really important that the teams still be friends afterwards. I think that's where the beauty is."

(3/98)

SUZANNE LUMMIS AND THE LOS ANGELES POETRY FESTIVAL
By Daniel McGinn

Some of you may remember the good old days between 1989 and 1994, when The L.A. Poetry Festival was a festival with events taking place all over the city. The L.A. Poetry Festival continues to exist today as an organization, but not as a festival. They still sponsor events but on a smaller scale. And they are planning to have a city-wide festival again in 1999, when we will need to party like it's 1999, because of the approaching millennium.

The L.A. Poetry Festival's director Suzanne Lummis, who explained all of this to me, is a charming and complex woman. A study in paradox. Lummis can be simultaneously sarcastic and serious. As a poet, teacher, editor, and promoter, she carries in her waif-like frame a quiet strength and authority that might be more at home in a world leader than in a starving poet. She is a poet by choice, a poet of national reputation. I asked her how long she had been involved in poetry. "I told my parents that I was going to be a poet when I was nine," Lummis replied, "and I did not know anybody who was a poet. So I couldn't have been influenced by anybody I knew, but my family had a great appreciation of literature. I don't know how I came upon the idea that it was possible to be a poet. I had a volume called, *Children's Poems: Old and New*, so I knew that there were people out there who were poets." Lummis holds workshops in her home and teaches extension classes at UCLA. In 1996 she was awarded the outstanding teacher of the year award for her work with the UCLA Extension Writers Program. Recently I learned that she was influential in the beginnings of the new and improved Valley Contemporary Poetry series.

The VCP Connection

"Brendan [Constantine] and Nicole [Harvey] were both in my class and you know that I recommended them to become the directors of The Valley Contemporary Poetry series. And then they brought in Robert Arroyo and Robert Wynne. That's because I had the sense that they were people who were really ambitious.

I pushed them and I gave them as much support as I could because I sensed that they had a vitality and a charm. An intelligence and a talent. I would like to see this become not only an energetic scene but one that's producing talent."

The Future: It Only Takes a Few.

I asked Ms. Lummis how she felt about the future of Los Angeles poetry. The extended quote that follows is her response.

"L.A. hasn't quite achieved respect. Respect, I think, is still a ways down the line. What's beginning to happen is a few terrifically well -informed adventurous spirited people out there beyond Los Angeles, all the way over to the East Coast and New York, are beginning to look toward Los Angeles and getting the sense that something interesting is going on here and they don't quite know what it is yet. Nobody is saying that the great poetry of the fin de millennium is emerging from Los Angeles but that there is a scene that is so dynamic and very distinctive. It only takes a few people to emerge from a particular literary world in order for many people to begin to say that this is a movement. You know, Charles Webb is having a lot of success, incredible success, the kind that really counts. The book that he just published came about because he won the Samuel French Morse Award, which is quite respected. It only requires a handful of people to achieve some very unusual success to shape peoples opinion of the whole region. I mean, how many of the beat poets were very interesting writers? Two? Maybe there were three that were doing really interesting work. Then, many, many hangers-on — people who just happened to be there at the time that something terrifically exiting was happening, so they benefited from that. Even the Black Mountain scene, you can mention a few legendary people that emerged from there but you probably can't mention a dozen. It only takes a few people."

Central Library Newer Poets Reading in April

The Los Angeles Poetry Festival will be joining hands with Beyond Baroque for Newer Poets III. This event will be held on April 22nd in the Marc Taper Auditorium at the Central Library in Los Angeles. Six poets will be showcased at this reading. The poets chosen by Beyond Baroque are Robert Arroyo Jr. of the Valley Contemporary Poets, Sara MacLay, author of *Weeding the Duchess*, and AK Toney, featured in the anthologies *Catch the Fire and Tough Love: The Life & Death of Tupac Shakur*. The poets that were chosen by L.A. Poetry Festival are William Archila, whose work appears in *New to North America: Writings by Immigrants*, Carine Topal, author of *God as Thief*, and Jan Wesley of the Hyperdisc Poets.

Illustration of Suzanne Lummis by Michael Paul

Newer Poets III will introduce "the people who will shape the community and the future of poetry in Los Angeles," Lummis explained. "Beyond Baroque picked people that they were championing and we picked people that we are championing. In this way we introduce new poets — not necessarily younger — to each other and to a larger audience. We're trying to champion people who are working very hard, writing well and who are involved in the community."

The Auction

I was invited, as a *Next...* reporter, to attend a fund-raising benefit auction to help finance the 1999 L.A. Poetry Festival blowout. It happened in an upscale neighborhood in the hills above Los Angeles under the shadow of El Nino clouds. I was greeted at the door that Saturday afternoon by auctioneer Brendan (cleanhead) Constantine. He was dressed to the nines in black trousers, big shoes and a spiffy Punjab that he claimed he had stolen from a waiter. In the room behind him there were people in suits and dresses sampling hors d'oeuvres and sipping coffee (pinkies extended) from china cups. I immediately felt underdressed. I was wearing thrift shop denim trousers and an old flannel shirt. Mr. Constantine grabbed me by the collar and warned me to remain calm because there were patrons of the arts in attendance. He knew, from personal experience, that they could smell fear.

This fund raiser was an experiment, Suzanne Lummis' idea. Rather than auctioning off paintings or cars, the L.A. Poetry Festival auctioned off poems, handwritten and signed by some of America's finest living poets: Tess Gallagher, Donald Hall, Robert Creeley, Naomi Shihab Nye, W.S. Merwin, Steve Kowit, Robert Hass, Diane Wakowski, Billy Collins, and Rose Styron to name but a few.

Unfortunately, Mr. Constantine lost his gavel in a yachting accident and was forced to use the blunt end of an ice pick to indicate when the bidding was closed. He never showed any fear, not for a moment. I've never seen anything quite like this auction. Each of the poems were performed before the bidding started. The pieces were read by Laurel Ann Bogen, Charles Webb, Suzanne Lummis and Alicia Vogl Saenz. Willie Sims, L.A.'s storyteller poet closed the evening by performing two original pieces that were also sold in the auction. Poems were auctioned off for as little as twenty five dollars and as much as four hundred dollars (for "The Art of Disappearing" by Naomi Shihab Nye). Before the event was over, I found myself bidding on poems although I had no intention of doing so. I was reminded of the days when I used to take my children to baseball card shows. I would get so caught up in the excitement of trading, I would come home with cards of my own.

After the auction, I was given a chance to sit and talk with Suzanne Lummis. I asked for her reaction to the event. She assured me that it had been a fiscal success but one thing surprised her. "By and large," Lummis said, "it was the poets in the audience who were the most fervent bidders. And that amazed me. I thought it would be some well-to-do people who came, who were maybe art collectors and had an interest in culture but weren't necessarily interested in poetry, but had a lot of money. Instead it was poets, who don't necessarily have a lot of money."

Personally, I'm not surprised. Unless I'm mistaken, it is poets who buy the majority of poetry sold in bookstores. If another poet's work has touched my life and influenced me as a writer, a poem, handwritten and signed by that author would be an invaluable and very personal thing to own.

I'd trade you my Kirby Puckett rookie card for a signed Billy Collins poem.

(4/98)

JEFFREY MCDANIEL

Interview by Victor D. Infante

Jeff McDaniel's poetry is marked by an unusual empathy for human nature and unrelentingly startling imagery. In his poem "Leonard," published in Volume II of *Beyond the Valley of the Contemporary Poets*, he writes, "The boy was bright, like the retarded girl/ he set on fire. No one predicted she'd ever be/ so understood." In these dark lines, McDaniel speaks volumes.

A recent transplant to Los Angeles, McDaniel quickly attracted attention as both a performance poet and a literary figure – being the first poet to have competed at the National Poetry Slam Finals as well as be published in *Best American Poetry*.

"I knew I wanted to be a poet when I was very young" says McDaniel, "although I had read very few contemporary poems. I wrote my first poem at 14. I was very bad at that point. I don't know why I chose to express myself in that medium — I hung out mostly with the delinquents at that time. I used a lot of drugs, and expressed myself in notebooks, mostly rhymes."

Born in Philadelphia, PA, McDaniel attended Sarah Lawrence University in Bronxville, NY, in 1986, where he studied with major poet Thomas Lux, author of the acclaimed poetry collection, *Split Horizon*.

"They had a very high power writing program there," he explains. "Freshmen can study right away with the big people. There's no hierarchy." He later attended graduate school at George Mason University in Washington, D.C. It was there that he first became exposed to the idea of "performance poetry."

"I loved to perform. I actually first performed my poetry in 1984, when I did a seven-minute poetry show with dance and music for my school talent show. I didn't do anything multi-media again until grad school — thought it wasn't my cup of tea or too artsy or something."

McDaniel was drawn to the D.C. Poetry Slam through a newspaper article in 1993. It was at the slam that McDaniel encountered the local poetry scene, including his future slam teammate D.J. Renegade, who appears in the *Catch the Fire* anthology.

"The slam was a very different atmosphere for me – you have people who do stand up, or are actors – you had people who are coming from different points of view… Going to Nationals really blew my mind — I heard a lot of what I thought wasn't poetry at that time… It expanded my consciousness… I couldn't conceive of the sort of things that people were doing."

It was at the Nationals in '93, in San Francisco, where the publishers of Manic D Press heard his poem "Following Her to Sleep."

"That's when Manic D offered to print my book, *Alibi School*," says McDaniel. "I would have never met those people if not for that." The poem appeared in *Ploughshares*, and was selected to appear in *Best American Poetry*.

Later, McDaniel had a chance to see the editor of that issue read. "I was surprised because his work is not at all like mine. I was pretty freaked out."

Press photo of Jeffrey McDaniel

McDaniel moved to Los Angeles in September of 1996. "One of the reasons," he says, "was that this isn't Tulsa. This is a big place and I thought that, when I'm 50 years old, I can say that I moved to a bigger city and tried to make something of myself. I was a big fish in a small pond in D.C., and I had lived in New York and I didn't want to live there again, so I moved to L.A. – a place I never thought I would live…

"There really are a lot of great writers out here that I'd never heard of. There's not enough connection between L.A. and the rest of the country. There's a real prejudice against L.A. — one of the worst things about L.A. is going elsewhere and putting up with some smart-ass making comments. It's like the slam. I don't mind someone who's done it making comments, but it's hard to take it from outsiders. If you go to one slam, it's very different than another. L.A.'s like that. If you don't like the poets at one reading, you might like them at another."

In addition to finishing his forthcoming book, McDaniel also produced a CD entitled *Meow*, which highlighted a number of poets from around the country. He is currently hard at work producing a follow-up, *Tongue in Both Ears*, which will feature himself, Beth Lisick, Justin Chin, Ellyn Maybe, Matt Cook, and Kenny Carroll.

"We'll need one of these parental stickers" he quips. "We'll sell them over time, 'cause it's a good product. It was recorded at Luna Park here in LA and at the Black Cat at Washington D.C., a big punk rock club that I used to do shows at – I miss that. D.C. was so simple, there's only a couple of everything, but here there's so much."

(4/98)

MATTHEW NIBLOCK
By Daniel McGinn

Matthew Niblock is extraordinarily gifted. I would imagine that Niblock's musical career began at birth. When the doctor held his feet and slapped his bottom he extended his arms and gave out a cry with perfect pitch. A cry that pierced the air, rising up into high octaves that lasted several minutes. I can't imagine it being any other way. Niblock sang in gospel choirs as a child. His debut, at age eight, was at the Angelus temple in an Opera called *Majesty*. Between the age of 9 to the age of 14 Matthew and his sister were professional Christian recording artists, singing on a number of children's records.

As Loudon Wainwright III once pointed out, there is yet to be a perfectly straight line. The road that led to the development of the band, Clear, and their recent CD, *Refrain*, was a long and winding one. Clear features Matthew as lead vocalist, songwriter, and "tyrant." In his secular lifetime Matthew Niblock has worked with numerous musicians, and bands "fraught with trouble." At one point, when Niblock was fronting the band October, there were deals, a demo disc and shows that sparked enough interest in Niblock's vocal ability that he was considered as a replacement for Natalie Merchant when she left 10,000 Maniacs.

October (the band, not the month) was looking for a new guitarist when they auditioned "this surfer dude from Orange County, named Marc Smith." Matthew left October to work with Smith. "He was great," Matthew said. "The other players in the band didn't like him and I was just stunned. I was like, what the fuck is the matter with you? I was trying to make this band rock a little harder because it certainly didn't. That, plus the pressure that was happening because of this 10,000 Maniac's thing — we just blew up in the course of an evening — and the band was over. I called Marc on the phone and said, well, we have to start a band together because you're the greatest guitar player in the land. We started working together, writing songs together, and we started playing at poetry shows of mine and etc."

According to Niblock, *Refrain*, Clear's CD, "is the product of two and a half years start to finish, with almost a year and a half in between of nothing. The record began with me and Marc and our hired players.

Everybody in our band is on that record, everybody in our band was a hired player, at some point or another, but they aren't any more. The great privilege of the whole thing is, with the exception of Jennifer [Hardaway], who's becoming less and less an exception to this rule all the time, everybody in my band except for me plays music for a living. Nobody in my band plays gigs for free. Nobody. But they are all in this band because they want to be in this band and nobody's making a dime. I think that's the most flattering and coolest thing that's happened to me musically in my life so far. What's happened, over time, is we've played lots and lots of shows together and we've written lots of songs together and we don't really sound much like that record anymore."

NEXT…: I was surprised by the record. I was expecting "Marianne," "The House I Live In," "Jealousy," "Boxing The Sky"… But I like it.

NIBLOCK: We recorded all of those songs. I didn't like them.

NEXT…: How did it get compiled?

NIBLOCK: We threw out half of what we started with, recorded a few new songs, but most of the songs on that record are at least four years old, except for "Blue Satellite" and "Nazareth by Rail."

NEXT…: "Nazareth by Rail" started out as a poem then it became a song. Is that the process? Or does it start with the music?

NIBLOCK: It happens either way. A lot of those songs started as poems. In fact, about half of the songs on that record have been published as poems. "Nazareth by Rail" happened because Jennifer Hardaway came over to my apartment one day with a guitar. She strummed a couple of chords in a tuning that she'd never played in before and I went, "Wow, that sounds cool, let's write a song around that." We sat there for half an hour and I sang a bunch of nonsense lyrics and da da da da da and tried to write something and I couldn't come up with anything. So I said, "uhhhhmmm, hold on!" And I dug a copy of *Caffeine* out of the bottom of a drawer and started adapting the poem into the song and it just happened to work. Now, and in the past couple of years, the music and the lyrics generally come at the same time. I write while they are playing the music to me. Most of the time.

NEXT…: Your song "On the Radio" was a most pleasant surprise. It gave me chills when Ellyn Maybe came in and began reciting "Tent." It's probably the clearest (no pun intended) I've ever heard Ellyn Maybe recite. How did that come about, getting Ellyn into the mix?

NIBLOCK: That was one of the songs left over from the original recording sessions. In our original mix the bridge was filled up with static noises and talking voices and it was cool but it didn't really kill me. I thought, I'd really like to have a spoken part here but I don't want to do it myself. I don't have a poem that short, for one, and I don't have

Illustration of Matthew Niblock by Michael Paul

anything that would fit into that context. I tried to write something and I wound up just sort of rehashing my own lyrics to the song. I'm never sure what my own songs are about, to tell you the truth, but one of the points I was trying to make in the song is that every voice is important and you have to hear everything. You have to listen to everything. I just adore Ellyn Maybe, she was amazing in the studio. That's the second complete take, with no overdubs. And the only reason we didn't use the first take is that the recording engineer wasn't fast enough to realize that she was going to get it the first time. She was astonishing. It was perfect. And I love that poem. And it was short enough. And I knew that KCRW would play it if we put her on it.

NEXT…: But they haven't, have they?

NIBLOCK: Man in the Moon played that song once. I think.

NEXT…: Another thing that struck me is that a lot of the CD is not radio friendly — it's more artistic than that.

NIBLOCK: That has been a big problem, so far. Record people are frightened of it. So they go, you know, if you would just write a song with pop guy, blah blah blah — and I go write a song with pop guy and it still sounds like me. I'm the issue, not my players.

NEXT…: You say, "I don't completely know what my songs are about." One person I know, a fundamentalist, Christian, he found your songs disturbing, a little offensive, a little flippant about things biblical.

NIBLOCK: Oh, then he's completely mistaken.

NEXT…: OK.

NIBLOCK: It isn't flippant at all.

NEXT…: Let me give you the contrast. I play it for somebody else. They react with, "That's awfully religious."

NIBLOCK: (Laughs.)

NEXT…: So you have two different people listening to two different CDs when they pop it on. What is your take on that? I almost feel that this is the obligatory question.

NIBLOCK: First of all, I'm sort of pleased by reactions like that. Because once I write a song, I don't really feel like I'm responsible for it anymore. It is what it is. It may have had some very particular meaning to me when I wrote it and there may be some hidden context of subtext that only I would understand. You know, I mean, seventy-five percent of that record are songs that were written while I was getting a divorce. They're about that relationship and about my ex-wife. "Nazareth by Rail" is not, for instance. People get to decide what they think it's about for themselves.

NEXT…: But you were offended by the word "flippant."

NIBLOCK: Well, I'll get to that in a second and I'll tell you why. I've always felt that way about any kind of artistic expression or creative expression that I've managed to force up. Once it's out of my head it's out of my hands. I've had people come up to me with the most astonishing interpretations of my poetry. I don't even know what poem they are talking about until they give me a couple of lines from it. That's OK. I like that. I think that means I'm doing my job well.

I am offended a little bit by that "flippant" idea. My faith and/or loss of faith is the most serious issue in my life. It's the most important thing that ever happened to me or that will ever happen to me. I don't have the slightest fucking idea what the truth is but I spent a long, long, long childhood convinced that I knew the truth. It was only as I got a little older and shot a little heroin… (Laughs.) I sort of was, you know, stricken with the idea that maybe I was wrong and so those things that might be interrupted as flippant are really painful. Having faith is a great thing. Being unable to have faith is a terrifying thing. It's not like I'm saying, "Oh gee, I don't feel like believing in God today." I frequently find myself unable to believe even though I'd very much like to.

NEXT…: What is it like to be Matthew Niblock? You walk into a poetry reading the reaction is, "Oh, he's here." How do you respond to that? Do you like that or do you not like that?

NIBLOCK: Well, of course I like that. I think that's cool, but that's because I'm such an arrogant son of a — no, that's not really even all that true. The dichotomy about that sort of thing is that, obviously, and this works for everybody who stands up in front of people and reads their poems, sings songs, or acts, or does whatever, we do want to be noticed and we want people to pay attention to us. We're definitely going for some sort of connection with the audience and we want them to clap when we're done. If they don't clap when we're done that's a bad sign, but on the other hand it still makes me intensely uncomfortable. I have incredibly bad stage fright in every context. I have stage fright when I'm singing in front of hundreds of people and I have stage fright when I'm reading a poem for four people at Sam's Book City. It's always a frightening experience.

NEXT...: You realize that if this gets picked up by a distributor and something happens with it, all of that is going to be intensified.

NIBLOCK: I hope so. I'd like very much to do this for a living, that's such a novel concept. It would be really cool.

(5/98)

UTAH PHILLIPS
By Victor D. Infante

As a long time fan of alternative/ folk/rock musician Ani DiFranco, I was delighted one day when I walked into the record store and discovered *The Past Didn't Go Anywhere*, an album credited to both DiFranco and Utah Phillips, a name which was, at the time, unfamiliar to me.

Much to my delight, I discovered that this was less a rock n' roll album than a Spoken Word Collection, with stories and tall tales by Phillips backed by melodic acoustic guitar by DiFranco. I enjoyed the CD immensely. Reading through the liner notes, I discovered that the spoken word recordings were all done at various times and locations, and that DiFranco collected them, and recorded the music separately — all in one sitting. It's a truly remarkable album — spontaneous, quick moving, solidly produced and captivating. Phillips is a consummate story-teller, with impeccable timing and a fun, conversational delivery.

Utah Phillips was born in Cleveland, Ohio, in 1935, although his family moved to Salt Lake City in 1947, where he was raised, and where he began making forays into the wilderness – the start of his affection for the natural world. Currently, he lives in Nevada City, California, with his wife, Joanna Robinson.

"I get away with whatever I can, wherever I am," says Phillips, in a recent interview with *Next...* "Whenever I do a story-telling festival, people say 'how come you sing so much?' and when I do a folk concert, people say 'how come you talk so much?' I can't win either way.

"Since I've gotten into this trade I've felt that what happened between the songs is as important as the song itself, that the song introductions are as important as the songs themselves."

Phillips left Utah (the state) in 1969. "There was a political blacklist, and I was on it," he says. "After that, a good friend steered me towards singing songs and telling stories." His career began at a place called Cafe Lena, in Saratoga, New York, which had a stage for musicians in the front, and a room in the back where they produced small plays. Phillips noted that one of the one man shows being produced in the back while he started was by spoken word giant Spalding Gray.

"I've always told stories," says Phillips. "When you're a little kid and you come home late, and come up with an excuse, that's storytelling. Some people give it up when they become 'blown-ups,' as we like to call them around here. I never did…

"A good story has a beginning, a middle and an end, some sort of incremental repetition and everything [in it is] related. You can have a whale of a good story, and if it's badly delivered, a whale of a good story can turn into a boffo. I want the house lights up when I'm telling stories so I can see the far corners. I decide whether they're quick or slow so I can adjust my timing."

For Phillips, it's important that he stays at a pace that's enjoyable for the audience. When he does a performance, he uses humor, absurdity and "blather," to use his own words, as a means of loosening up the audience. He claims he likes to keep things loose and friendly. "Then we have time to talk about why I'm really there."

To date, Phillips has ten albums and has appeared on seventy-three audio anthologies, doing both music and spoken word. He claims the reviews on his music are mixed, but a 1992 appearance in Orange County received glowing praise from then LA Times journalist Jim Washburn.

The Past Didn't Go Anywhere finds its origins with Phillips and DiFranco, who share the same agent, being boarded together in the same house in Philadelphia. "She kind of skipped out with a tape I made in Ithaca, New York." Claiming, "I want my younger audience to hear these stories," she asked Phillips to send her all his recordings so she could record them.

Although he's made his career as a folk musician and storyteller by touring across the United States, a recent heart attack has forced him to reduce the amount of time he spends on the road. Currently, he has a talk and spoken word radio show on KVMR in Nevada City, which is syndicated and plays on KPFK, Los Angeles, KPFA, Berkeley and WABI, New York.

He also continues to perform at storytelling festivals from time to time, and continues to MC events for the Redwoods Alliance, an environmental group dedicated to Redwood Forest preservation. He is perpetually working on a recorded "song book," but has no idea when it will come out. He has a storytelling album, on Redhill Records, which is about half completed.

Although his material is highly enjoyable and layered with depth and social observation, Phillips sees himself as a poor writer — that is to say, the physical act of writing. As such, he has no plans to sit down and publish a written book. Says Phillips, "The world I've created is one of speakers and listeners."

(5/98)

Press photo of Utah Phillips

PATRICIA SMITH

Interviewed by Charles Ellik

Patricia Smith is a monument. For those readers who haven't witnessed her, especially in heated competition, there are no words to do her justice. I saw her win her fourth National Slam Championship, sending 1,700 plain folks to a standing ovation. In Chicago and Boston her name is synonymous with the Slam, and is often used as an exemplar of what this form can be. It should be no surprise her poetry also stands solid on the page. She is extensively published and has three books to her credit — all in multiple printings. Many Slammers don't realize she is also a well known journalist, and likely better recognized as one. I suffered a delicious jolt of recognition when I saw her face on the side of a bus while in Boston — advertising her column in *The Boston Globe* — but her eyes were closed, her head thrown back, her mouth wide open — her expression was pure poet. You'll have a chance to see her this year in Taos.

NEXT...: Thousands of people have seen you perform, but you are a columnist in a paper which circulates tens of thousands. Do you think more people know you as a performer or as a writer? Does this perception affect your work?

SMITH: It's hard to say. I travel in two completely different spheres which overlap in some very odd ways. When I first came to *The Boston Globe*, my editors were very supportive of my creative work, which I guess is rare in journalism circles. They understood that if I was to be a happy and productive newshound, I had to be a happy and productive poet. When I did a poetry/theater performance for eight weeks in the theater of Boston University, the two worlds collided once and for all. The lights came up on opening night, and every single editor at *The Globe* was in the house. They understood from the beginning that poetry is not something I do recreationally; it's an essential part of my total voice.

The fact that I'm a poet greatly influences my journalistic signature — I'm always looking for risks, always keenly concerned with rhythm; and you've noticed that many of my poems are rooted in real people, real stories. That's me drawing from what journalism has taught me.

Since my poetry/journalism careers grew side by side in Boston, most people who know about the paper know about the poetry. And it helps that *Globe* management continues to nurture both sides — for instance, every New Year's Day, I write a poem that takes up the entire Editorial page. When I'm asked to speak, the topic is often the intersection of journalism and the creative arts. I guess I'm a pretty intriguing hybrid.

NEXT...: Is your personal focus as a poet more on performance or the page?

SMITH: It's moving increasingly toward the page. I got my start on stage at the Green Mill, cutting my teeth on the slam, and I don't regret a single second of that experience. It gave me the guts I needed to open other doors and check out what was behind them. But the longer I write in other ways, the more I see the magic of being able to share those words with other people, many of whom would never and will never set foot in a poetry venue. But I try not to "set" my focus — one poem I write may be begging the take the stage, the next one languishes quite elegantly on the page. Usually I let the poem decide.

NEXT...: What does performing do for your writing, and vice-versa?

SMITH: Constantly performing my work makes me search for the unexpected perspective whenever I sit down to write. I want to take an ordinary thing — something everyone may be talking about — and make it extraordinary. So I have to turn my poem, my short story, my theater piece, upside down, inside out, until I know I've found the side no one's ever seen. What does my writing do for my performance? Not much. It's up to the voice to give the words life, very seldom the other way around.

NEXT...: Is there a difference in the way people who know you as a Slam Champ only treat you vs. people who know you only as a writer?

SMITH: There's more than a little unwarranted celebrity attached to the Slam — a bit of the rock `n' roll. It's a rush, but it helps to keep it in perspective. People who know me as a Slammer often want to challenge me in some way, break through what they see as a veneer developed for performance. Or they snap their fingers and want me to do somersaults. That's understandable — if I run into David Copperfield, the first thing out of my mouth would be "Do a trick." People who know

me as a writer want to have long, technical, imaginative discussions. They're hungry for craft. And I learn more from the community of writers than I do from the community of slammers. But it wasn't always that way. Much fire has been siphoned from the slam's belly.

NEXT...: We in this country still generally think of poetry as a written art. Do you agree?

SMITH: Nope. I'm a storyteller, and I've always considered poetry an aural, and oral, art. When you read a poem on the page, the poet's intention is always open to a number of interpretations. When you hear that poet do that poem, there's usually no room left for questions. That's why I'll never stop reading aloud, no matter how mired in the page I become. I've seen the faces of people who hear real, live, can't-back-away-from-it poetry for the first time, and there's nothing like it. I think poetry is why we have ears.

NEXT...: What is the difference between performance and the page?

SMITH: The page gives a poem legs; performance gives it breath.

NEXT...: Your new book — why isn't this a novel?

SMITH: It isn't a novel because it began with a newspaper story. Every year a statistic comes out that says, "A black male child born in this year won't live as long as a white male child." The statistic is released, every year, as regular as clockwork. And every year the media reacts in the same way. TV folks grab their mikes, newspaper folks grab their notebooks, and they all go rushing into the black community, go up to the first available black man they see, wave the statistic and screech, "Howdoesthismakeyoufeel?" So in '91, I decided to do it differently — I took my tape recorder and just interviewed as many black men as I could, just about their lives. Once the story was finished and in the paper, I still had all those myriad voices on tape, chilling me, encouraging me, haunting me. So I began

Photo of Patricia Smith by Michael Brown

to write poems, all with black men at the center. That was genesis of the book, although I've gotten ideas from it for short stories and plays.

NEXT...: Have you written a novel? If not, why not?

SMITH: I was right in the middle of one when I got a chance to write a companion book for a PBS series. I jumped at the chance to do a nonfiction book, and my novel — and, for all practical purposes, my poetry — took a back seat. Since the PBS project is a historical book, I'm dealing with scholars, massive revisions, nitpicking NYC editors. But it's an invaluable experience. And the novel will always be there.

NEXT...: Your work is very prose-y. Is this a conscious decision on your part? Does it come from a specific source/influence?

SMITH: It's not a conscious decision. I guess I love the "completeness" of a poem, and that means substance, rhythm, forward movement. We're all storytellers—and if you find every place where light touches down in a story, you have a poem.

NEXT...: Much of your work is written in the vernacular of the people you portray in your poems. Sometimes it sounds like your voice, but mostly it sounds like you, as a poet, are performing a sort of embodiment of this character, describing them as if they were describing themselves without any regard to who might be listening, sometimes even as such a person would never dare to describe themselves. A possession of sorts, or channeling, maybe. What do you call this voice/device?

SMITH: I don't really have a name for it. I think it comes from being a reporter for over twenty years, and teaching myself to see everything lurking behind what a person actually says. We're trained to look inside a person almost immediately, to put ourselves in their place, to tap into their motivations. So persona poems come naturally to me. When I sit down to write a newspaper story, I turn the expected upside down, inside out, to look for an unexpected perspective. And I usually find that perspective by stepping into the shoes of everyone involved in the story. When those babies feel the most uncomfortable, I start writing. Thus a poem like "Skinhead." Being "inside" that poem really scared me, but how else could I share that man's heart?

NEXT...: When you are on stage performing, it does not feel like acting, you are Patricia with this voice in her head, not only saying what they might say, but making Patricia's own choices, passing her own judgments. On the page it's not so clear, there is no physical Patricia there, you are more transparent. Sometimes it seems odd to have your characters describe themselves as if they are seeing themselves through Patricia's eyes. Is this a conscious choice?

SMITH: If your poem is going to come from a honest place, at some point you've got to let the character take over and lead both voices where he (or she) wants to go. At that moment, I let go of the choice. And you're right, on the page that's risky. But it's a risk worth taking.

NEXT...: Are all these voices yours?

SMITH: At the beginning of the writing, no. By the end of the performance, yes.

NEXT...: Many of your poems are based on specific people. Do you ever conduct interviews for your poems?

SMITH: I'm getting into that more lately, because I feel the need to approach many poems from a knowledgeable place. I don't conduct "formal" interviews — but I know I couldn't write or perform a poem about an undertaker without talking to one. Oh, and since I was an entertainment writer for a number of years, some of my poems are based on interviews I did long, long ago.

NEXT...: Race is an issue you confront in your work. Do you have goals you are working toward through it? What are they? What obstacles have you encountered?

SMITH: I just want people to look at each other. That doesn't mean a constant sympathetic portrayal of blacks and biting indictments of whites. It means daring to break the surface of our touted "dialogue on race." One of the ideas I'm tossing around for a new book is "White Men," a book of persona poems from that coveted place of privilege. Obstacles? Only those I create. And they're only created to be knocked down.

NEXT...: How are the issues of race and racism different in performance vs. print?

SMITH: When I perform, my perspective is unmistakable — because everyone can see that I'm a black woman. Sometimes it's hard for an audience to get past that. In print, I can screw around with perspective, play mind games, whatever I need to do to get my point across.

NEXT...: How do you feel race or ethnicity affects the voices of poets?

SMITH: You can't separate yourself from your skin, your ethnic background. Everything I do, say and write is through the lens of a black woman. I can move away from that by stepping into other shoes, but the feet in those shoes are always my own.

NEXT...: Many of your poems are about Black-ness, even White-ness. Is it possible to be a poet in this country and not reflect issues of race?

SMITH: Sure. Poets can ignore race just as easily as many of our countrymen ignore racial problems. It's probably a mistake, but it happens.

NEXT...: Where are you from?

SMITH: I'm from the West Side of Chicago, the part of town everyone tells you to stay away from. Proud of it.

NEXT...: Any road trip stories?

SMITH: A painting fell on my head in East Berlin. Michael and I had to read in Milwaukee to a bar full of bikers who were mourning a fallen comrade (and not expecting poetry). Expecting to die on the Autobahn. Reading to 25,000 Japanese businessmen. The trip to San Fran for the first National Slam Championships in 1990 was the best road trip ever. I am one of the few people alive who has seen Marc Smith gleefully jumping up and down on a bed, his head covered in shaving cream.

NEXT...: What projects do you have in the works?

SMITH: Hoping to record and tour with a jazz band I'm working with locally in Boston. The video of "Undertaker" was part of the Lifetime Network Women's Film Festival and won a Cable Ace Award — I'm dying to do more poetry videos, preferably with those angels at Tied to the Tracks or the inimitable Kurt Heintz. My novel is tapping me on the shoulder. And I'd like to release a volume of collected works sometime in the next year. And I'm a finalist for the Pulitzer Prize in commentary this year — by the time this runs, I will either have won or lost. If I win, they'll be chances for other projects.

NEXT...: How has your latest book done?

SMITH: I can get exact numbers if you need, but it's been reprinted. The previous book *Big Towns, Big Talk* is also in its second printing, and my first book, *Life According to Motown* is in its fourth reprinting.

NEXT...: Most poets come to the Nationals and to poetry readings with their books. You don't. Why not?

SMITH: I usually have my books somewhere — in the trunk of the car, stuffed into my suitcase, just not as visible. I guess the difference is that I don't rely on the sale of my books for income, so I don't push them as much. I usually have them available if someone asks.

NEXT...: Many performance poets have tapes of themselves to sell. Do you? Why/why not?

SMITH: I have a tape my publisher did a couple of years back. It was a recording of a live performance. I liked it, but he priced the tape too high, and I didn't feel comfortable asking audiences for eleven dollars. It's that simple. I'm also on several compilation CDs and tapes, but I don't have enough of a supply to sell. I guess I just haven't focused too heavily in that direction. With the jazz band, I'm starting to give it serious thought.

NEXT...: You are an active part of the Cantab [reading in Boston] when present, often motivating the crowd. What does running a reading do for your poetry?

SMITH: You get to listen to so many different voices — and, consciously or unconsciously, you draw from them all. Running a reading is beneficial because you gain access to so many worlds beyond your own. What's fascinating about hosting is the fact that everyone who walks through the door is a poet. That's all you know about them — no more, no less. And through the course of an evening, a month, a year, you see the real person emerge through his or her poetry. I've met some of my best friends that way.

NEXT...: Can you remember a favorite night at the Cantab?

SMITH: The first time we held a regional slam a few days before the Nationals. (Well, not exactly "regional" — there were teams from London, Detroit, Syracuse, etc.) Ten teams competed, both upstairs and downstairs, and came together for a grand finale at midnight. I've never felt so much excitement in the place, and it gave the locals a good taste of what national-level slamming was all about. Now, of course, we've made it an annual event.

NEXT...: A favorite feature, if different?

SMITH: Tim Seibles, during our annual Erotic Poetry Night. He's one tall, dark drink `o water, his poetry was luscious and languid, and inhibitions dropped all over the place. Mention the night, and people still sigh.

NEXT...: How do you feel about Slams?

SMITH: I think they're great, for some people. They're not for everyone. For instance, if you're looking to legitimize yourself as a poet, and you're counting on the "score" of some randomly-selected person to do it, then you're asking for trouble. A high score doesn't necessarily mean you're a good poet, and a low score doesn't mean you stink. It's just a delicious little crapshoot.

I also think the slam is invaluable for introducing the masses to poetry. Folks hear the buzzword or read some article on "trends," get together and say "Hey, let's go laugh at the poets." Then they find energy, talent and passion they weren't expecting. And they become bonafide members of the poetry posse.

NEXT...: What has Slamming done for you as a poet?

SMITH: It's made me more comfortable on stage, more aware of the audience, and it's taught me to draw deeply from the well each time I step on stage. It's also a tremendous confidence builder.

NEXT...: What makes Slams different from "normal" readings?

SMITH: The competition. The feverishly responsive audience. The promise of monetary reward.

NEXT...: How do the politics of the slam scene affect you? Does it ever influence your writing?

SMITH: I've tried to stay out of the politics by holding tight to memories of the early days. Marc and I get together and cry on each other's shoulders all the time. But when you have an influx of new, energetic people — who don't necessarily care that the slam has a "history" — and the slam is blanketing the country and moving abroad, there has to be system of management and there are bound to be power plays. I'm not crazy about it, but it's the price you pay for growth. If I let he-said-she-said-but-she-did-and-he-didn't affect my writing, then I'm definitely writing for the wrong reason.

NEXT...: How did you start writing poetry?

SMITH: In 1986, I went along to a poetry reading in Chicago with a colleague from the *Sun-Times*. He'd been assigned to write about the city's first-ever "Neutral Turf," with fifty poets reading in a blues club over the course of a winter afternoon. To be honest, I tagged along just to see what kind of losers would spend all day reading poetry to each other. But when I got there, it was electric.

Gwendolyn Brooks was there, as well as teenage poets, poets performing with music. The language was immediate and accessible, and the topics were things normal folks talk about (instead of that indecipherable hearts-rocks-flowers stuff I expected). I met a guy named Michael Warr (Chicago's foremost literary organizer), and he introduced me to a vibrant literary community I didn't know existed. Since I consider myself a writer (and if you're a writer, you should write in as many ways as possible), I felt like another door was opening for me. I couldn't wait to try getting up on stage and communicating. Michael Warr also introduced me to Marc Smith, who introduced me to the Green Mill and the Slam. The rest, as they say, is history.

NEXT...: Why do you continue?

SMITH: It's like breathing. If I stop doing it, I drop dead.

(6/98)

ANNE MACNAUGHTON
AND PETER RABBIT

By G. Murray Thomas

Whatever you want in a poetry festival, chances are you'll find it in the Taos Poetry Circus. Intensive workshops, relaxed open readings, powerhouse featured poets of both local and national acclaim, plus a little competition to create excitement and draw crowds — it's all there. Add in friendly locals, a gathering of poets from across the country, and clear mountain air, and what else could you want?

"We always had in mind living up to the concept of the Circus," says Director Anne MacNaughton, "by presenting poetry in all its variety." MacNaughton and Peter Rabbit started the Circus in 1982, and have directed it ever since. Its tone and evolution are the direct result of their vision.

The centerpiece of the Circus is the World Heavyweight Championship Poetry Bout, a ten round, head-to-head, poem-to-poem competition between two of the world's top poets. This year, two-time Champion Jimmy Santiago Baca will go up against Sherman Alexie. As with slams, the point of the competition is not to determine who is the best poet, but to attract a non-poet audience.

Rabbit emphasizes this point. "This is a poetry reading. This is two of the best poets we can find, whose work will work together, or be such a contrast as to be interesting. The competition aspect is just to drag these huge, raging crowds in. The only way you get 1,000 people is to put on a competition. We push [the competition aspect to the poets], so that they will give the performance of their lives."

"I've always seen the Circus as a way to bring poetry to the non-poetry community," echoes MacNaughton. "Every time we do this, there are these average Americans who stumble out, grab me by the elbow and go, 'Oh! I didn't know it could be like this!'"

Of course, competition creates controversy, especially in the world of poetry. Last year's Bout, between Baca and four-time National Slam Champion Patricia Smith, ended in a tie, with Baca retaining his title, despite the fact much of the audience thought Smith had won. "Controversy is not new to the Bout,"

notes Rabbit. "There have only been one or two which didn't have some kind of controversy surrounding them."

Still, controversy has its advantages. Rabbit continues, "People are still talking to me, in the check-out line at the supermarket, in the post office, or on the street, they're still talking about poetry. As far as I'm concerned, we've done our job."

Photos of Anne MacNaughton (with G. Murray Thomas) & Peter Rabbit by RD Armstrong

Another goal has been to create a situation in which poets get paid for their work. They emphasize that all of their headliners get paid. Much of this is because they are able to draw in an audience of the general public. To do this, they try to keep prices low, under six dollars for most events. "We're competing with the price of a movie ticket," says Rabbit. "Poetry is good cheap entertainment." With the emphasis on "good."

As with all poetry events, funding has been a problem. Rabbit and MacNaughton credit the Peter and Madeleine Martin Foundation for the Arts with providing the funding which enabled the Circus to succeed.

Also important is the formation of a community of poets. They see this happening in repeat visitors to the Circus and the connections they make there. Many of these connections are made in the Poet's Living Room, the round-robin style open reading which takes place every afternoon.

But they want more than just poets meeting their contemporaries, they must learn from them. "The continuous poetry conversation is really important," says Rabbit. "One of the things which gets missed in this time of computers and TV is the plain study of the art, which takes a lifetime. And then, mostly, we still don't get it.

"I'm afraid there's a lot of looping going on, people saying the same shit over and over again. There's still much to be said, but you've got to find out what's already been said first."

Much of this teaching takes place in Mexican Bob's Poetics and Performance Camp, a ten-day workshop seminar held every morning of the Circus. "What we wanted was a way of passing on this information," explains MacNaughton. "Contemporary poetics doesn't come from academic training, it comes from a long line of primarily 20th century Americans. It's valid information which needs to go from poet to poet, from master to student."

MacNaughton also sees another tradition being upheld in the Circus. "The Circus has always come from an understanding that poetry is essentially an oral art form. Writing it down afterwards — that's your script."

Still, she has reservations about some of today's performance poetry. "There is a certain kind of performance occurring which is much more stand-up than it is poetry. If you're doing stand-up, you're going to be spending a lot of time on temporal stuff. You'll get a great audience — for a month or two.

"Poetry deals with universalism. After a lot of working on just contemporary events, you should be able to pick out a universalism in that. If you want your work to last, it has to be understandable to people who haven't seen the latest version of some movie.

"Word art is the culture speaking to itself. As we all do in our private lives, the first thing we talk about is all the little temporary things that occurred to us today. Eventually we get around to 'What a wonderful sunset.' Poetry needs to do that — get beyond the tax collector and on to the sunset."

When asked which carries the Bout, the words or the delivery, she emphasizes the amateur status of the judges. "The judges frequently protest that they don't have any technical knowledge. We go, 'Good. You're supposed to choose what you like.' [Therefore] I think performance holds a lot of weight."

One final mission of the Circus is to prove that poetry can be fun. If the blend of serious poetry, raucous competition, and an occasionally uncomprehending public seems rather contradictory, MacNaughton has a ready explanation. "Irony is the heart of poetry." Rabbit concurs, and takes it a step farther. "The problem with poetry has always been: Not enough jokes."

(6/98)

HENRY ROLLINS

Interviewed by LOB

Henry Rollins has been in Los Angeles for over fifteen years now, moving here from Washington DC in the early 1980s. In that time he has made a name for himself as the vocalist for the monumental L.A. punk band Black Flag, as an actor appearing in over ten major films, as a publisher owning and masterminding 2.13.61 Publications, as record label president (co-running the Infinite Zero label with producer Rick Rubin), as a spoken word performer, and as a writer, on the verge of the publishing of his thirteenth book of stories and thoughts, *Solipsist*.

NEXT...: How did you get involved with spoken word?

ROLLINS: In 1983 I started doing "talking" shows here in Los Angeles. Harvey Kubernik would have these nights where he would get all these musicians like Jeffery Lee Pierce, D. Boon, Exene Cervenka, Chris D., John Doe, Dave Alvin... all of these 'band types' of people and he would tell them "... you can do whatever you want... but you just can't play your music... sketch, or sculpting live... read poetry, journal entries, anything, but get out of your element..."

He used to have them down at the Llasa Club... I would go to these shows because they were a lot of fun... One night Harvey sees me there and says, "You should get on one of these. You're in a band, you could do this." So I went up there one night and told a story about band practice in Long Beach and how rough it was down there. I did my ten minutes, and afterwards all these people rushed up to me and said like, "That was great!" and I was like "Huh?" because I was just sorta hangin' out on the stage ya know? I feel really at home on the stage, I was really relaxed up there. I've never really been nervous going up on a stage. So anyway, this guy says, "When's your next gig?" and I say, "I think that was just it." "How long have you been doing this?" and I say, "Tonight..." There was this really intense response from all these people, some patting me on the back.. and saying, "That was so cool."

Then Harvey said, "Do you wanna be on another show?" and I said "Yeah!" I liked the money, I got ten bucks ... I was like "Fuck Yeah!" 'cause that was a lot of dough back in the Flag days. (Laughs.) It was like, "I'm gonna eat and have a real meal." I think I blew most of that on a full-on Mexican meal at this place near Black Flag practice. I did another show and then Harvey asked if I wanted to do this a little more regularly. He said I seemed to like what I was doing and that I was really good at it.

So then I started opening for all these L.A. poets, and within a few weeks they were all opening for me... and then within a couple of months from the first show, this would be early 1984, I was doing my OWN gigs. We had them out at this place in Reseda... and we would have like around twenty paying people to start with... then I was selling the place out. I started doing two sets... The venue managers would ask me, "So what are you doing two weeks from now?" and I would say "starving," and they would tell me to come on back, and so I would... and then a Black Flack tour would happen.

Photo of Henry Rollins by Phish Blackler

NEXT...: Where did the notion for starting 2.13.61 Press come from? How long did it take to make it work?

ROLLINS: I put together this fold-and-staple book. It took me like six months of saving money from my touring to be able to put out a fold-and-staple book from Kinko's... I had hand written all the pieces and the book was called *20* because there were twenty pieces in it... I had to hand write everything because I didn't know how to type and I didn't have a typewriter. I was living at Richard Pettibone's place so I had him give me some crazy art that we used for the cover (a drawing of some hippies holding up these people in a house with the quote "Your children on summer vacation")... and we did an initial run of five hundred copies.. sold them. Did another run of five hundred, and sold those. We gave away a lot.. and sold a lot at two bucks a pop... took that money and made a paperback.. a little red paperback of that book and sixty other things.

So Harvey says you have to have a D.B.A., a "doing business as." You have to make up a company name. I said, "Why?" and he says, "Otherwise you'll end up with trouble regarding copyright infringement." I said okay. We'll call it 2.13.61, 'cause that's my birthday, that's me, and there's only gonna be this one little book on this label... the name just sorta stuck.

Fast forward through many years of really arduous work just trying to keep the label alive... and we signed Don Baima, an excellent poet from up north, and we signed Nick Cave. I called Nick's manager in England, who is a friend of mine, and told him, look, we can't get Nick's book *King Ink* over here in the US. We are being forced to buy import hardbound copies for $30 each, why don't we bring it out here for like $12 and make it affordable for the fans?

Since then we have renewed Nick's contract regularly, and we did *King Ink II*, and with those releases, this thing started to grow... it went from my bedroom to a small apartment to a bigger apartment where I shared living quarters with the office... I literally woke up to the staff of 2.13.61 outside my bedroom door. Eventually we got a nice space to work in... The label is doing well...

The ideology behind it, as far as a bigger thing than just my books, is that I'm interested in publishing the voices, primarily American voices, that might not otherwise get heard... because my heroes are the Hubert Selby's, the Nelson Algrin's.. the people that aren't prime time, but are very vital and are kinda the voice of the disenfranchised, or the people who aren't clean and beautiful and racing by in nice cars. I wanted to give them a voice too, because those are the kind of books I like to read...

The books on the label are decidedly edgy. I mean like the stuff on the label that is funny is really funny, but sorta giving you an Indian burn at the same time... there's nothing really mainstream on the label. My books are certainly not mainstream, nor are Exene's, or Ellyn Maybe's... she is a great poet, but that is not mainstream poetry. She wouldn't be taught at Princeton. Which is too bad, because some writers could really learn from her. But her work is challenging and does have an edge to it. She is brilliant... like a prodigy or something. She has this weird radar instinct, this built-in "something" that causes her to have almost a "sense" regarding poetry. It is that "thing" that true artists have. It is what makes the difference between, say, The Doors and Doors clone bands...it makes it "the real thing."

NEXT...: So, let's talk about your new book, what's it called?

ROLLINS: *Solipsist*... It's basically one who thinks the world is an extension of themselves. That nothing exists, it only exists because you're there. It's all just a function of your existence, which is how I feel when I am living in New York — when I am in a city, or on a subway... like, okay these people are just here to get in my face, or traffic exists just to piss me off — which makes it easy to get into that headspace. Easy to be outside of yourself... I took that word and I wrote a whole book around it...

I did a few pieces about me and the audience... ya know... I'll do a talking show... I'll be on stage for three hours, sometimes longer... come backstage... I'm just hammered and tired, and then I have to meet people before I can go to the hotel and get my five hours of sleep before my 7 a.m. flight...

They all have to tell me something special... I'm thinking, "How come you wont let me go home? Didn't you already get enough from me? I didn't like just rip out all my entrails and just hand them to you from the stage? For 15 bucks you got me for three hours, I made you laugh 'til your side ached." I don't hate these people. I actually really love them, but I'm like, "What could you possibly want from me?" If you really liked me you would get in your car and go home and say, "God, that guy must be really tired. Let's leave him the fuck alone." But I will sit there and I will meet every single person until they leave, because they came to the show. So I wrote this one thing, that I really like, where they come after the show and this guy says, "Hey, my girlfriend wants to cut your head off, because she cut your head off in '85 when you played here and she wants to have the other head for a bookend, so can you do that?" and I say, "Yeah," so she whacks my head off and another head sprouts out; and another guys goes, "Man, I really like your tattoos" and I go oh yeah, here's a cleaver, hack my arm off, you can have them; and another guy wants my intestines and he pulls them all out.

There are a lot of super distorted views of myself and distorted views on how I look at other people in the new book. It was one of my cooler concepts… I felt like, "Wow, I'm on to something here." It was really fun and really harsh to write, really traumatic at points. Then finally it was done in the summer of 1996 and for most of 1997 I just let it sit… I came back to it like six or seven months later and re-read it to see if it was any good at all.

NEXT…: Do you have any new audio projects coming soon?

ROLLINS: Yeah. I am editing down a talking record right now, a double CD scheduled for September 1998 release on the Dreamworks label. Then I want to start doing some other talking records, some really weird ones, with some reading and some weird music and some strange recording techniques with different found sounds… And I have this tape of me, Don Baima, and Hubert Selby sitting on the floor in my old apartment in Venice, taking turns reading things. It's a really great tape and I wanna put that out someday.

NEXT…: You have mentioned Hubert Selby a couple of times now, do you wanna talk about him for a few minutes?

ROLLINS: I think that he is just one of the great unsung American voices, I mean those who know, know! He gets major respect, you'll see his name in Cortland liner notes. Let's put it this way, I met David Bowie last summer… we played this festival together… So I talked to him a couple of times that day.. and we had dinner… and we were eating and he's talking to me…

and quoting me out of interviews… saying, "So in this magazine you said… blah blah blah..?" and I am like *woah!*… and he asks, "So how's the book company?" and I'm like, "You know I have one?" and he is like "Oh yeah, I've got a few of the books." So we were talking about something and he immediately switches subjects and turns to me and says, "You know Hubert Selby!" I go, "Yeah," and he goes, "God!" He's a genius!!" …so I was like, "He'll like to hear you say that." He was just really impressed with Selby's work.

NEXT…: What would you say to an aspiring young teenage writer, who is just getting into poetry to give them any guidance or inspiration?

ROLLINS: The most important thing to remember is the one thing that always fucks everybody up… if you're a young writer and you're just getting started… Find your own writer's voice. Be inspired by other writers, don't be influenced by other writers. Find your own voice from the get go. All the great writers have their own way of doing it. There is nothing like John Fante, he write likes nobody. There's nobody like Henry Miller. There's nobody that used language like Hemingway. There is nobody like Thomas Wolfe. They are great in their own way… they had the guts to find their own writer's voice, and they didn't try to be the next Bukowski. Man, if I had a dime for every manuscript that gets sent in here trying to be me or Bukowski, please.

But a guy like Selby… look at his use of grammar: no apostrophes, a slash, no quotation marks. He has his own vocabulary of like eighty words per book that you've never seen before.. Shakespeare came up with 1,500 words that are "Shakespearean." That he wrote. And if it takes, like, three years of writing and you trash it all to find that thing that's really you… that is the only reason you should be writing, to be original.

NEXT…: Do you think there is any power for social change with spoken word?

ROLLINS: No. I mean I am not down on it… but you are reaching such a small audience… and on the spoken word circuit I speak to more people than most. But look… no poet is drawing 1,000 people a night… you can put across some change, but it won't do much. People will always be themselves.

(7/98)

JOHN SINCLAIR

Interviewed by G. Murray Thomas

I interviewed John Sinclair, poet, blues historian, political activist, etc., in the cafe of the Border's Books on La Cienega. While we talked, his band, The Blues Scholars (which tonight included the legendary Wayne Kramer on guitar, Brock Avery on drums, and Doug Lunn on bass), set up for their show, hauling the paraphernalia of a full rock band into the tiny space between the tables and the windows. It looked like it was going to get loud in this normally quiet store. In a few minutes, it did. They subjected the book store customers to a combination of blues, jazz, and rock which had said customers boogieing in the aisles. While John Sinclair works in traditional forms, he does nothing in traditional manner.

Sinclair's history is too long and multi-faceted to describe in detail here. It has included stints as a poet, journalist, manager of '60s rock experiment the MC5, founder of the White Panther Party, federal drug prisoner, and counter-cultural hero. Now he has reemerged as a spoken word artist, telling tales of pioneering jazz and blues musicians, backed by the very music he describes. His compelling performances set a standard for "music and verse" (his phrase) composition.

NEXT...: Do you see a thread of continuity through all the various things you have done?

SINCLAIR: Absolutely. It's all one thing to me. When I was a political activist, it was what I needed to do at the time. There's no dichotomy to me between politics and culture.

Music is the main thing which goes through everything I have done. I grew up listening to blues and R&B on the radio in the '50s, just prior to and immediately after black music crossed into white stations and the pop charts. After that I started listening to jazz. I was passionately involved with avante-garde jazz through the mid-'60s.

Then when I got with the MC5, we fused all these different things together, and added a lot of electricity. Also, they were explicit in how much they hated the way things were, and how much they wanted them to change. Moving the music another step forward, into direct confrontation with authority.

NEXT...: Can music still confront authority?

SINCLAIR: I think anybody can confront them all they want. I don't think they do it now, though. I did everything I knew how for ten years, and then I realized the things I wanted to happen weren't happening. They weren't going to happen. And if they were, they weren't going to happen as a result of what I was doing. I thought the only sensible thing to do was withdraw and assess personal damages. Then I went back and started over where I left off, which was as a poet, writer, and cultural organizer.

In the mid-'70s, it had gotten to where people, in a mass way, weren't too concerned about changing things that much. This was disappointing to me. Looking around, and finding oneself and a few other people standing there, and everyone else and had turned around and gone to a picnic.

NEXT...: Do you have any intention of putting the stories of the '60s into musical form?

SINCLAIR: I don't know. If I write them. All [my] stuff comes out of my music research, trying to understand the music I listen to better. That's much more a burning interest to me than what I did thirty years ago.

NEXT...: Is there a process of adapting these stories to musical form?

SINCLAIR: I'll be reading about somebody, and I'll want to save [a story] in a notebook. I'll start copying it out, and it'll come out in verse. Since I mostly perform with music, now when I compose I'm aware that ultimately I'll be standing in front of people with some music to deliver it. That shapes the composition.

I beat my verses up a lot. I beat the shit out of them. I take them up an stage and read them, and I'm always attuning myself to things that aren't right. Then I'll go back and beat up the manuscript some more, until finally I get it to where it's permanently fixed.

NEXT...: Do you have the music in your head beforehand?

SINCLAIR: Yeah. Or playing. If I work on a poem, I'll play the tune. If I was going to write a poem to a song, I put it on, use the repeat function of the CD, and play it over and over again. So I'm in the right rhythm, and what I'm composing will fit. It's not writing lyrics to a song, but it's kind of an abstraction on that.

I have a big jazz work, dedicated to Thelonious Monk. It's called *Thelonious: The Book of Monk*. I'm trying to write a poem for every piece he ever recorded. I've got about 80 of those. They each go to a different song.

NEXT...: Anything new coming out?

SINCLAIR: I've got a cut, a piece on Charlie Patton, on a project by James Mathias, of the Squirrel Nut Zippers. He recorded a tribute album to Patton's daughter, called *Songs for Rosetta*. He found out that the lady who was housekeeper for his aunt and uncle, this woman who helped raise him, was Charlie Patton's daughter. He flipped right out. He got his lawyer to look into royalties, but the company Patton had recorded for went out of business in the '30s. The Squirrel Nut Zippers were starting to get popular, so he figured a record with his name on it might sell something. So he made the record, and he dedicated the profits to her.

NEXT...: Any comments on "the state of the art" today?

SINCLAIR: I listen to a lot of blues coming out today… black artists that couldn't ever get recorded commercially. You've got this world. It's the world I live in, with most people in roots music, or poetry. I call it the World of 2,000. I'm not referring to the Millennium, but the number of people who inhabit this world. A blues record, a poetry record, a jazz record, any product like that has a potential sale of about 2,000. Then there's the world of mega-sale, and they're selling two million. Or thirty-four million.

I'm pretty attentive to what's going on [in the World of 2,000], and I stay out of the pop world completely. I'm trying to preserve a little world in my head, and not have to live in the world I abhor so much any more than I have to.

I'd like to see more people enter the World of 2,000, make it 5,000 or 10,000. I don't think we're going to get anywhere in the Mass World. It's too stupid. You have to dummy down too much. Things with intelligence and feeling, things which come out of intense, idiosyncratic human experience, aren't going to get in the mainstream. I'm just trying to make a living and exist in the World of 2,000.

NEXT...: What do you call what you do — poetry, spoken word?

Sinclair: I like to call it "music and verse." I don't care if they say poetry, or spoken word, whatever. I want them to think of it as a band, to go out for some musical entertainment for the night.

(7/98)

Photo of John Sinclair with Wayne Kramer (guitarist) by G. Murray Thomas

MIRANDA JULY

Interviewed by LOB

Miranda July is a spoken word/performance artist from Portland, OR. She combines spoken word/ sounds/and video to create a multi-media presentation of her words. She has produced several short films for her on-going video chain-letter project *Big Miss Movieola*, has performed with the indie pop/new wave band The Need, and recently has released a new CD called *The Binet-Simon Test. Next...* Editor G. Murray Thomas and I went out to see one of her SoCal tour appearances in support of this new CD, and I had the chance to ask her a few questions....

NEXT...: What you are doing is very "different" for a spoken word artist. What can you tell us about your current "spoken word" tour?

JULY: Well, it's really more than a spoken word tour. It's really like a movie... a movie performance piece. It's kinda what my world is... which is entirely mixed between movies and performing... and really not seeing too much of a line between them. Because a lot of my influences are more cinematic, and a lot of the people around me are movie makers, and I am also. The fact that I am "live" when I perform is really just happenstance.

NEXT...: It was an amazing show. I've heard people talking about using video production in spoken word performance, but have never seen it done... and especially so well. Have you considered maybe approaching more galleries and art spaces with this performance style?

JULY: Yeah, I'm moving sorta into being much more in the "performance world." Because it takes so much to do each show in a certain way, I mean the amount of preparation for the show tonight was like five or ten minutes, right before we started... and it could have easily been done in over three hours with a lot less stress in terms of technical problems. So I am much more wanting to set up a performance where I play for two nights, and a lot of people come and I can really give it everything I have. I have a lot more that what you saw tonight. This was like a little sampler.

NEXT...: So, you have three different projects going on in your life... you have this live performance work, and you have a huge video/movie project, *Big Miss Movieola*, and you have audio CDs and recorded material... do you like doing the movies better than the CDs?

JULY: No, the CDs have their own thing... with this last CD I was like, "Wow!" because it is starting to get to the point where it is a really interesting form, to me, to work in. It isn't like I'm just taking things from the way bands record things. It's more like, in my mind, making up doing it in a way that works for me, which is something I kinda had to teach myself. I had to look at it with the thought, "How do I make this totally visual?" and start there.

NEXT...: It works, the CD is really good, I listened to it today..

JULY: Wow, cool...

NEXT...: Are there any other spoken word artists in the U.S. that you like?

JULY: I don't really listen to much spoken word, I mean it's not really something I grew up with.... but I like the stuff that Slim Moon and Sue Fox are doing, but they are really IN my world a lot... just because they exist and are right now so focused and supportive of me, and of spoken word in general, it's really great.

NEXT...: Who in cinema influenced you?

Photo of Miranda July by G. Murray Thomas

JULY: Well… Todd Haynes, his work is really great. Also a lot of paranoia movies from the 1970s …and a lot of times it will just be like a little gesture in something, and I will be, "Oh why is that so resonant?" …And it's just that little gesture, or that certain way that someone says something, and it just makes everything stop, and I have to incorporate that into my being, so that every time I use it, it will be like pushing a little button in everyone, because they will recognize that certain gesture, and everything that is attached to it.

NEXT…: How long did it take you do get from the ideas and concepts of what you wanted to do, and to be able to do what you are doing now? How long have you been performing?

JULY: I've always sorta been doing what I wanted to do… I started writing plays and stuff when I was in high school, and then I started to perform with bands, and then those two things kinda just mixed and became this. It always made perfect sense. It wasn't anything I really strove towards, I just did it in the moment.

NEXT…: Do you have anything to say to anyone who is just starting to do creative stuff…?

JULY: Just to constantly remind yourself that there isn't anything that you "can't," there isn't anything that isn't "allowed." There isn't anything that you should have to repeat, you should create what is exactly in your head.

(8/98)

JERRY QUICKLEY
Interviewed by Jeffrey McDaniel

When I moved to Los Angeles two years ago, my poetry friends in San Francisco told me to check out a guy by the name of Jerry Quickley. The first time I saw him was at a little coffeehouse in Orange County, but it wasn't until the 1997 National Poetry Slam in Connecticut that I experienced Quickley at full volume. He is one of the rare poetry performers who can expand and excel in a venue big enough to hold a thousand people. He was overwhelming. My pals and I were rooting for him, but, as is typical of slams, the judges screwed up and scored him fifth – not a bad finish considering there were over one hundred and fifty poets in the competition.

Photo of Jerry Quickley by Phish Blackler

NEXT...: When did you write your first poem?

QUICKLEY: After a friend of mine of mine was killed by a drunk driver.

NEXT...: When was that?

QUICKLEY: October of 91.

NEXT...: Well that must have sucked.

QUICKLEY: There are actually a couple of things that happened. I was a DJ in high school and college. That's how I put myself through college. Even after college, when I got an office job, I was still working as a DJ. When I stopped working as a DJ, I became more disciplined about my writing as a whole. At the same time, the accident happened to my friend. I had a need to create something.

NEXT...: What is the scope of your creative writing?

QUICKLEY: An as-yet unfinished novel, several screenplays, re-writes on several big studio projects, short stories and plays and poetry.

NEXT...: You had some plays done in New York, right?

QUICKLEY: Yeah, I was the playwright-in-residence at the Tiki Ti Theater company in New York.

NEXT...: When you watch actors perform your material, do you ever want to push them off the stage and say, "let me do this"?

QUICKLEY: More often than not I'm just amazed and overjoyed when I see my words coming out of actors, because they create things that I didn't even know was in the writing; they find moments and emotional beats that I wasn't aware I had created.

NEXT...: What were you like as a child?

QUICKLEY: Overly sensitive and overly militant, which makes for a really bad combination.

NEXT...: You seem to have a natural gift for performing — was it present as a child?

QUICKLEY: I had this strange childhood that ran the gamut from extreme poverty to relative wealth. I went to the United Nations International School, and I also went to jacked-up ghetto schools deep in the hood. I had this weird, schizophrenic ability to connect with whoever my peers of that particular week were. When I got to public school, my first thought was "Oh my God, I've landed among barbarians," because I was getting my ass kicked every day. My parents were pacifists. That was the first time I realized my parents fucked up sometimes. As a result, I ended up taking martial arts for eight years. No amount of verbal reasoning or impassioned speeches was gonna work; I had to do some ass kicking.

NEXT...: What are your literary aspirations?

QUICKLEY: After the second Nobel... (Laughs.) My literary ambitions are not well defined at this point. I try to keep the focus on my work. The vast majority of my time is spent wrestling stanzas in the dark of my den at night. One project seems to flow into another — I'm just barely beginning to make a living from it.

NEXT...: What are some of the projects you're working on?

QUICKLEY: My first full-fledged book, Core Samples. I'm in discussion with several publishers.

NEXT...: How about audio stuff?

QUICKLEY: One of the audio things is top secret only 'cause I'm trying to pull out of it and don't want to piss anyone off. I'm doing a CD with a large label. I'm not happy with the process, or the people involved. I'm trying to put the brakes on it, and do it as an indie and just use a major label for distribution. The other recording project is to raise cash and awareness for Mumia Abu Jamal. It's a whole CD about freedom, or some aspect of freedom, or lack thereof. Some of the people I'm recording with are Saul Williams and Mike Ladd and some other hepcats. The producer, This Kid Named Miles from the local band Breakestra, has a great ear for beats.

I just edited my first anthology. It's called Juke Joint Magic. It'll be out in September. It's got about fifteen poets, including mostly local poets and some folks from around the country, like Beau Sia and Taylor Mali. The NCAA wants me to come to the Final Four this coming March and perform.

My latest play is a one-act play called Color of the Day, about police corruption and racism, and it's going to be produced this fall here in Los Angeles.

NEXT...: I could see you popping up one day in a movie. Have you ever thought of acting?

QUICKLEY: Not really. I acted in a couple of plays in New York. I wanted to get a small sense of what it's like to be on the other side of the process, to have a director telling you what to do, so it could maybe help me become a better director.

NEXT...: So, do you think you're gonna win the Slam Championship this year?

QUICKLEY: The National Slam Championship is kind of random. I think anyone who finishes in the top 25 or 30 could be the champion. There are so many intangibles. If I finish in the top 30 or 40 I'll be happy. I think it was a fluke I made the finals last year.

NEXT...: Any closing words?

QUICKLEY: Poetry is really important to my life. The main reason is because poets continue to clamor for the emancipation of the human spirit. We prove over and over again that we're connected, that we're not laboring alone. Our struggle is noble. We're building a cultural resistance.

(9/98)

DERRICK BROWN

By Jaimes Palacio

At first sight you might think: "Oh, they crossbred (once Olympic hopeful) Prefontaine with George Clooney." You might notice the thick eyebrows, the long biker sideburns, the bowling shirt. You might be afraid. He is, usually, very quiet. Sits in the back. Intense. Doesn't heckle much. Maybe he is a stalker, a serial killer, white trash, a rejected member of the Village People, an alien, an Amway product salesperson.

Then you actually meet him and he is goofy, friendly, amazingly devoid of ego. A damn nice guy who also happens to be a simply amazing poet (or is it the other way around.)

Derrick C. Brown was born in 1973, in San Francisco. His father made gaskets for the Navy base. (Even though he was a civilian, he had been a butcher in the Air Force.) Derrick claims that, "I was raised very... very, strangely by my father..." His mother developed Chronic Fatigue Syndrome and now mostly stays at home. His father moved to Texas where he farmed Emus (a flightless, three-toed, Australian bird). Derrick's poem on the subject is called "A Few Things You Already Knew About Humping Emus."

Lately Derrick has achieved a certain hometown notoriety. He has a CD (*It's a Jolly Holliday*), and, as a member of the Laguna Beach Slam Team, won second place in the individuals category at the Nationals.

His work is varied; transcendent of genre stereotyping. For example, at his Sept. 9th feature, at Alta Coffeehouse, he was backed by Freeze Peach and began by noting, "There comes a time when all poets must write a poem about sticking cigarettes in their eyeballs." He also read a raucous Christmas piece and attempted a country song. Sandwiched between all that were several subtler pieces. Poetry. He moved from one to another with stunning grace and even was asked to come back for an encore!

The following interview took place in Long Beach, California. The walls of the room are plastered in collages, movie posters, and various other eclectic nonsense. He is seated on a broken office chair. One beer in his hand. A band provides muffled background from the adjoining living room. Talking into a borrowed tape recorder this is how we begin:

NEXT...: Ladies and gentlemen, I'm sitting here with possibly a significant figure in future poetry history.

BROWN: (Makes flatulent noise which continues unabated for several minutes.)

NEXT...: That may have to be edited. So, Derrick, tell me a little about yourself. You know, all the boring stuff.

BROWN: Well, in order to be long-winded, like all the interviews I've read; I kissed Monique Powell [the lead singer of Save Ferris] in high school.

NEXT...: She's gorgeous!

BROWN: Changed my life. (Pause.) Left the high school to jump in the army for the 82nd Airborne Artillery. Did that for three years, no joke. I then escaped – with an honorable discharge – and lived out in Temecula, California, to become a better writer. It didn't work. I then got a scholarship to go to Northern Arizona University.

NEXT...: Your work is very performance based, but it is not what you would call shallow work by any means. One of the things that ties your work together is colorful characters, whether it is Amelia Earheart (tenderly rendered in "Waltzing Amelia") or the exaggerated parody of Reverend Budgreen ("Church on a Monday").

BROWN: Right, I believe the last line from that piece is: "Why don't you just kill yourself?" When Mr. Heckle, my P.E. teacher from Pacifica High School, told me… uhm …when I asked him how to shoot a free throw, he said: "Why don't you just kill yourself?" And I took his advice.

NEXT...: So you are actually dead?

BROWN: Right.

NEXT...: That's very interesting.

BROWN: Yes, it's very sad actually.

NEXT...: I see, moving on; have you been inspired by other poets?

BROWN: Yeah, Jeff McDaniel has a line that really twisted me. You know, certain people write things that burn a hole in you. He's got this line: "In some other

world gigantic seashells hold humans up to their ears and all they hear is the echo of machinery." That stings me.

NEXT...: That's a beautiful line.

BROWN: I started writing to make fun of poetry and then I started reading Robert Bly and Anne Sexton.

NEXT...: I notice you are really into music. I've heard you sing. You are not bad.

BROWN: I'll kill you!

NEXT...: Do you get inspired by music? I know you're a big fan of Radiohead.

BROWN: They ride the rollercoaster, as far as hitting emotional levels. Thom Yorke could put out a book without ever having sung a thing and I think he'd be a hit. It's so…it's so… wonderful on many levels.

NEXT...: Going back to the performance angle. Do you think being in speech helped at all when it actually came time to take your poetry on the stage, perform it at coffeehouses?

Photo of Derrick Brown by G. Murray Thomas

BROWN: Well the interesting thing about speech performance — and almost every college has its Forensics' team — is that every round you do, someone judges you and writes comments about the piece and about your performance. So you've got… twelve different editors a day giving you critiques. This stuff is probably pretty boring and no one gives a damn about it, except Forensics geeks.

NEXT…: Which I was one of.

BROWN: Yes. I do believe you did *Hitchhikers Guide to the Galaxy*. You used a book that was so big it covered your upper torso.

NEXT…: Ok, on to…

BROWN: …Big…

NEXT…: …other…

BROWN: …Real big.

NEXT…: …avenues. Is it true that you are now deluged with women calling you, offering you their bodies and other sexual favors?

BROWN: I don't know if you know this, Jaimes, but ever since I was a little boy I've been offered women's bodies. I'm very confused on how to handle it. So what I mostly do is I just say: "Chill baby! Chill baby! Daddy's gonna come home and bring you a bowl of biscuits!"

NEXT…: Is that code for: "I'm afraid of commitment?"

BROWN: I really wish my relationship scene was… very different.

NEXT…: Are you a religious man? Do you have a religion of choice?

BROWN: Yeah. Free Methodist. Though the term kind of sounds funny to me.

NEXT…: Free Methodists! Are there more expensive Methodists?

BROWN: Yeah, don't let the enslaved Methodists know I'm cracking jokes about them. They don't take kindly to that.

NEXT…: Do you think extraterrestrials have a religion?

BROWN: I do know for a fact that E.T. was Mormon.

NEXT…: Really? What about Alf?

BROWN: It's funny you should bring up Alf because I was a big fan of Alf and, if anyone asks, I do an Alf impersonation. I hope that's how I am going to make my riches someday.

NEXT…: You heard it here first! Derrick someday will make his living doing Alf impersonations.

BROWN: (Magically transforms into Alf.) Hah! I kill me! — I think that will look good in print. Here kitty, kitty, kitty! Here kitty, kitty, kitty….

NEXT…: Where does your inspiration come from?

BROWN: My inspiration comes from the way I see things. I try to put all five senses into my work. I will twist that and bend it… not just surrealism — I'm not trying to do Pink Floyd —I'm trying to do poetry that people connect with.

NEXT…: So basically you take a real moment and try to make it relatable and real to someone else.

BROWN: Well, now I feel dumb because it's kind of like I'm bragging about my life being wacky but I don't know if that's what I meant at all.

NEXT…: You seem to be uncomfortable with certain aspects of your life. Is this a fair perception?

BROWN: (Very carefully.) I think the moment you let yourself fall into the trap of… being comfortable you stop… trying to push your art. There's a constant sort of searching going on, not just with women, but with seeking…happiness, you know the things you can read about in… What's that book by Gandhi — not the Kama Sutra… No, Gandhi didn't write the Kama Sutra.

NEXT…: What is your ultimate goal personally, for poetry?

BROWN:. I'm tired of being hungry. If I can get a job writing advertisement copy…

NEXT…: Some people would call that a sellout.

BROWN: Well, getting a real job is a sellout. I think survival is more important than smoking pot and growing my hair long. Wait. Why am I talking about pot? I've never smoked pot. Did you know that?

NEXT…: You heard it here first: Derrick Brown has never smoked pot! This seems to be a very tough question for you to answer.

BROWN: I'm probably, actually, very scared that I've fallen into a passion that's a poor man's passion.

NEXT...: But if you could make a career in poetry financially and spiritually satisfying? Could this possibly be a future goal?

BROWN: You've just announced my lofty dream, and if I can find a gal…

NEXT...: Well, those are the lofty dreams of…everyone.

BROWN: Then I guess there's nothing new to learn from me.

(10/98)

THE POETRY SCENE 1994 - 1998

SCENES · REVIEWS · CALENDAR

+plus: Miranda July and Jo-ann Mapson

Cover Illustration by Charles Ellik

POETRY BRIDGES ACROSS CULTURAL GAPS

By G. Murray Thomas

I moved to Southern California for beaches and sunshine. I stayed (no bullshit) for poetry. But these days, what excites me most about L.A. is its multicultural character. As a WASP from purebred northeastern suburbs, I am constantly fascinated and intrigued by the variety of cultures here and their interactions.

But, to be honest, my own interaction with these cultures is often limited to eating Thai food and listening to Mexican music on my car radio.

Except at poetry readings. There, people of all races, nationalities, cultures, ages, classes, political leanings, sexual orientations, etc., – that is, people from every set and subset of this jumbled city, come together as equals. The only judgments made are on the quality of the poetry.

Poetry does much more than provide an equal footing, however. Since poetry is self-expression, it is one of the easiest and most enjoyable ways to learn about these other cultures. When listening to the poems of a black, or a Mexican, or a lesbian, or a homeless person, or a screenwriter, I hear their lives. I hear their rituals and traditions, I hear the accents which color their days, I hear their perspectives on life. I hear their values. I am transported, for the duration of the poem, into their culture.

I also hear individuals. I hear people of the same (supposedly) group or class disagree wildly on issues, political and personal. And I hear people from wildly divergent backgrounds agree on beauty, love, and the meaning of life.

I learn what is probably the most important lesson of human interaction — the differences which seem so important on the surface are really irrelevant. We are all more the same than we are different. Yet, simultaneously, there is a deep and important difference between people — that of individual identity. Each person is unique. Each person is an individual spirit, and is therefore important.

Thus, in my more optimistic moments, I see in the poetry community a bright flash of hope, a model for the diverse yet tolerant community that Los Angeles, and the world, could someday be.

(5/ 94)

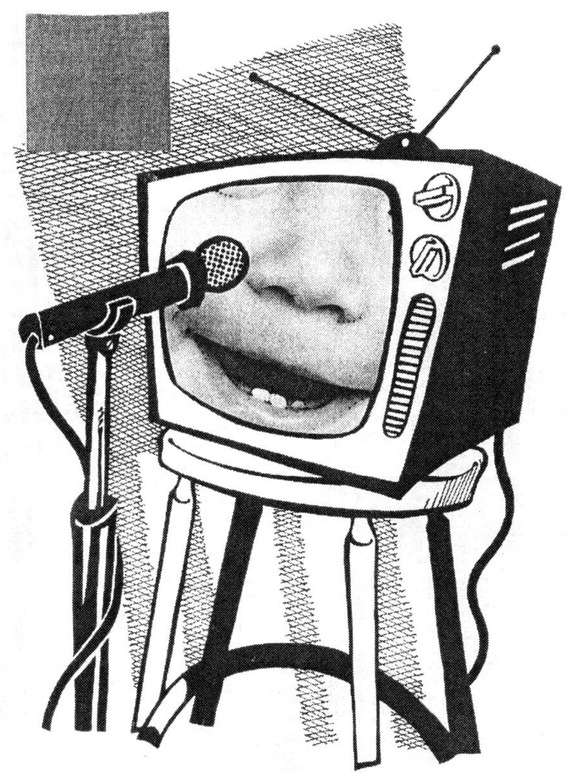

MCPOETRY

MTV "Free Your Mind" spoken Wurd Tour
Ellyn Maybe, Reg. E. Gaines, Maggie Estep, John S. Hall,
Gil Scott Heron
Monday, Feb. 12, 1994 • Doug Weston's Troubadour
Reviewed by Charles Ellik

The hand-stamp says "hip," and does not lie. Walk in and, Surprise! a local is on stage wandering through a long stream of clever conscious. How did she get up there? After she ends, the monitors start and ask us to detach our heads. Many bright pixels of faceless mouths speaking much political correctness.

The video then moves on stage by possessing warm bodies (and is not referred to again). The first performer is a racial/political/predictable black man with a jazz/rap/

Illustration by Charles Ellik

black thang rhythm. Chants much anger at symptoms of social sickness, with bass and keyboardist. We are surprised by all the musical instruments on stage, but here it works. This preacher delivers no revelations, however. Good delivery though. Poet says it may be MTV but not censorship. "Fuck that!" he says. There doesn't need to be. He avoids eye contact with the audience.

There is a long empty gap between performers filled with music. A barmaid asks if we want booze. We do, but at $4 for domestic beers, we pass.

A ratty hair vamp chick with cigarette and power suit comes on stage and tells us she wants to be a vampire. Recites many words about victimization backed by three-piece punkish band. (Can punk ever be "-ish"?) Her armpits are strangely naked — shaved. A barmaid in tights often blocks the view.

After that set, a friend wonders aloud how the director decided what demographic niches were to be filled. We argue whether the performer was a singer trying to be a poet, or a poet trying to be a singer.

The third up does goofy-misunderstood-alternative very well. His set is almost a comedy routine, and the interaction is well-received. He asks someone up on stage to read his infamous piece titled "Detachable Penis" while he does back-up vocals. The drummer from the last set comes back out and works with the poet better than any other word/music combo of the evening. After he ends, someone brings up a good point: the only performer so far who is actually in a successful band chose to come out without one.

He actually comes out to talk in the audience after his set. Very friendly, shaking lots of hands. "Better listeners than New York…"

Long set-up for last performer. A bluesy slurred-voice street-wise black sage type. Anthem songs sung over the world's most extended play of four chords. Works with very intense percussionist. His advice to poets: "Try not to be deep." (The other performers must have listened.) Those who are very interested stay that way, the rest leave. A very sad barmaid with an empty tray wanders through (lots of thirst, no money). The performer congratulates the others and ends. Long applause.

A few stay and talk. We agree the performers know how to use their microphones. It is noted that most memorized their work. Yet it is obvious that it is no better content than any good open reading. Why so popular?

We steal posters and leave.

(4/94)

LUMBERING DINOSAURS
By G. Murray Thomas

Orange Ocean Press attended the American Booksellers' Association (ABA) Convention at the L.A. Convention Center last month. There were some 30,000 people there, representing all major and many minor publishers, distributors and bookstores from across the country and even around the world. And there were almost NO poets!

Sure, there were a few — Bob Holman from New York, Jennifer Joseph and Bucky Sinister from San Francisco, booths from City Lights and other small publishers that dabbled in poetry scattered around. But we were one of the few booths dedicated solely to poetry. More important, there was no sense that poetry was a vital part of the publishing industry.

Now, I'll admit I'm biased in this matter. Extremely biased. But I do feel there is a poetry explosion going on in America right now, and these giants of publishing were blissfully unaware of it.

One scene stands out for me. Many booths had promotional gimmicks, such as costumed characters. While wandering the aisles, I spotted a Velociraptor chasing Barney around. This seemed an apt metaphor for the convention — dinosaurs chasing each other, while ignoring the mammals which will replace them.

It's not just poetry either. The primary mammals here are electronic books. While there will always be a place for print, it is clear to me that the future of publishing is in electronic books. But here were the publishing giants of the world, paying lip service to e-books only because they could ignore them no more. It was obvious they had no understanding of their potential, and were frankly afraid of them. The only booths displaying any innovation on e-books were small, new companies.

This is, I believe, because the giants have no vision of the future. They base their decisions on what sold last year, not on what could sell next year. They are dinosaurs in denial.

If they are in denial about something as huge as e-books, it is easy to understand how they are oblivious to something as grass-roots as poetry. It is also clear that we cannot look to them to break poetry.

There will be poetry bestsellers in the near future. Huge poetry best-sellers. But they will not be books. They'll be CDs or videos, and they will catch these dinosaurs totally by surprise.

After all that, I will close on a humble note. I may be wrong. We poets may not be mammals. We may be dinosaurs ourselves, but of a smaller, more tenacious variety. One that will evolve into something like geckos — an amusing sidelight in the animal kingdom, but irrelevant to the main action.

But not if we can grasp our own fate, instead of leaving it in the hands of these ancient monsters.

(7/94)

THE NAKED WORD

Directed by Kennon B. Raines
Christian E. Elder, William McLain, Mauro W. Monteiro,
Merilene Murphy, Mark Pomeroy, Kennon B. Raines,
Cynthia Toronto
Tuesday, July 26, 1994 • Hollywood Moguls
Reviewed by G. Murray Thomas

There were three big questions going in to this reading. Would the poets really be naked? Would that gimmick fill the room? Would the poetry transcend the gimmick?

Yes, it filled the room. It was literally standing room only in the 99-seat theater at Hollywood Moguls. And people were standing in the aisles for the show. The anticipation was high.

Yes, they were naked. They did the first piece ("The Flesh and The Word," about, well, nakedness and poetry) draped in sheets which they removed by the end. Then they performed the rest of the ninety-minute show, with a few carefully planned exceptions, all in the all together.

And the most important yes — Yes, the poetry transcended the nakedness. After a few minutes, the nudity ceased to be an oddity, became just another chosen costume. The poems were very well chosen; each piece was enhanced by the nakedness. Poems about personal identity, sexuality, racism, politics and religion all acquired a new level of meaning by the poets performing nude. This was not just poetry performed naked, but poetry interacting with nakedness.

Listing a few of the highlights of the evening will probably make this clearer. The chosen costume added extra dimensions to these poems, as you can probably well imagine: William McLain's "Dirty Old Man;" Mark Pomeroy's ode to narcissism, "Me;" Kennon Raines's "Rock My Chakra" (I mean, how can a piece about the liberating power of sex be honestly performed any way other than naked?); Christian Elder's "Racism Is;" Mauro Monteiro's "Pour Me a Dream;" and Cynthia Toronto's "Thank God." It all climaxed (pun intended, of course) with Kennon B. Raines's "Love Created My Soul."

The few times "clothing" (perhaps "covering" is a better word) was applied, it too made further comment on the poetry. Cynthia Toronto performed "The World Is a Virus," about obsessive paranoia about germs and other forms of infection, wrapped fully in plastic wrap. William McLain followed, with his safe sex warning "In These Times" with some selective plastic wrapping of his own. When Merilene Murphy performed her "It Still Runs" wrapped in an American flag, it was a not-so-subtle comment on the freedoms African-Americans have yet to achieve in our society.

For by that point it was obvious these poets had freed themselves, and not just of a few bodily inhibitions. By freeing themselves of their clothes, and all the societal restrictions they carry, the poets liberated their bodies, their minds, their power of expression, their poetry.

Be free. Get naked.

(9/94)

LOLLAPALOOZA: POETRY MEETS THE MASSES

By G. Murray Thomas

We've gotten some comments to the effect of, "Why are you guys wasting so much space on Lollapalooza?" The answer is basic and, to our eyes, obvious. The poetry program at Lollapalooza is the most serious attempt to present poetry to a mass audience which we have yet seen.

According to Liz Belile, poetry coordinator for Lollapalooza, the attempt is working. They are not only presenting poetry to large crowds of people, but connecting with them. She says the connection is especially strong in "oppressive police-states" like Florida, Indiana, and Kansas, where "poetry is keeping the tent [the Revival Tent, where the poetry stage is located] packed to the rafters." The audience, she says, "is starving for poetry."

She gave numerous examples of poets who "rocked the house" from the third, second, and even main stage. Tom Peters, in Denver, had the whole stadium chanting along with his words.

It hasn't all been a rave, however. Las Vegas and, surprisingly, New York gave less than enthusiastic responses. She described the general Lollapalooza crowd as a tough audience, and said reading poetry to 30,000 "wasn't really that great an experience." (She quickly followed that statement with the prediction that, nonetheless, poetry tours of stadiums are in the near future for us.)

In fact, poets are no longer appearing on the main stage. (Sorry, all you slam winners.) The reason is not poor reception, but rather the requirements of rapid set changes for the bands. (Imagine reading your words into one mike while a roadie is shouting "Mike check!" into another one.)

Another positive result of the tour has been to link up poets across the nation. Poets who have only heard each other's names, or seen occasional samples in print, are meeting each other on the road. Networks are being set up to facilitate national poetry tours.

This all hits Los Angeles on Sunday, Sept. 4 and Monday, Sept. 5, at Cal State Dominguez Hills. Tons of local poets will be performing. This includes slam winners Jim Bolt, Danni Bonaducci, D. Knowledge, Rick Lupert, Trey Nichols, Arash Saedinia, Manuel Schwab, G. Murray Thomas, Tom Foster, Jamal Holmes, Ross Rubin, William P. McLain, Kennon B. Raines, Cynthia Toronto, John Kinney and Mark Pomeroy. There are still three slam slots to be chosen. Two will be picked at Luna Park, on Sunday, Sept. 28, and the final one will be filled at Iguana Cafe on Thursday, Sept. 1. *YOU* still have a chance.

New Alliance recording artists make up another significant portion of the roster. On Sunday you can hear Liz Belile, Iris Berry, Luis Alfaro, Pleasant Gehman, Steve Abee, Danny Weizman and Joel Lipman. Appearing on Monday are Liz Belile, Julie Ritter, Jack Brewer, Kathy Martin, Linda J. Albertano, Lisa Freeman and Paul Body.

There will be many more poets, including those who have traveled the country with Lollapalooza. And there will an open reading, so come show your stuff too.

Poetry is booming at Lollapalooza!

(9/94)

Illustration by Charles Ellik

LOLLAPALOOZA: WHAT DID IT ALL MEAN?

By G. Murray Thomas

Having poetry at Lollapalooza was one of the most exciting things to happen to SoCal (and national) poetry in recent years. However, it is easy to blow up its significance, or even dismiss it. Let's put this event in perspective.

Lollapalooza was not an isolated event. It was one step in the ongoing evolution of poetry and its presentation to the public. Many developments in the poetry scene over the past decades lead to poetry at Lollapalooza.

The Lollapalooza spoken word tent this year should be seen as an experiment. It was the first large scale attempt to present poetry to a rock'n'roll audience. Many approaches were attempted. Some worked, some did not. It is important to focus on the lessons learned, not on specific successes or failures.

HISTORY

Q: Where did the idea of poetry at Lollapalooza come from?

A: Who really knows? — Liz Belile, director of poetry at Lollapalooza

If it is hard to pin down whose idea it was, that is because it came from so many directions as to seem inevitable. Perry Farrell, Lollapalooza mastermind, has often expressed a desire for spoken word at the show. Farrell himself contributed a track to the New Alliance spoken word CD *HollyWord* in 1990. The 1993 Lollapalooza included spoken word videos by Robyn Hitchcock and Henry Rollins, among others, in the Forum Tent. Meanwhile, poets have been on MTV and working with bands all over the country.

What it took, apparently, to translate desire into reality, was someone willing and able to do the work. Mud Baron, who ran the Forum Tent in 1993, came forward. He was later joined by Liz Belile and Juliette Torrez. A poetry program was put together.

None of this, of course, occurred in a vacuum. Poetry is exploding all over the country. Slam poetry, the Nuyorican poets, our growing SoCal scene, and similar scenes across the continent contributed three vital factors: excitement among the poets, public interest, and a huge pool of talent.

Harvey Kubernik, head of New Alliance records, puts it in perspective, "If you subtract Lollapalooza, you can tell there has been a lot of foundation and root work done… Lollapalooza was one small layer of positive, concrete work."

FIRST MEETING

If seen as just another step in the development of poetry, this was a big step. It was the first meeting between poets and a huge new audience. On an animal level, they were just sniffing each others' butts. To both parties, this was a major revelation.

Charles Ellik, who slammed at an L.A. show, says he felt, "People were expecting a freak show, yet heard stuff they liked… 'Hey, this isn't telling me how stupid I am.'"

Liz Belile states that, across the country, "This generation is starving for poetry, and digging it."

Not only did many poets find themselves facing a crowd larger than they were used to, but one untrained in listening to poetry. Liz Belile says, "Performance chops count a lot. This is a tough audience." Charles Ellik elaborates, "We are all used to reading to a poetry crowd. It's a much different dynamic in front of others."

The first lesson the poets who traveled with the show learned was how to grab the audience's attention. The poetry audience constantly changed throughout the day, and its attention needed to be grabbed again and again. As Kubernik puts it, "Nobody shows up for seven minutes to see two Beastie Boys songs and then splits." Shappy, a Chicago poet who acted as emcee, lamented the need to constantly perform the same loud, angry poems, and not the rest of his work.

If the poets did succeed in grabbing the audience, they rarely got to the next step, delivering substantial work. In fact, some of the poets with the most substantive poetry had the hardest time holding the crowd.

Liz Belile did provide examples where that was not the case, such as Tracie Morris, from New York City, who read from the second stage and riveted the audience of 2,000 with "gorgeous poetry." Hopefully, we will soon see audiences willing to give more of their attention and poets will be able to move from grabbing to holding that attention.

NETWORKING

Networking, according to Kubernik, "is where the real influence of the gigs lie… People that never met each other before will be working together." Poets not only met a new audience, they met each other. Present at the L.A. shows, in addition to locals, were poets from Seattle, San Francisco, Texas, Chicago, New York, and, well, we didn't get everybody's address. All these poets were exchanging books, addresses, and information.

Probably more important than individual connections was the awareness that poetry is going on everywhere. The same events of your local scene are being repeated all over America. This knowledge is empowering, letting us know we are not alone, encouraging us to expand our horizons.

MEDIA ATTENTION

Lollapalooza also helped alert the media to the strength of the poetry scene. (As with everything else here, it mostly accented an already growing awareness.) According to Kubernik, "It helped serve as a real icebreaker event." He cited many examples of national newspapers calling New Alliance for stories, and of radio stations looking for CDs.

A key change is media taking poetry seriously. Most reports presented the poetry tent as a significant part of the show, not just a bunch of bongo-beating weirdoes. (Though we did overhear someone at the KROQ booth dismiss it as "an excuse to get on stage and say the F-word a lot.")

PROBLEMS & COMPLAINTS

With media attention, however, come personality problems. The smell of blood is suddenly in the poetry waters, and the sharks are coming out to play. We heard comments such as "star-fucking" tossed around with a frightening casualness.

In fact, over the past three months we heard many negative comments on Lollapalooza. These ranged from a general attitude that a rock concert is no place for poets, to specific complaints about the judging at various slams.

One oft-heard complaint concerned favoritism in picking the performing poets. Some poets had to slam to get a slot, others slid in the back door. When asked about the methods of choosing poets, Liz Belile responded, "It was back-breakingly difficult. The national poetry community is huge — lots of emerging talent. We wanted to show that diversity."

Without a Billboard Top 100 of Poetry, how does one select poets? Liz Belile listed four factors for the Road Poets: Talent, Team Player, Connections and Product (books, CDs etc.) to sell. Slams were included so other talented poets could have a chance. Let us not forget that, in the larger scale of American culture, almost all poets must be considered unknowns. There were no obvious choices.

A question which pops up here is: Did Lollapalooza change that? Did any of the hundreds of poets who crossed the Revival Tent stage find new fans?

It is too early to tell. It may never be possible. The standard method of finding out such information would be sales figures. Liz Belile attempted to include poets with product to sell, but that, too, often meant self-published chapbooks. Harvey Kubernik, whose New Alliance records many poets who appeared at the L.A. shows, including Liz Belile, said he did not expect any dramatic changes in sales figures from the shows.

THE FUTURE

If it is too early to tell how Lollapalooza will affect the future of poetry, we still feel that is where the focus should be. Rather than rehashing what happened this summer, we should be asking: What now?

Lollapalooza was an experiment, and much was learned from it. Most conversations we have had about the experience often turned to what was learned.

Many poets learned performance techniques — how to use a mike, how to approach a large crowd, how to grab their attention. We hope not too many learned negative lessons, such as shock is more important than substance.

The producers obviously learned much about putting on poetry shows of this nature, but they declined to share those insights with us. Nonetheless, we anticipate new, powerful poetry shows in the near future.

Most important, and the hardest to determine, is what the audience learned. Did they realize the vitality of poetry today, or did they conclude this was a freak show after all? We may find that out in the months ahead, as they do, or do not, vote with their feet and dollars. (That is, assuming someone gets some product out there for them to buy.)

Perhaps the best conclusion is a quote we heard, attributed second- or third-hand to Liz Belile: "The point was just to get the crowd to take the bait. We can worry about reeling them in later."

(10/94)

POETRY FOR THE MASSES

By Manuel Schwab

(Manuel Schwab has been impressing poetry audiences since he was thirteen. He managed to travel with Lollapalooza for a couple of weeks this summer. He won the slam at Lollapalooza on Sept. 4.)

"You wanna come back here and say that to my face, or are you afraid of a 6'2" drag queen comin' after you and kickin' your fuckin' ass?" With these words another braindead alternative rocker for beer (who came to Lollapalooza looking for anything but this) bites the dust. Torment, a man in six-inch stiletto heels and a dress made of Fender guitar picks, walks away with a dry "thought so."

Welcome to the Revival Stage! Welcome to Lollapalooza's bombardment of vision and word! We're taking every city by storm, and, in our wake, the alternative masses are left drowning in their brain-waves! Here are the poets.

I'd been touring with the Spoken Word poets since Houston. I was unbathed, I hadn't slept. A few of us were sitting on the lawn next to stage left, watching the Spam eating contest from a safe distance.

The man next to me was grinning. A 50 year-old local poet from Dallas had just eaten ten tabs of acid when he was called up on stage where he howled like a dog through ten minutes of derision.

That was what we were there to do: force-feed the American population from Houston to L.A. with angry sound bites tinged with all the humor and bitterness that

Lollapalooza goers could take for a year.

The run-down at each city was the same. All the poets would meet at 10 a.m. to get their passes and become acquainted. There were three types of poets at each city. The Road Poets were paid to travel and had the ever-coveted laminated pass that took one backstage. The Slum Poets (to which I belonged) were unpaid but were guaranteed a place on stage and a pass in as long as they showed up at each city. In addition, there were local poets at each venue made up of the Slam Winners from that particular city.

At about 10:30, we would meet to discuss rules and "etiquette" on stage. At noon the doors would open, and the show would begin with a reading of all the invited poets. We would also send out poets to hassle the crowd with megaphones and soap boxes. At 2:15 there was usually a slam for $100. At 6:30 the stage would close and we could (if we chose) see the shows.

I quickly learned some survival tips. Reading a poem would get you a free cup of coffee, a smart drink,

Illustration by Brian Hagen

or some food. Also, in the great portable city of vendors and nonprofit groups, poets were family.

I spent the first night in Houston walking from stand to stand, offering gas money and work for a ride. After an hour's search, I had a ride to the next city. Those rides were the magical hours of the evening.

I was eventually dropped from the Seattle and Vancouver shows because of my age. The interstate travel of minors was a serious problem for the producers. It's that kind of bureaucracy that I think inevitably develops when an event like Lollapalooza gets so big the organizers have no contact with the smaller stages.

There is nothing, however, like reveling in the insanity of the Spoken Word, and perpetuating it. There's nothing like seeing the alternative nation realize how much they have left to learn. There is nothing like pure, naked, aggressive thought.

(10/94)

SLAMS COME TO SOCAL

By G. Murray Thomas

Did you know that the national poetry slam finals were held in Asheville, North Carolina, on August 18-21? They attracted poets from all over the U.S., Canada, and Europe. The finalists competed to a packed, 200-seat auditorium. As well as competing, poets got a chance to meet each other, and form friendships and national networks. But no poets represented Los Angeles.

It looks like that may finally change. Slams, long the backbone of performance poetry elsewhere in the U.S., are coming to Southern California. The various Lollapalooza slams have stimulated interest among the local poets, producers and audience. Midnight Special, in Santa Monica, and Sacred Grounds, San Pedro, are both running monthly slams, and we hear rumors of more slams to come in Long Beach and San Diego.

Next... Magazine welcomes their arrival.

The slams we have seen go far to combat some of the standard open reading problems — boring poets, uninvolved audiences, and the dreaded "read-and-leave" syndrome. Additionally, slams could provide a much-needed connection to the national poetry scene.

Don't get us wrong. Slams are not perfect, and we are not advocating that every open reading be turned into a slam. There are plenty of faults with slams, from individual cases of lousy judges to the whole notion of competitive poetry. But we're going to rely on you, our readers, to tell us about those. We are going to tell you why we like slams.

The most important aspect of slams is that they encourage poets to be at their best. Poets are going to bring out their best material and perform it with an extra punch. You will rarely hear, "I just wrote this today, and I'm not sure if it's any good," at a slam.

Only poets sure of their work will compete. That confidence will increase the quality of the night. (As a snide aside, we would like to say that, in our experience, many of the poets who are afraid to put their work up to be scored have good reason for that fear.)

Slams encourage audience participation. We have all experienced, and participated in, polite applause which has no relation to the poem's merit. At a slam, if the audience likes a poem, they let you know. Likewise if they don't like it. Almost all the slams we have seen have had enthusiastic, energetic, involved audiences.

Enthusiastic, energetic, involved audiences that stayed to the end. Not only do the participating poets stick around to see who wins, so does the crowd. The Lollapaluna slam, which took place at Luna Park on Sunday, August 28, lasted six hours, and hardly lost any of its crowd.

Our conclusion from all this is that slams are a way of presenting poetry that the non-poet public can, and does, enjoy. Isn't that what we've been searching for out here? As a final bonus, by linking into the national slam network, we can make Southern California part of the national poetry community.

It's about time SoCal started slamming!

(10/94)

ALLEN GINSBERG

Saturday, Sept. 10, 1994 • Long Beach Promenade Amphitheater
Reviewed by Gwynne Garfinkle

First of all, the outdoor promenade amphitheater in Long Beach is a terrific place for a poetry reading, particularly a large one, as this was — hundreds of people sitting on blankets under the darkening sky. However, I heard numerous complaints from people who had waited in line, some for hours, to get a good spot, only to not be let into the amphitheater until after 6:30, when the show was supposed to have begun. (I also heard complaints about conflicting information as to when the show was supposed to start – many thought 6:00.)

When we were let inside, One Percussion and Lilly de la Mora performed brief, entertaining sets of music and dance before Allen Ginsberg took the stage. Ginsberg interspersed songs and poetry. For the songs, he played harmonium, ably accompanied on violin, guitar, and banjo by Steven Said. Ginsberg's songs are mostly humorous, at their best political, and often too long. Among the most entertaining were an improvisation that must've been taken straight off a flyer by the Friends of the L.A. River, a gay lib song, and "Put Down Your Cigarette Rag."

While enjoyable, Ginsberg's songs, even at their best, don't compare to his poems. He read several from his new book, *Cosmopolitan Greetings*, along with new work, and showed himself still one of the best readers of poetry around, being true to American spoken idiom, with impeccable Jewish comedic flair. When he reads, his voice has a true music that his songs lack, and his voice becomes a powerful instrument. This was especially noticeable when he performed the anti-war chant, "Hum Bom."

Ginsberg read a poem consisting of one-liners, advice to young and old, including "Stay irresponsible," "Catch yourself thinking," "Maximum information, minimum number of syllables," and my personal favorite, "If we don't show anyone, we're free to write anything." He also read a hilarious paean to the salty, sugary, and fatty foods of Western culture, followed by a poem about excrement which made many audience members groan. He concluded the evening with a sing-along of Blake's "Nurse's Song," followed by his own "Father Death Blues."

While I would have preferred more poetry, fewer songs (or at least, shorter songs), the varied program allowed the audience to listen better to the poetry. I'm all for combinations of poetry and music, but where Ginsberg's concerned, the poetry should be preeminent. (10/94)

COWBOY POETRY IN ELKO NEVADA

By Scott Preston

Cowboy poetry embodies the most important and vital literary culture to have emerged in this country since the Beat Generation.

Most of this country's literary history centers around New York, San Francisco, and a handful of academic outposts. Cowboy poetry has put places like Durango, Wickenburg, Salmon, Nara Visa, Silver City, and Ruidoso on the poetry map. The poets themselves live in even more obscure locations. They are people who've been generally disenfranchised from typical writing scenes in this country, yet the hands-on experiences of their actual working lives gives them as much or more to write about as anyone grooving on big city alienation.

The core of Cowboy Poetry, spiritually and practically, lies in the annual gathering every January in Elko, Nevada.

Like the old rendezvous of the fur trappers, everybody makes Elko a priority, and a greater location for a poetry gathering can't be imagined. The local casinos make 24-hour action naturally available, yet gambling is way down on the list of activities. Poetry and music in concurrent sessions fill the day time hours, ticketed event night shows run to midnight, then after-hours jam sessions, cabaret performances, and visiting at the bar goes on 'til dawn. Over the years, Elko has hosted international ethnic ranch-life performances, including Australian bush poetry, Native Hawaiian cowboy songs, Mexican and Peruvian vaquero stories and music. This year is focused on Native American ranching traditions. At Elko, as throughout Cowboy poetry culture, poetry and music are virtually inseparable.

The Elko Gathering was originally assembled in 1985 as a fabulous one-shot event, a chance for Western American folklorists to document a cult folk-life phenomenon of their very own, to assemble an archive and write a few essays. Something else happened, a virtual explosion of unharnessed inter-poet activity that academic folklorists had no real understanding or experience to grasp for years. They kept the event going, yet only gradually have come to the realization that a genuine literary culture was midwifing itself in the very midst of the carefully orchestrated traditional recitations they thought were the basis of the form.

I don't want to disparage the traditional poetry. After one hundred years of practice, ballads handed down from the mid-19th century to the present day give Cowboy poetry an authoritative grounding that has more practical value in the lives of the writers than any Norton or Oxford genealogical anthology can ever hope to engender in its bored student readers. Reciting traditional ballad poetry is also a way to allow the inclusion of a lot of folks who don't necessarily write their own stuff, but still have a claim to participate.

Elko is not, and has never been, a contest. There is a screening committee that makes the necessary decisions of who gets formally invited, no mean task given there are only funds to underwrite sixty or so poets out of hundreds of applicants. And consider that the Cowboy poetry network, extending from Texas and Oklahoma to the Great Plains of Canada, and every rural area west to the coast, covers a vast range where gas money and a motel room are simply part of the gig. There are now hundreds of Cowboy poetry events held in the Inner West, from regional versions of the Elko grandsire, to sets at county fairs, auctions, barbecues and wagon rides.

A spirited open-form movement has taken hold, and a new anthology edited by John Dofflemyer, *Maverick Western Verse* (Peregrine Smith, 1994) makes one hell of a statement as to where this poetry has come from, where it might be going, and who else might conceivably be included as stylistic compadres.

Cowboy poetry puts a heavy emphasis on participation, and a basic enjoyment of what's happening, and leaves the questions of immortality for a later time. It doesn't hurt that a tradition already exists. Besides, show me a poetry movement in the history of the world where even half of its published output made the cut into the next generation's interest.

So who's hot? For starters, the work of Paul Zarzyski, a former student of Richard Hugo, whose attempt to merge his academic poetry training with the bucking rhythms of his mutual love, rodeo, has resulted in a body of work that revolutionized the acceptance of free verse at the same time that his experiments with traditional forms launched Cowboy poetry into a verbal space age. Zarzyski is one of the most original poets in the United States right now, and the pure fact that the Cowboy circuit has embraced his writing far more avidly than the MFA culture that Zarzyski originated from stands alone as a mark of the validity of this folk movement as a creator of important American poetry. But there's a hell of a lot more.

There's a NamVet contingent, poets like Bill Jones and Rod McQueary, whose early success writing traditional verse under the protective umbrella of Cowboy poetry enabled them to take the risk of writing about Vietnam, resulting in *Blood Trails* (Dry Crik Press, 1993), a time capsule of raw war writing that's almost disappeared in the advent of 20 years of NamVet workshop experience. There's a brilliant Crow from Montana named Hank Real Bird who performs a kind of Native American rap Cowboy poetry.

There's a powerful grassroots feminist segment, including Sue Wallis, Peggy Godfrey, Thelma Poirier, Linda Hussa, and many others who have begun telling their side of the story sans male approval, and it too offers a time capsule of anger and repressed emotion that reads as fresh and immediate as any innovative American poetics based in the vernacular idioms of the language.

I understand there's a group of unemployed Hollywood actors who formed a Cowboy poetry troupe after hearing the real thing at a show in Visalia. Apparently they do well enough to actually pay a residual performance royalty to some of the living poets whose work they rely on. It's to their credit, but it's still as close to the authentic energy as a shrink-wrapped T-bone in the meat department is to a live herd mowing grass in the shadow of the Rockies.

So come to Elko. Like the major leagues observed from the minors, it's "The Show" in the West right now. The various spin-off and complementary events are no comparison.

(12/94)

NEWS CLIPS & EGO TRIPS

By G. Murray Thomas

It's been a great month for readings/parties… The ABA Convention provided multiple opportunities for partying, as the big publishers poured the booze wooing the masses… maybe someday Orange Ocean Press will be able to host such smashes… One of the best was a slam organized by New York's Bob Holman at Book Soup on Sunset, featuring Wanda Coleman, Ishmael Reed, Luis Rodriguez and Miguel Algarin… a few weeks later, Book Soup was home for a reading organized by Justine Bateman. We missed that one, but we do wonder what has inspired Ms. Bateman to get back into poetry after a five year absence… another big name is rumored to be entering the world of coffee houses and spoken word, but my computer keyboard doesn't have the fancy little symbol he uses for a name these days… yes, the Purple One is said to be opening a coffee house on Melrose, and it will have poetry…

Tommy Swerdlow held a release party for his new CD *Prisoner of Gifted Sleep* (New Alliance) at Luna Park in West Hollywood. He put on a good show, backed up by David Zazloff's band, but no one actually had any copies of the CD… We finally found Tommy's CD in Tower Records' steadily growing spoken word section, sharing space with Linda Albertano, Reg E. Gaines, Jack Kerouac and *The Best of Penthouse Forum*… Go figure…

(7/94)

THE YEAR MADONNA BECAME THE PATRON SAINT OF POETRY

By Lawrence Schulz

Let's face it: Poetry in SoCal is the ugliest kid on the block. You can dress the kid up…it's still the ugly kid. You can ask the kid to dance…. yep, still ugly. You can take a picture of it with the homecoming queen or the football hero… you know what they say about how cameras don't lie.

But 1994 will be known as the year when the ugliest kid on the block dusted off the old Madonna records, listened to "Like a Virgin" and decided it time to get touched for the very first time. It set up a little shrine in its ugly closet and said to itself, "She can't sing, she moves like a cow, and she's still rich, famous and has lovers galore…"

Then came the magical question that either makes a difference or drives a person totally crazy. "WHY CAN'T I?"

She just markets herself, the Ugly Kid decided. That's all she does different. That's what I'm going to

Illustration of Lawrence Shulz by Charles Ellik

do. In 1994, the Ugly Kid decided it was time to market itself.

Coffeehouses sprang up like joints at a Grateful Dead concert. There were open poetry readings, open mikes and featured readers all over SoCal coffeehouses. Next to the O.J. trial, the press gave great coverage to coffee house poetry readings. So what if it wasn't as glamorous as the Michael Jackson case, at least it wasn't as complicated as Orange County losing two billion dollars. The Ugly Kid thought this would be a great place to show off. So, armed with copies of *Next... Magazine*, Ugly went to as many poetry readings as possible and found one thing it wasn't getting from real life.

Acceptance.

Acceptance is a poor substitute for getting touched for the very first time, but when you're ugly, you go for what you can.

Just about this point, when the Ugly Kid was feeling good about itself, some clever promoter-types decided that the Ugly Kid might have a following. In an ever desperate search for a label, they called it "alternative" and decided to match it up with the Lollapalooza concert. They held Lollapalooza slams throughout Los Angeles and Orange County. The Ugly Kid might get a chance to make it "Big Time" at a major rock concert. There was energy going!

(Meanwhile, there was a voice that said "Lollapalooza" and "alternative" were the biggest pieces of commercial crap hype since Pet Rocks and Bell Bottoms. But the Ugly Kid didn't listen.)

Lollapalooza comes.... Lollapalooza goes. The Ugly Kid still hadn't gotten laid yet. But now there was a "strong possibility." The L.A. Poetry Festival somehow got swallowed up by the earthquake or eaten by Godzilla, but that was okay. The Ugly Kid didn't care, it was now everywhere. Writing for magazines, at poetry readings, on cable, on compact disc, on video tape. The energy level was at an all time high and just when it looked good…

The year came to an end. The Ugly Kid looked back and said "I did all the right things…what happened?"

1995 is about to come around. Who knows, this could be the year the Ugly Kid will get laid… but it's doubtful that it will ever be loved.
(1/95)

OFF THE HIGHWAY
By Lisa Verlo

Being "red tagged" in the Santa Monica earthquake became a catalyst for hitting the road last January, and the growing number of poetry venues has kept me on it ever since. This past year was spent touring the country in my Chevy Blazer, performing and making gas money doing the poetic thing. Hit several festivals, slid into a few coffee houses and made the poem run. Collecting every oooooh I earned for working my puns off, I gathered enough change to make it back to the sunset without an attitude.

After checking out the scene in Colorado, I made my way down to Taos for the Poetry Circus and was inspired by a reading of Bobbie Louise Hawkins enough to participate in a workshop of hers the next day. While reading in the Poet's Living Room and attending the Championship Poetry bout, I was slightly surprised that the only Californians present were event winner Quincy Troupe and some guy who was kinda snobby cause he was covering the bout for the *LA Times*. What happened to vanpooling fourteen hours for the literary cause?

So I go up to Boulder for the week-long tribute to Allen Ginsberg and there again, very few L.A.ites besides Midnight Special cutie-pie Ryan Vincent who was checking out Boulder as a college choice and catching a whiff of the reconstructed Beat scene at the same time. The event started off with a super inspiring performance by Meredith Monk and continued with seven days full of panel discussions, lectures, film and slide shows, with readings and jamming by the likes of David Amram, Sharon Olds, Antler and musical festivity by the man himself. Allen kept reminding everyone about how they all just did everything themselves. Didn't wait around to be discovered and published, but created their own venues; reading everywhere, jamming till the wee hours, making chapbooks. Meanwhile all these people are attending this huge event, more worried about keeping their laminated pass from being punched so it would be worth more intact as a collector's item. No one was hustling any self-published paper, so being the only choice, I made out pretty good, and went running back to Kinko's for second editions. An open reading was held outside under a big tent, where I tried my material out on the beat crowd and got a few pieces in at the West End Tavern as well.

Next, I was featured at the Denver press club, opening for a monthly slam, the first I'd ever attended. I was then asked to judge. Hearing about the National championships being held a week later, I thought, why not go to Asheville, North Carolina, and check it out. Twenty-five teams of four from all over the U.S. (except California!) presented their creamiest crop. They even displayed my hand-bound book on the Slam merchandise table, even though I wasn't competing. There were plenty of open mics staged around town during the four day event, which helped with promotion and sales. The best part was meeting all these wonderful poet-types from all over the country, and exchanging info, interest, and food at three in the morning in one of Carolina's supreme literary haunts — the Waffle House.

That is how I ended up at the Insomniacathon '94 in Louisville, Kentucky. Three days of nonstop poetry and music organized by Kent Fielding of *RANT*, who gave me special billing as Lisa Pillow. Serves me right for making the arrangements without spending two dollars on a follow up fax confirming the facts. So it costs half the price of a chapbook, do it anyway. It's real disappointing when you pull into town, and they have these beautiful posters plastered all over with somebody else's last name on them, which is the only original part of yours anyway.

Ohio was the best, it was! I was all set up through the most receptive network of referrals anywhere. Every venue had a super attentive attendance, and a very supportive response, as well as the best chapbook and tape sales ever — $90 one night at the Classique Cafe in Lorain, and only thirty people there! Kaldi's in Cincinnati is also a must-stop for any touring poet. In Cleveland I caught up with four-year road veteran Ray McNiece, who may be in your neck of the woods as you read this. He has been driving cross-country so much, his ears pick up freeway frequency.

Did Detroit and made some more gas cash at the Ann Arbor Poetry Festival. Read at the legendary Lili's in Hamtramck among many other motor city stops, including Rabbles in St. Clair Shores, and Gotham City, downtown. Ann Arbor will be hosting this year's National Poetry Slam in August, so Michigan will be bursting with the genre in no time.

November brought me back to Los Angeles again, to record some Spoken Word for an upcoming CD. Visiting the area gave me a whole new perspective, venturing to farther reaches, and discovering some great down home venues. It is one big wild and exciting world out there. The corners of this country are calling, gotta get going again before the car craps out. Maybe I'll see ya out there. If you are just getting by in L.A., you can just get by about anywhere else. As long as you keep your eye on the gauges.
(6/95)

Illustration by Charles Ellik

THE TAOS POETRY CIRCUS

June 11 - 18, 1995 • Taos, New Mexico
By G. Murray Thomas

The Taos Poetry Circus is a week-long series of poetry events up in the glorious mountains of northern New Mexico. It was started in 1981 by Anne MacNaughton and Peter Rabbit, and has grown steadily since then. This year it attracted poets from across the country, with a crowd of nearly three hundred attending its final event.

That final event, the "Main Event," is the World Heavyweight Championship Poetry Bout, where two poets go ten rounds, matching poem for poem, while being scored by three citizen judges. The 1995 bout pitted defending champion Quincy Troupe against challenger Bobbie Louise Hawkins.

This year also marked the first time National Slam Poets were a strong presence at the Circus. The goals of the Bout and the slams are the same; they both use the competitive format to add an extra level of excitement to a poetry reading, and thereby to increase the audience. However, until now the two formats have kept their distance from each other, focusing on whatever differences existed. Whether the meeting was a success or not depended on who you talked to.

The Slammers headlined the Friday night show, in the form of Bob Holman and Patricia Smith. Holman is the host at the Nuyorican Poets' Cafe in New York, one of the most successful slams in the country. Amongst many other credits, all related to increasing the poetry audience, he is currently producing *The United States of Poetry*, a PBS series which (judging from the episodes we were privileged to preview) should set a new, high standard for the video presentation of poetry. Patricia Smith, from Boston, is a three–time National Poetry Slam winner.

Their performance was a great demonstration of the strengths of slam poetry. Bob Holman uses rapid-fire delivery and wild word play to comment on the politics of communication. His primary concern is the potential for words (i.e.: poetry) to change things, from our society to our thoughts. "You know things!" he commanded. "Think them!"

Patricia Smith clearly showed how she wins slams. Every word of her tightly crafted poems hit like bullets. She covered topics (gang violence, South Africa) which we have all heard turn to mushy cliché in the mouths of far too many poets, yet she stayed consistently fresh and original. She found a unique perspective for each poem, distinct details she could use to express her larger ideas. Her delivery was sharp and clear. Craft and performance combined to astounding effect.

The energy and quality did not let up for the Main Event of Troupe vs. Hawkins. Quincy Troupe, now a professor of American and Caribbean Literature at UCSD, came out of the Watts Writers Workshop, and his work reflects the rhythms and realities of urban Southern California. Bobbie Louise Hawkins grew up in West Texas, and writes about the people she grew up with and their relationships. Both are meticulous crafters of words and powerful performers.

It was an extremely close competition, but the difficulties of judging it lay more in their differences than in their strengths. The styles of the competitors were so divergent that there was little crowd for comparison. Troupe used the rhythms of jazz and R&B and verbal repetition to fuel his emotional collages. Hawkins' poems were structured on a conversational tone, and focused on the details of human interaction. Put another way, Troupe dressed his ideas up in elaborate verbal costumes, while Hawkins used spare language to express her ideas as sharply as possible. Whichever style a listener preferred would, in their ears, win.

The judges acted accordingly, producing the closest Bout in the history of the Championship. Quincy Troupe squeaked his way to another title by a mere two points. However, the audience, polled for the sake of curiosity, voted almost two to one for Hawkins. Myself, I rated six rounds as ties, and two as narrow wins, one apiece. Only on two rounds did I see a clear winner. Hawkins won the final, improvised round, using the challenging phrase "bearded iris" (drawn randomly by her) to inspire a gorgeous piece on waiting for blossoming and joy. Troupe, given the word "militia," stalled with repetitions of "Militia! Rat-a-tat!" but still failed to come up with anything compelling.

The Bout had already been decided for me, however, during Round 8. Then, Troupe read a moving short piece called "Changes," which was written in a style much more like Hawkins that his own. In a battle of styles, he demonstrated that he could do her style, and do it well, while she never came close to his.

This battle of styles did provide a perspective for the whole festival. Throughout the week there was much talk about conflicting notions of poetry. There was slam vs. bout, performance vs. print, rural vs. urban, establishment vs. grassroots, and everyone present vs. Cowboy Poetry. The debates were many, and they were exemplified in the Championship Bout, which came down to a personal definition of poetry.

All that, however, was mere talk. The action of the week told a different story. It involved poets coming together, without attitude or judgment, and nourishing each other. There was an ongoing series of workshops, large and small, where the headliners helped the audience work on their poems. There was an open reading every afternoon, which was attended, with some regularity, by Holman, Smith, MacNaughton, and Peter Rabbit, as well as Michael Brown (husband of Patricia Smith, and head of the National Slam Organization) and Al Simmons (one of the originators of the concept of competitive poetry). There were poets from all across the country, meeting and inspiring each other. The whole festival proved poetry is very alive, despite, or perhaps because of, its differences.

As Holman, who emceed the Bout, announced, "The winner is always poetry!"

(7/95)

NATIONAL POETRY SLAM

August 9 - 12, 1995 • Ann Arbor, MI
By G. Murray Thomas

"Judge #3 gives that poem an 8.7," the emcee announces. The crowd boos.

It's the final night of the 1995 National Poetry Slam. The 1,700-seat Michigan Theater is packed, and the audience is wild with enthusiasm. There is no polite applause here; instead, there are repeated standing ovations. 8.7 is not a high enough score for this crowd. They think these poems deserve at least a 9.5.

For the most part, they are right. The quality of the poetry is exceptionally high. Over the past three days, twenty-seven teams and over 120 individual poets have been narrowed down to four team and six individual finalists. Tonight, the best slam poets duke it out with their best material.

If there is any doubt that this poetry has appeal beyond a narrow group of literati, it is dispelled when Marc Smith, originator of the Poetry Slam and emcee for the team competition, asks the poets in the house to stand up and applaud the audience. The poets who stand are vastly outnumbered by those who have just come to listen. Through the slam, poetry has found its long-lost audience.

Four person teams came to Ann Arbor from all across the continent — Portland, Oregon, to Portland, Maine, Seattle to Key West. Among the ten additional individual poets (all team member also competed for the individual title) are representatives from Sweden, Pakistan, South Africa, the Mohawk Nation, and the sole official SoCal contestant, Roland Poet X. Mark Pomeroy, also from L.A., filled a last-minute opening on the Las Vegas team. First prize was $2,000 for the winning team, and $500 for the top individual.

The 1995 National Slam was run by local Ann Arbor poets Larry Francis, Steve Marsh and Deb Marsh. They did an exemplary job. The various slam bouts all ran smoothly (what few complaints there were centered on judging disagreements), and all events were organized and promoted quite well.

The week started with a registration ceremony, where each team did a group introduction of themselves. These pieces, some carefully rehearsed, some improvised, were all entertaining, and gave everyone, participants and audience, a chance to size up the competition.

Preliminary bouts were held Wednesday and Thursday at coffeehouses and other small venues throughout Ann Arbor. Attendance hovered around 150-200 for each location. Each day there were nine three-team bouts. Because of wide discrepancies in the scoring between the different panels of judges, teams advanced based on their rank (first, second, or third) in these bouts, not on their actual scores. Eighteen teams and ten individuals advanced to the semi-finals on Friday, which further narrowed the contestants.

With some two hundred poets in town, there were many other poetic activities scheduled, including a softball game, a head-to-head haiku contest, a round table for newsletter publishers, and an assortment of midnight open readings. The open readings proved very popular, with most sign-up lists running over forty names. A reading of poetry about sin and vice, held in crowded, non-air-conditioned bar, featured a naked poet and another poet, fully clothed, chasing a waitress through the kitchen while screaming about "Toad Venom." There was also the expected informal partying, schmoozing, networking, and exchanging of addresses and info.

The final night opened with a selection of audience favorites — poets whose work resonated with the crowds at the preliminaries, but who did not score high enough to advance to the finals. These included Trinidad Sanchez, Jr. and the Albuquerque team; Evert Eden from South Africa; Holly Hunt (Athens, GA); Beth Lisick (San Francisco); Ava Chin (on the Las Vegas team); Crystal Williams from New York City, who scored a perfect thirty in the semi-finals; and the hometown favorites, Ken Cormier and the Ann Arbor team, whose strong performances during the week couldn't quite carry them into the finals.

The final four teams were Boston, Cleveland, Asheville NC, and Portland, Maine. The six individual finalists were Patricia Smith (Boston), Taylor Mali (Maine), Wammo (Austin), Boogieman (Cleveland), DJ Renegade (Washington, D.C.), and Justin Chin (S.F.). The competition was fierce and the atmosphere was tense. The crowd, as was mentioned earlier, was excited and involved.

Asheville emerged victorious, largely on the strength of group pieces, followed closely by Cleveland, Boston, and Portland. Patricia Smith took her fourth national championship, narrowly beating (in order) Wammo, Boogieman, and DJ Renegade.

Of course, not everyone in the audience agreed with the final results. That was part of what made it an exciting and memorable evening. Everyone had their favorites among the poets (and their anti-favorites). By cheering on their choices, they formed a connection with the poets far beyond polite listening. I'm sure everyone in that theater walked out with some poem fixed firmly in their mind which they thought was the best, some poet they felt deserved to win.

(9/95)

PATTI SMITH

Ed Sanders & Bobbie Louise Hawkins
Thursday, Sept. 7, 1995 • Long Beach Promenade Amphitheater
Reviewed by G. Murray Thomas

The When Words Collide Festival opened with a bang. Over 750 people packed the Promenade Amphitheater to see Patti Smith, Ed Sanders, and Bobbie Louise Hawkins. The show was entertaining, at times quite powerful, yet not completely satisfying.

Hawkins, who opened the show, presented herself as a storyteller. She entertained the crowd with finely detailed accounts of romantic and family relationships. At one point, she revealed the foundation of her talent: she is a listener who wants "every last detail." Those details then show up in her poems.

Ed Sanders's many credits include the '60s band The Fugs, *The Family*, a Manson bio, and a just-completed bio of Anton Chekhov in verse. He came off as a minstrel entertainer. He accompanied himself on a long-necked lute, and with prerecorded musical tracks. His main theme was continuity: there has always been a "Rebel Cafe" and a "Lost Generation." There was a yin-yang contradiction in this: one of the things which never changes is that there are always people who change things.

The crowd greeted Patti Smith, in her first Los Angeles area appearance in fifteen years, with a standing ovation. She then spent much of her set seeming to deny that acclamation, trying to reduce herself from a rock star to just another human. It could be described as an "anti-performance." Smith wandered almost aimlessly through a selection of her poems, often losing her train of thought and spacing out on the setting. She offered a series of excuses for her lack of energy, including exhaustion and, primarily, "I miss my kids."

The irony is that Smith's work was something beyond human. It attempted, and often succeeded at, the highest goal for poetry — to express the inexpressible. Her themes were dreams, death, and redemption — the moments when the spirit rises above and away from earthly reality. Such moments, by their nature, cannot be put into words. Her meandering stage manner emphasized this; there was a feeling of walking around something without quite touching it. Her difficulty in completing a thought echoed the difficulty of expression inherent in her poems.

Still, she did, at times, hit that center. In poems such as "Georgia O'Keefe," "Land" (the printed, not the recorded, version), and her ode to the Dalai Lama, Smith's spirit suddenly inhabited her words; her voice became strong and sure, and we were all someplace else for a few moments. This was especially true when, at the end, she sang a few songs. Everything she had been attempting came together in her version of "Dancing Barefoot." It was the most powerful moment of the night. A little music can sure help the inexpressible.

In all, it was a very entertaining evening, although occasional flashes of brilliance from all three performers hinted at an intensity which was rarely delivered, and was missed by at least a few in the crowd.

(10/95)

DAVE ALVIN, G. LOVE, WATTS PROPHETS

Friday, Sept. 15, 1995 • Long Beach Promenade Amphitheater
Reviewed by Lawrence Schulz

Two performances rocked the spoken word show of "When Words Collide" on Sept. 15. Dave Alvin, reading from his book *Any Rough Times Are Now Behind You*, and the Watts Prophets, fusing rap, poetry, and music, both showed that spoken word poetry can be as potent and powerful as any rock concert.

Alvin, rock veteran through his work with the Blasters and X, started his set with a tribute to the Long Beach bars. With a nod to his mentor Professor Gerald Locklin of Cal State Long Beach, Alvin took the audience through a tour of heartbreak in "After We Had Sex," to life and hard times on the road with "My Brother." His concluding poem "Song" took a look at what drives artist to produce in the face of hard times. To refer to the title of an early Blaster's album, Alvin's performance of Sept. 15 was nonfiction poetry that hit as hard as an ending power smash cord at any rock show.

Blues-rap guitar player G. Love interspersed the spoken word shows with his slide guitar work. Unfortunately, it did not carry a strong enough impact to move the audience. His "been down that road

before" voice failed to catch fire. Songs like "Special Sauce" and "She Got That Soul" could have hit harder if they had been delivered in a different venue.

The evening belonged to the Watts Prophets. This legendary rap group call themselves the Godfathers of Rap. Because of its history, this group (which started in

the 1960s) could well claim to be the predecessor of all current rap music. It is good to see the Watts Prophets get the recognition they deserve. They combined showmanship, music, and a great poetic delivery for a strong performance. The group's background musical accompaniment of conga drums and flute underscored their show, never overpowering their performance. Works like "Money" and "All is Vanity" at times took on a Sunday church revival service with its zest. "After I Had Died" pointed out the relevancy of who your true friends are. The Watts Prophets brought it all home

Illustration by Walt Hopmans

with "Do You Remember Watts?" and "Change is Overdue" to show that rap and poetry are brothers and sisters in the same house of cool.

The Sept. 15 show showed that words can rock.

(10/95)

WHITE TRASH APOCALYPSE TOUR DIARY

By Pleasant Gehman

In June of 1995, Iris Berry, S.A. Griffin, and I decided to go on a spoken word tour, to promote our various books and CDs. We didn't want the tour to be "ordinary," so we treated it like a rock'n'roll tour, leaving a wake of flabbergasted audiences and wild, hedonistic ruins. Dubbed "White Trash Apocalypse: Words on Wheels '95," we had 8x10 glossies, T-shirts with our logo, and even a freshly recorded studio cassette of our work. We began booking in July, for an October tour, which paid off: advance press and promotion meant sold-out houses, which translated into gas money for S.A.'s 1971 metallic burgundy Buick Riviera, our tour vehicle.

Our objective was originally to read in a diverse cross-section of venues (everywhere from theaters, rock clubs, and java joints to art galleries) and meet fellow poets. As the tour progressed and got crazier (that just happens with no sleep and endless driving y'know?), we also began a quest for The Hope Rhinestone, the worst polyester clothing on earth, the cheesiest tourist attractions, and the most psychotic party animals we could find. Thankfully, we fulfilled every goal to the T!

October 5: We began last night in Long Beach, at Living Planet's Poetry on Wednesdays. Good show, good open readers. We were very pleased. Stopped by Incommunicado Press when we got to San Diego and picked up our publisher, Gary Hustwit. Read tonight at The Rita Dean Art Gallery, which had a very graphic Erotic Art show up, and an even more graphic Museum of Death in the basement, complete with 1940s police photos of train wrecks and car crashes, serial killer paintings (quite a collection of John Wayne Gacy) and other sick things. Apparently, the gallery was once a mortuary. They also had a live two-headed turtle and a huge pig named Chaos, who got into a fight over a stick with gallery's dog.

Oct. 7: Drove all night from San Diego to Tucson, arrived as the sun was coming up at Hotel Congress, the ancient hotel they captured the John Dillinger gang in. Our rooms are right above the club where we performed, opening for the Geraldine Fibbers and Tucson legend Al Perry. The small crowd we had was enthusiastic, but the after-party was wild — culminating with Iris and I dancing on the bar in the club's Tap Room (the bartender's only admonition was, "Be careful of the ceiling fan!") and continuing upstairs in the Geraldine Fibbers rooms. The "sober" room was playing gin rummy, and the "party" room was cross-dressing, singing seventies hits, jumping on the beds, and doing shots of tequila out of (sorry, mom) my belly button. Yes, indeed! The bartender even signed my ass… the scary thing is, nobody can remember if it was his idea or mine. Today we're all hungover and driving to Albuquerque, where we're performing at the Andaluz, the brainchild of Juliette Torrez, whom Iris and I met at Lollapalooza.

Oct. 9: Juliette is a goddess and Andaluz was an amazing show. The papers in Albuquerque gave us three huge write-ups, and the gallery's phone was ringing off the hook all day. There was standing room only, and in honor of White Trash, Juliette hosted an all-you-can-eat Saltine Buffet. Virginia slam poet Julia Delbridge was staying at the gallery, in the midst of her own tour, and did a few great pieces. Left ABQ at dawn this morning, and arrived in Boulder just before dark. Our Penny Lane reading was a bit low-key, though S.A. wowed 'em with his "Sunny Riviera" character (we all have new road names), and his by-now honed a capella lounge rendition of the Red Hot Chili Peppers' song "Little Pea" is hilarious. The show's host, Tom Peterson, of the Beat Bookshop, took us bar-hopping, but we're all dead from driving, even though S.A. does it all.

Oct. 11: Played Denver's Mercury Cafe tonight, an eclectic club full of crazy lamps, stained glass and plants. Poet Ed Ward hosted the reading, and his nine-year-old son opened for us doing a Nirvana cover on guitar, to the delight of the crowd, who were really fun and rowdy. Sold tons of books, chaps, T-shirts and tapes. On our way back to Ed's house, he gave us the Beat Tour of Denver — Keruoac monuments, Larimer

Street stories and the like. Woke up again before it was light in preparation to drive through the Rockies and into Utah.

Oct. 12: On the road again. Right before we got into the mountains, the electronic window switches shorted out, and there were no fuses at the one remaining gas station. Drove through Vail and Steamboat Springs in the sub-zero weather (yes, kids, there was snow — lots of it — on the ground) with the windows stuck all the way down. Iris and I huddled in the backseat, our leopard coats gathered around us. We looked like Zsa Zsa Gabor Goes to Antarctica! Twelve hours of freezing wind, and of course on the way down from the mountains, it began to rain. Utah is like Stepford-land. We keep getting weird looks from redneck and/ or conservative Mormon types when we stop to pee. Totally "Ya ain't from around here!" Deliverance!

Oct. 15: Viva Las Vegas! It was insane. People drove to meet us from New Mexico and Los Angeles, including S.A.'s girlfriend Lorraine, and Honk If Yer Horny's Lovely Connie Rubbermaid, a beautiful, 6'2" raven-haired transvestite, who sold our swag and did a wild striptease down to a marabou bikini and pink fishnets while S.A. was reading. S.A. is somewhat of a legend in Vegas, because he plays "Dr. Osirus" in the Luxor Hotel's virtual reality ride. During our afternoon show at the amazing Benway Bop Records (the hippest store in town) and at night at Cafe Coppio, Vegas performance poet Dave Figler read. He was great — hilarious, literary, hip and with terrific dead-pan delivery. Poems about *The Weekly Reader* and fourth grade, and taking heroin. Whacked out! Later that night he, the Benway Bop crew, and a fez-wearing fellow who emceed our show called simply "The Professor," took us out to party and gamble. We totally tore up the Hard Rock Cafe casino, and everyone kept thinking we were in a band! Iris and I coveted the waitress's leopard hotpants.

Oct. 17: … Some time in the morning… we're on our way home from San Francisco. Last night did Bucky Sinister's rowdy-as-always Monday Night Reading at The Chameleon, a crazy little bar full of velvet paintings and weird patrons. Bucky, whose great book *King of the Road Kills* just came out on Manic D Press, is always a great host. Some guy wouldn't shut up during my set, and I invited him up onstage and then continued reading while sitting on his face — the only way to keep

him quiet! It was Connie Rubbermaid's birthday, so we all went to Hotel Utah afterwards (they have readings there, too) and ended up dancing on the bar! A perfect way to begin and end a tour!

Oct. 22: Home for a few days, then did the "official" last date of the tour at Eagle's Coffee Pub in North Hollywood, on Poison Ivy night, hosted by Cornboy. Great local poetry — Scott Wannberg, Doug Knott, Rafael Alvarado, Kennon B. Raines, and Boomer Maverick all read. The backdrop was a wall-sized photo of Tom Selleck, which S.A. presented to Rafael. There was cake, and a good time was had by all.

It was nice to be home — but give me the road anyday! You never know what might happen. Anything can happen… and it usually does. I highly urge you to get your butts out on the road. Contact any of the places mentioned in this article, and I'm sure they'd love to showcase your talents. As they say in Vegas, "What do you have to lose?"

(12/95)

NEWS CLIPS AND EGO TRIPS
By G. Murray Thomas & The Troll

The *Next…* All Night Marathon Open Reading was a tremendous success. It did go all night, ending with a rapid round of thirty second pieces just past sunrise. Some sixty-five poets read a total of over 130 poems. The energy level was extremely high, as far-flung poets from across SoCal encountered each other for the first time. The resulting synergy has already produced new cooperative projects, such as "Tearing the Curtain," a series of readings exchanging poets between The Iguana, in NoHo, and Java Garden, in Huntington Beach, which will take place in early August…

–GMT

(7/95)

How a magazine evolves over the course of its life is one of the yardsticks I use to measure its worth. The more it changes and grows, the better I like it. *Caffeine* is one such magazine.

When I first came across it by accident just under a year ago, it was very interesting but hard to read. Often the publisher would publish the text of a poem or story in dark letters against an even darker background picture which just about strained the juice out of this poor troll's eyes. Since then, they have gotten better with this particular technique and you can now enjoy excellent poetry against a backdrop of fine art or photography. In perusing issues nine, eleven, and twelve (don't ask what happened to ten) some of the standout poets were Michelle McCarthy, Brent T. Leake, Fred Voss, Steven Pelcman, Rex Butters, and Geoff Farr. There was also a really cool short story by Robert Steven Rhine that is especially worth checking out in issue eleven.

–Troll

(9/95)

The second *Next… Magazine* All-Night Marathon Open Reading, held at Watson I Presume, Long Beach, on Friday, Sept. 29, was a bust. Literally. Shut down by the police at 2:30 a.m.. It seems that some of the participants, despite repeated warnings not to, insisted on drinking on or near the premises. One poet, who prefers to remain anonymous, showed up intoxicated and eventually passed out in the alley. At that point the police were called. (Remember, an entertainment license is an expensive and fragile thing for a coffeehouse to maintain.) The police entered the coffeehouse, where the audience was valiantly trying to keep the reading going by calling out "Who's next?" One policeman announced, "There is no next!" and it was over….

–GMT

(11/95)

We finally got a look at Esther, the new "magazine" from Temporary Vandalism. It consists of poems stuck in the windows of Alan Cohol's car, and has been attracting attention everywhere it goes…

–GMT

(12/95)

DANIEL X. O'NEIL
Wednesday, Nov. 15, 1995 • Living Planet, Long Beach
Reviewed by G. Murray Thomas

Chicago poet Daniel X. O'Neil rolled into town in mid-November for a series of shows with the Dylan Morgan Orchestra. I caught him at Living Planet, and was quite impressed.

First I was impressed with his businesslike approach to a poetry tour. He spent a week in SoCal, and had a show every night, in venues ranging from Midnight Special to Tower Records. These weren't "show up with a full notebook and fake it" shows, either. He had two musicians and a full set of material, which he could vary in length from half an hour to an hour and a half, depending on the demands of the venue.

His work was of a quality to merit this approach. The poems were a bizarre combination of death and humor, surreal snapshots of our current culture. A favorite topic was the absurd tragedies of the modern workplace (as exemplified in "Plant Number 10" and "Local Girl Lands a Job"). The centerpiece of the show was "Boilerplate: Being a List of Eight Ways in Which the Dead at Waco Were a Lot Like the Rest of Us," in which the siege of Waco became a metaphor for the impositions of bureaucracy and government on everyday life.

The Dylan Morgan Orchestra (Dylan Morgan on drums and cello, and Bob Christy on saxophone) expertly complemented and expanded O'Neil's words with jazz and classical accompaniment. This was a true case of synthesis of poetry and music, where the two fed off and built on each other, rather than just words overlaid on music which we hear so often.

In all ways an impressive show. Now O'Neil has gone back to Chicago, and the Orchestra is in Santa Cruz, and we are left wishing for more, but glad they made the effort to drop in and entertain us.

(1/96)

1995: THE YEAR POETS GOT HOOKED (UP)
By G. Murray Thomas
With Lawrence Schulz, Charles Ellik and Victor Infante

We almost passed on the "Year in Review" idea. While there were plenty of noteworthy poetry events in 1995, we could arrive at no consensus on what was important (Seamus Heaney to one person, Rita Dove to another; slams to him, high school students to her). However, as we looked back, one thread emerged to link all the disparate developments. That thread was the very notion of linkage. Poets were eager to connect

— with each other, with other artists, with a growing audience — and used every tool at their disposal to accomplish that.

The first tool, we feel obliged to admit, is in your hands right now. We encountered many writers in venues far from home, and their newsprint-smudged hands gave them away before they could even say, "I saw it in *Next…*"

This increased contact lead to events such as Tearing the Curtain and Words Xing the Line, in which veritable busloads of performers invaded distant venues en masse. New friends were made, and the words celebrated in fresh atmospheres. It began to feel as though there was actually a community of poets in SoCal.

Next… was not working alone. Every month brought some new poetry newsletter to our PO Box, from New York (*The New York City Poetry Newsletter*, which expanded from a single dense sheet to a sixteen-page magazine this year) to slam headquarters in Boston (*Slam*) to surprises such as Minneapolis (*Shout!*) and Dallas (*The Word*). There was barely room left for such favorites as *Poetry Fly* and *Speer Presents*.

Not everyone relied on Kinko's to get in touch. The Internet has swept up a number of artists, who are now out there hanging ten with all the hackers and techies. Web pages and BBS's are being set up by writers and publishers so rapidly we've lost track already. Web pages combine all the publishing options of a newsletter with instant links to other pages. Unluckily, those of us with ancient technology (computers with a pre-1994 vintage, say) missed much of the fun.

Ma Bell to the rescue. Even such ancient technology as the telephone provided new outlets for poetry, such as The Daily Word, a local phone line with a new poem every day, and other similar lines around the country. Leaving a message was like submitting to your favorite 'zine!

Ah, yes, 'zines. Again, we've lost track. They are out there in droves, stacks of new freebies in every coffeehouse. And we wonder why paper prices are going up. (Like we have any right to talk, we just doubled our circulation to 10,000).

Of course, most poets were not satisfied just reaching others like themselves. They wanted new audiences, new readers, new fans. As soon as they got together, it seemed, they put on a big, dramatic show, or even a festival. There was at least one festival per county in SoCal this past year. When Words Collide, the largest of them, brought in crowds of up to 1000 to hear local and national performers. Other festivals across the country, such as The Taos Poetry Circus and the National Slam Finals in Ann Arbor, produced audiences of similar size.

The second urge which hit poets this year was to travel. They were drawn by the festivals, or the knowledge that there was a coffeehouse in Dallas, Denver, or Seattle that would give five minutes or maybe the moon! Tours were suddenly the thing to do; even our own editors joined in. Many of these tours were set up using the networking tools (newsletters, e-mail, phone lines) already discussed

Illustration by Charles Ellik

here. Not only is our local community developing, there are hints of a national scene!

While Bill Moyers's PBS special, *The Language of Life*, brought poetry to a national TV audience, many poets continued to use a more primitive method to reach their audiences: publishing chapbooks. This lead inevitably to marketing. We've seen poets go from saying, "This is my chapbook, please buy it," to "Buy this sucker… Cheap!" in less than a month. While many of the chapbooks we've seen this year are in serious need of editing by another set of eyes and ego, it is great to see this kind of initiative. And some of them have been quite good.

On a larger scale, 1995 saw some impressive anthologies of and by SoCal writers. Primary among them were *Grand Passion*, edited by Suzanne Lummis (Red Wind Books), the anthology of the L.A. Poetry Festival, and *Revival*, edited by Mud Baron and Liz Belile (Manic D Press), the Lollapalooza anthology, which included many local names. More are promised in 1996, starting with Midnight Special's *Foreshock*. We have even detected hints of an informal competition to see who can produce the definitive SoCal poetry anthology. We say, "Good luck in trying" and we'll just enjoy them all.

Finally, to many poets, just the word seemed insufficient, and they established links to artists in other genres. One of the primary goals, and successes, of When Words Collide was to bring poets, musicians, and storytellers together in one place, to share and celebrate their similarities rather than segregating themselves over their differences. Spoken word has linked firmly with music, and most of those putting out chapbooks feel obliged to include artwork. Even most poet web pages have some graphics on them.

What all this will mean in 1996 is still unclear. Maybe, together, we can all inject some new excitement into the scene, producing larger audiences and inspiring new leaps in our art. Or perhaps, like the Balkans, we will suddenly decide we can't stand each other.

In any event, we hope you hooked up this year, and that your connections, whatever they were, will last long and serve you well in the future. And we hope we remain one of them.

(1/96)

THE UNITED STATES OF POETRY
Our Reader Reactions.

Wow. I knew this was going to be good, but I had no idea how good. To tell the truth, the video medium seems to lend itself beautifully to poetry. Poetry achieves its objective through tone and imagery, rather than literal context (which is the domain of fiction). Video works about the same way. This is best illustrated through Sparrow's poem, where he thanks the people in the city for looking out for him. In the video, the crowd he stands in is completely oblivious to him, illustrating the poem's ironic tone without hammering it over the head. Beautiful.

On a side note, I really hope L.A. was watching this. Nobody does film better than us Californians, and maybe this will be enough impetus to get Hollywood looking at our own poets. I can't believe our plethora of film and TV companies would let themselves be upstaged by, of all things, a New Yorker. The gauntlet's been thrown: is anyone in Tinseltown willing to pick it up?

— Victor Infante

I had the great pleasure of viewing *The United States of Poetry* on PBS last month, and all I can say is the spoken word, cafe style, never had it so good! It was truly a treat to see such wonderful production values bestowed upon what has always been a video stepchild. It was like MTV meets the Mother of the Muse, and those video artists showed her a really good time.

I'm a visual person first, so *USOP* grabbed me where I lived. I realize that the "theater of the mind" provides images as infinitely varied as the listeners, and that some folks may not care for ready-made images while listening to spoken word. But the production/creator team of Joshua Blum and Bob Holman, along with director Mark Pellington, showed a true sensitivity to the Word through insightful imagery.

Pictures aside, *USOP* was billed as a showcase for cafe poetry, and that is what it was. From coast to coast, the poetry was marked as much by its diversity as its quality. Their motto: "If it ain't a pleasure, it ain't a poem." [From William Carlos Williams.] I kinda like it.

— J.L. Silas, KCBS TV News

I was only sorry that it isn't a regular series. Each installment left me wishing it would have lasted longer. The concept could have been disastrous but the excellence of the visuals matched the visions of the poetry. It was nice, too, that each poet appeared in his/her poetry video. I once was told, by an actor, that actors should perform poems rather than poets (why? because we're not "visual?"). *The U. S. of Poetry* proved we can be stars.

— Lynne Bronstein

Overall, *United States of Poetry* was interesting but flawed. Definitely a MTV Generation product. Images were beautifully orchestrated, I liked some of the music, but some of the poets were not very good and young poets were barely acknowledged.

— Jaimes Palacio

Yeah, I tuned in to KCET for *The United States of Poetry* broadcast. Three whole nights of poetry on television (on the same channel that brought us *Sesame Street*). Underwhelmed. It tried too hard to be hip. Universally, the poets on the show lacked drama and humor both in their poetry and their performance (the outstanding exception was Maggie Estep's performance of "Emotional Idiot"). What I did see was a bunch of better-than-average poets in MTV-like video clips with music background. I kept on waiting for the "wows" to show up, but they never did. Later, the ad came out to buy the entire package for my video collection. I went out and purchased the Claudia Schiffer Workout Video instead. It was less pretentious and more interesting to look at. Also the music matched the performance. Most important, it did not try to be hip or cool.

— Lawrence Schulz

Some thoughts about *The United States of Poetry*:

• MTV poetry at its best.

• Larry Eigner was a pleasant surprise.

• Johnny Depp needs to practice on his Kerouac impersonation.

• Allen Ginsberg should leave his clothes on.

— Ed Jamieson Jr.

I think my expectations were a little high for Monday, but I was impressed with Tuesday's episode. I personally have a bit of a bias against videos that simply show what the poem is saying, even if it is shown beautifully. Also, I think shots of the poet speaking can get old fast, although Leonard Cohen, Amiri Baraka, the guy in the chef's hat stirring the bowl [John Wright], and the guy shouting out over the umbrellas [Sparrow] were among the exceptions, the first three partly because the pieces were so good. Thursday night's was my second favorite (Tues. being best for me). I liked the overlapping voices of Michelle T. Clinton, and the two girls [Emily XYZ and Myers Barlett] talking about Las Vegas, though I think this could be used to greater potential (e.g. different words or speed or style of vocal delivery, more than two voices, etc.). Also liked the use of text in what I think was in-between (or interstitials as I guess they're called) segments.

— Mark Schaefer

I thought *USOP* was excellent. It was a watershed event. Such people as Maggie Estep, Sparrow, and that guy from Milwaukee [Matt Cook] will become the household names they deserve to be. The video was generous in spirit and open in its taste and accomplished its ambitious task.

— Blake Nelson

This series will excite a new generation of video makers. It is like a successful test detonation of a new bomb. *The U.S. of Poetry* is sure to offend someone but the free-flowing joy it creates is a vibe even a child that hasn't learned the language can understand. It speaks like art walking out of the museum. Yes.

— The Beatlicks.

(4/96)

SAVE US FROM THE CYBER-POETRY THUGS!

By Raindog

The coffeehouse poetry "scene" continues to move along. The state of the art-form seems to be pretty shaky, indeed, at least in one arena.

Many poetry hosts/promoters complain about the glut of poetry readings that have recently emerged in the SoCal area. The audience hasn't grown to keep pace with the volume of readings. In the resulting stagnation, poets are beginning to lose interest and are searching for a way to reach a wider audience; and vice-versa. Poetry is about, among other things, the communication of ideas, and it does seem pointless to reach only a few people at a shot.

Enter the Internet and World Wide Web and a potential audience of millions! This is an ongoing theme that I hope will continue to expand to include more than just theorists and the academic, but will eventually draw in poets of all types. The following conversation includes Mike Bruner, poet/writer, a theorist in language and communication (University of Washington); myself, Raindog, poet/writer/promoter of things poetic and publisher of the *Lummox Journal* (a monthly magazine that explores the creative process); and Steve Meloan, writer/poet/musician/web developer,

who has written extensively on the Internet and its ever-evolving cutting edge technologies, including CU-See-Me (which allows you to actually see the person on the other end of the line!)

NEXT...: From a purist's point of view, the Internet serves to provide open access to (nearly) free forms of expression. By free forms, I mean, censor-free expression (there is always an inherent self-censorship involved in any conscious act of communication — we aren't too far removed from the "club first, ask questions later" mentality). In the ideal world of pure science, where there is no need for standards or rules, in other words, in the realm of Burbank's or Schweitzer's brainpan (a gray land that you and I will never get to experience), in that world, the free exchange of ideas, facts and information is never sullied by petty human frailties. Unfortunately, most everyone, including poets, lack the discipline to travel in the rarefied climate of such a "site."

BRUNER: In pre-modern times, before the rise of literacy and the industrialization of society, prejudices were even more taken for granted and identities might have seemed even more "natural." With the dramatic communication explosion over the last half-century, contemporarily exemplified by the Internet, I believe we have witnessed a "drive to the surface" (Frederick Nietzsche) away from deeply ingrained, unself-conscious, relatively simple identities, toward highly complex, self-reflexive, and superficial identities. Now what these new identities are good for, or if they are good for anything, is not clear. It could be that we are being divided in order to be conquered, but conquered by whom, or what? What individuals are continually aware of the intricate communication powers enacted by certain kinds of political bureaucracies? Whereas once, we were animal spirits with secret names and lice in our hair and dying at 33 with rotted teeth, at least living was "magical." But today everyone has become a clerk, an expert at finely differentiated language games with more and more leisure time, yet everyone is still simply being pulled along by the energy of it all and no doubt the "magic" will return, Internet or not.

NEXT...: If it was only true, then we could sit around like poets of old and make with the beautiful/ugly words that would move an entire planet! But, alas, this isn't the case. Most everyone acknowledges that the world is round, but they're still afraid to go in "over their heads." We are, by nature, first and foremost, dreamers, and then, when we feel it's safe, we act on the dream.

MELOAN: The Web is quickly evolving into a strange new mixture of the computer, the television, and the telephone, and will soon do all of what each once did by themselves, and many new things that have never been seen before. There's the added impact upon telecommunications as we now know them. It's already possible to make international phone calls for an unlimited amount of time (and for the price of a local call) over the Internet. This has profound implications for Ma Bell. It's currently not a major threat to the phone companies, but will be soon. The same is true of Internet Radio. If you can broadcast CD-quality sound to millions over the Internet, who needs radio stations, advertisers, record labels, and "hits?" Further, how do you quantify listening, and thus royalties? It's like when Edison invented the lightbulb. That was just the half of it. You still need power plants, wiring, relay stations, etc. And what did that do to the gaslight industry, the coal industry, the ice industry? If the Net evolves into a TV, radio, phone, and computers all rolled into one, it will profoundly impact these other industries (and their related industries).

BRUNER: Bottom line is it's all romance. I would expect that if we had some kind of war break out that the Internet would be mined. That is, go to the wrong location and be identified. Identity for me is the issue. As long as some large group of people somewhere (anywhere!) can be mobilized into mass belief then trouble is afoot.

MELOAN: In fact, technology has more often than not been the antidote to totalitarianism. In places like Tianammen Square, and the brief Gorbachev coup, things like fax machines and e-mail were the prime communications medium of the underground resistance. That's why Red China is very fearful of the Internet. They know they need to get on board as a country, in order to stay competitive, but they want to be able to regulate access in some way — and that flies in the face of the entire paradigm of the Internet. This is even an issue for the US government. They want forms of encryption that they have the key to. That way, they can perform the equivalent of a cyber-

wire-tap. Otherwise, it will be virtually impossible to track crimes on the Net. Cyber-libertarians say, "so be it." In reality, a RAND Corp. study found that the ultimate current big-brother facility is the ATM! With that, the government can track your physical whereabouts (most now also have cameras), and they know your financial dealings, to boot!

NEXT...: Poets are not technophobes by nature, but, they are eccentrics and, oftentimes, outcasts. The nature of poetry as a craft or art-form (as distinguished from poetry as a hobby), demands a single-mindedness, a focus of attention that is comparable to any Olympic gymnast's (mental gymnastics?). The act of creating poetry requires an ability to move easily (relatively speaking) between the two spheres of the brain: right and left, linear and non-linear. It is, to put it simply, to live in a waking dream. Cyberspace is the mother of all waking dreams. Or, at least, it has the potential to be so. The very act of declaring oneself a poet, a maker of words, is to take a stand (significance notwithstanding). This stand falls somewhere on the continuum between pure poetry (an ideology where poetry exists for no other reason except itself — an altruistic act of creativity, if you will) and self-serving dogma, designed to garner the most of whatever your personal greed requires. Between these two extremes lays the bulk of the poetic world, a mixture of altruism and desire. It's not that desire has to lead to greed, or, more importantly, that we are greedy by nature; it's just that it takes cash to pay the

Illustration by Brian Hagen

bills, and "if you ain't got the do-re-mi, then you'd better go back to beautiful 'wherever' you came from" (to paraphrase the old song). Most of the poets who have been doing this for any length of time will tell you that they'd never make it if it weren't for their day job. Many are involved in the performing arts, but many more are teachers, truck drivers, trades people, students; even a few lawyers have managed to redeem themselves (as poets). Very few poets can survive in this world, let alone the Cyber world, without some sort of cash. Our world (20th century America) is just not geared for that kind of support.

So, does Cyberspace become an oasis where we go to share our interpretations of the waking dream? Or does Cyberspace become an interactive amusement park where you "pays your quarter and takes your chance?"

MELOAN: It's both. The future will look like *Blade Runner* — high tech mixed in with scum, crime, and poverty. It's not going to change basic human nature. Some argue that the Net is like an evolving global brain, like a baby whose neurons are wiring together into a sentient, new, global being. And I suppose that's true to a certain extent. It does bring people together. But it also facilitates cancerous pockets of cyber hate groups which already exist in droves out on the Net. And there are also the avenues of sexual pleasure, which are taking off in quantum leaps — CU-See-Me cyber-swinging, pay-per-view video table dances, etc. These all already exist out there. Which is not surprising. Sex has been a primary driving force in any new medium — from the printing press to the VCR.

BRUNER: Ideally, the problematization reflected by the Information Superhighway could lead to peace, inasmuch as it increases perspective, and lessens the chances of monological thought. Some argue that we are already witnessing a move from nationalism to internationalism, a move away from militarization and toward market warfare. I don't buy it. But the Internet could contribute to the kind of information sharing required for an intelligent citizenry (something American democracy has not shown much respect for in the mass media, whose power in mobilizing mass beliefs is more insidious and less capillary).

MELOAN: But there's also a lot of time wasting to be had out there. Many reports are coming in of people who've become addicted to the Net — forsaking normal human contact for chat lines. Of course if it wasn't that, it might just as easily have been something else. There are plenty of addictions out there. But there's something to be said for going to a cafe and talking to people, rather than burying your face in a TV screen.

(9/96)

THE PROBLEM WITH SLAMS
A Rebuttal
By James "Boomer" Maverick

There is no issue more divisive in the poetry community than whether slams are of value to the art. You either love them or hate them; there is no middle ground. Those who advocate slams say that it brings a heightened level of excitement to the art, and gives poetry a higher profile.

Others say that better poets are needed to generate more excitement to poetry, not competition, which is better relegated to the football field. If poetry needs a higher profile, then we should promote ourselves more aggressively — as aggressively as, say, a slam promoter.

In entertainment, competitive slams are prevalent only in the poetry community. One outraged artist railed: "You think Bukowski or Kerouac or Lorca would do slams?" One might well ask: "Why is poetry the only art form where we must pit ourselves against each other? How is poetry served by such competition?" Poetry slams degrade the art, making Winning Poets idols while Losing Poets are, well, losers. Not a way to promote an art form where personal expression is its lifeblood.

Slams alter an artist's creative focus. The poet's focus shifts from living in the moment to writing for a specific outcome: to win a slam. It makes an artist judge their work differently — from charting their place in the creative process to whether their piece is a "slam" piece, and what they need to do to make their poem a "slam" piece. Some artists attend readings for the specific purpose of perfecting their "slam" presentation. The moment an artist focuses on a goal or end result is where that creativity ends. Slams take an artist out of the moment, out of the creative process, to fixate on the end result. In that moment, the artist is no longer true to him/herself, and their work as a result has become manipulative, derivative, ultimately untrue to the art. Why place such shackles on creativity?

Slams do not make poetry entertaining. Good poets do. It doesn't matter if the poet is featured in a slam. Is the work of a Pleasant Gehman or Lynn Manning less entertaining because they aren't in a slam? Is the appeal or influence of Kerouac or Ginsberg attributable to the slams they performed? What about Maya Angelou or Ntozake Shange?

Often poets ask whether one of their works is a "slam" piece or not; my response is: "What does a 'slam' have to do with what you're trying to express?" If you want to measure your success as an artist, take an unbiased ear and eye to your work at a reading and see if what you're trying to convey crosses the gulf to your audience. Every artist has a thread of universality to their work, no matter how personal they believe their work to be. Anyone can dance and kick through their poetry like Van Damme on speed, but it's a rare talent that can look into the eyes of their audience and find captivation rather than complacency, inspiration rather than indifference. Attaining that intimate level of communication with strangers in scant moments is where success as a poet should be sought, not the use of words as a verbal backdrop to an elaborate dog-and-pony show.

Your words and your expressions dictate how good a poet you are. If your audience doesn't understand you, FUCK 'EM!! Did you understand Bukowski or Shakespeare immediately after reading their work, or did such appreciation come after reading and learning more about the writer? You're not any different. Keep writing; keep reading. Find different ways of expressing your thoughts. Have you written something you think is too personal? READ IT. This is the very type of honesty that good poets convey to their audience, and successful readings are about honesty. What attracts people to a reading is the lack of fear and absence of the bullshit that has permeated every other art form; the reason why poetry still survives as an art.

The bottom line is this: winning slams has nothing to do with your success as an artist. They are slick, well-publicized placebos, offering an artist little more than a moment's validation that their art is worth something.

Keeping the honesty in poetry is what will cause it to thrive. Remain true to yourself in your art and you stay within the creative process, each piece you write taking you to a higher level of expression. Write toward an end and your creativity will do the same.

(9/96)

ALL THE SCORES
By Victor Infante

Note to editor: *I never thought, in my wildest dreams, that I'd end up doing sports writing. —VI*

By all accounts, the 1996 National Poetry Slam Finals, held in Portland, Oregon, were marked by upsets and changes from the Slams of previous years. Orchestrated by Portland Slam Master Jeff Meyers and funded in part, for the first time ever, by corporate sponsors, the slams drew poets from around the country (as well as Canada, Sweden and the UK) to read to packed venues around the downtown area and, for four teams and ten individuals, to an audience of nine-hundred-plus at the Performing Arts Center, where this year's champion team, Providence, R.I., and this year's individual champion, Patricia Johnson of Roanoke, VA, took first-place honors.

The event began informally at Powell's Books, a massive bookstore that takes up the better part of a city block, with readings by Marc Smith, the man who originated the concept of the slam at the Green Mill in Chicago, and Bob Holman, who until recently ran the readings at the Nuyorican Poets Cafe in New York, and who produced *The United States of Poetry* video series for PBS. There, old friends were re-acquainted, newcomers were introduced, and bonds were formed that eventually led to a casual, albeit festive tone that maintained throughout the rest of the Slam. Afterwards, participants left to observe a viewing of *USOP* or attend a local open reading, wherein visitors were welcomed by the curious local poets.

As the slams progressed, it became obvious that the results would not be a mirror of previous years. Former four-time champion (and author of the recent book *Close to Death*) Patricia Smith, from Boston, to the shock of all, did not qualify for the individual semi-finals (note: all contestants compete as teams *and* as individuals, therefore allowing some individuals to progress whereas their teams do not, and vice versa).

While other former front-runners, including Taylor Mali from Providence, Wammo from Austin, and DJ Renegade from Washington D.C., did progress to the finals, the prize went to Johnson, who not only was generally considered an underdog, but was actually the lowest qualifying placer in both the preliminary and semi-final bouts. Johnson's winning poem, a hauntingly sad lament of the burning of black churches in the South, received immense applause, and upon the announcement of her victory, Johnson received a standing ovation. While the victory was well-earned, it should be noted that, had they not exceeded the time limit, Renegade would have tied with Johnson, and Mali would have won, a turn of events which only added to the intensity of the experience.

The upsets continued in the team competitions, with last year's champions, Asheville, N.C., being knocked out at semi-finals, and two other traditionally high-scoring teams, Chicago and Boston, being defeated in the prelims by San Francisco, a team that few present would have put money on. San Francisco was not the only "black horse" to do surprisingly well, however. The home team, Portland, moved into semi-finals before being defeated, and freshman teams such as Los Angeles (who progressed to semi-finals) and Berwyn, IL (who progressed to the finals), had remarkably strong showings. Most amazing was the victory by Providence, who had been ranked dead last in last year's slams (although the composition of that team differed greatly). Other finalists, Austin and New York, were generally considered front-runners all along, with Providence being a strong outside possibility. (I would like to note however, that former *Next...* Assistant Editor Charles Ellik *did* predict their victory during the car ride up.)

While there were some serious issues being discussed, such as the ever-growing "style vs. substance" issue that's even echoed here in SoCal, a dispute about the presence of corporate sponsors, and some serious complaints about the judging, the event was enjoyable and an overall success. Still, with the number of upsets, strong upstart teams, and fallen mainstays wishing to regain their titles, the playing field looks leveled for next year's bout, scheduled to be held in Connecticut, and who knows what will come of that.

(10/96)

HOW I SPENT MY SUMMER VACATION

By Daniel McGinn

OK, I'll admit to being hooked. I've been slamming the stuff. This is the strong stuff. I can't stop, I've hardly slept for days. Wish you were here. Portland is a beautiful city for a poetry competition. It's been warm/ Even humid/ Everything is green/ And clean/ I'm doing poetry/ Line after line/ I'm having a wonderful time/ At the national slam/ Where everything rhymes. The flyer says 120 poets from 27 cities (The Ozarks? Is that a city?), but it's bigger than that. I've run into William McLain, Victoria Locke, Mark Schaefer, bowerbird, Deborah Edler Brown, Mud Baron and Sara Raymond. Every team brought their friends and their friends all seem to be poets, too. Poetry addicts are everywhere.

I knew the competition would be tough but I had no idea how tough. All of the monsters have come out of the closets. Yes Virginia, monsters are poets too. (Is Virginia a city?) It feels good, real good. I've never seen my teammates perform on this level before. They've been squeezing every ounce of meaning out of every word. These venues are sold out, packed to capacity. People are waiting in line to pay to watch the poets. People are waiting in line to pay to watch the poets. That's the best part. The audience has to get here early or they can't get in.

Long Beach is cheering for us and we are cheering for Long Beach. Hey Homes, when I talk about teammates the lines are blurred. Long Beach is red hot and so is Los Angeles. Everyone performing here is red hot. Except the judges. These judges wouldn't be able to find their own fat asses if they jumped up and tapped them on the shoulder. I'm not bitter or anything. Slams at every level are nothing but a crapshoot. About as predictable as a roll of the dice. Slams are just as addictive as any other form of gambling and a much bigger head rush.

Look what's happened to me. I can't stop. I go to bed at five or six a.m. and I get up just before noon and start doing poetry; free verse, sonnets, cowboy poetry, bad poetry, back-to-nature poetry, lyric poetry, haiku, limericks, '60s protest poetry, and yes, even killer clown poetry. They have it all here at the poetry motel.

There are poetry faces staring out of every window. The doors are open. Poets are singing German opera from the balcony. The police drop by three or four times a night to say howdy. They try to get poetry to

cease and disperse. They remind us that we should be watching TV. We have cable. Poetry ceases and disperses in room 411 but it moves to room 309. We start exchanging verse again. Poetry is roaming the hallways with a beer bottle and/or a bong until sunrise. 411. Long Beach is in 411. The emergency room, these poets are in critical condition. They never sleep.

Who won the slam? Rhode Island, I think. How did Los Angeles do? Somebody told me we placed seventh. I'm not sure. I only read three of my poems in the formal competition. But I got to do my complete works at the park and the motel and in the streets of Portland. I may look a little spaced but I've got the words of over a hundred poets orbiting my brain right now and I couldn't be happier. I found it difficult to pay attention to the scores and the ranking with so many diverse styles of verse in the house. I couldn't even keep track of who was on which team.

I remember the people and the poems. After being around so many poems and poets I can hardly wait to get back to my computer and encourage you to do the same. I wish you were here. Having a wonderful time. I've had my fun. Next year it's your turn. In Cleveland. I think they said it's going to happen in Cleveland next year. Or was it Cincinnati? Or Connecticut? Yeah that's it.

(10/96)

NEWS CLIPS AND EGO TRIPS

By G. Murray Thomas

We had a great time at the Ringling Sisters 10th (and last) Annual Fun-Raiser at the Palace on Mon. Dec. 18. Highlights included the Ringling Sisters' (Pleasant Gehman, Iris Berry and Annette Zilinskas) own set of their poetry set to rocking lounge music (interpreted by Mona Jean, our favorite ASL poet); Henry Rollins's description of meeting a young fan dying of leukemia; Flea's acoustic set which put the focus on some twisted lyrics; Mike Watt's explosive bass-playing; and S.A. Griffin's version of Santa Claus. But our personal favorite was Phranc ("just your average all-American Jewish lesbian folk-singer"), who demonstrated catchy tunes, a great sense of humor, and attitude all at once. We're sorry to hear this was the last Fun-Raiser, but we can understand the Sisters' wishes to reclaim the time it consumed…

(1/96)

Work for *Next…* and meet the stars! Somehow we found ourselves at a special reading of Pablo Neruda's poetry at Wolfgang Puck's on Sunset, sponsored by Miramax and The American Film Institute, to honor the movie *Il Postino* (it is Oscar push time). We scarfed free food and wine (very tasty) and listened to stars such as Rod Steiger, James Woods, and Jacqueline Bissett read Neruda's work. While a few overdramatic performances

Illustration by Walt Hopmans

had us struggling to restrain unmentionable antisocial impulses, others were quite impressive. Tops on our list were Patrick Stewart (Neruda's words and Capt. Picard's voice — how could we go wrong?), Esai Morales, the one performer who read in Spanish and thereby demonstrated the beauty as well as the power of the poetry, and Melissa Etheridge, who put real feeling, as opposed to mere emotion, into the piece she read. (When we later remarked on this to Ms. Etheridge, she replied, "It's been my favorite poem for ten years. It was easy.") Michael Radford, the film's director, also gave a moving, yet humorous, tribute to the star, Massimo Troisi, who died almost immediately after filming…

(2/96)

Those of you who watch TV (we know there are one or two) may have noticed slick, seductive ads for Poeme, the new fragrance from Lancome (which means that Poetry is now held in the same esteem as Obsessions and Opium). But are you aware that they are sponsoring a "Poetry of Love" competition, with a first prize of a $15,000 trip to Paris? As for the fragrance itself, the official *Next…* perfume correspondent filed this review: "An indefinable combination of flowers, a touch of the aristocracy, subtle spices and the bubbles of champagne, balconies on Florentine buildings, somebody's mad fixation cured by a jeweled dagger. Aw, heck, it smells good. Funny, it costs $80 a bottle. Wonder if any poems (minus the e) written by anyone we know will ever make $80…."

(4/96)

CONNECTION

By James "Boomer" Maverick

It was just after Thanksgiving when I received some e-mail from Murray. He told me that the final free issue of *Next…* was the February issue, and asked me for my opinion on the poetry community for that issue.

A grin played across my face not unlike that of Ren Hoek. In the back of my mind, a Peter Lorre-type voice spoke: "Oh, what I could say about the poetry community." I sauntered home with the grandiose vision of waxing Fitzgerald-esque — describing in vivid detail the tale of a world within a world, weaving a spiral of literary majesty that would evoke tears from a loan shark.

I drew a blank.

As Christmas neared, I sat at my desk wholly expecting another *Great Gatsby* or "Snows of Kilimanjaro" to flare from my fingers like a Phoenix resurrection, setting my telephone line aflame as the tome blazed across the ether to NextMag@aol.com, spurring the readership to yet another multi-page multi-issue letters column while patting myself on the back like some cartoon coyote exalting haughtily upon my genius.

Nothing.

Each day, I would sit at my computer and think: "Here we go" for thirty minutes, then fifteen, then five, finally vowing to sit at the terminal "tomorrow" and type something "acceptable."… my expectations lowering with every passing day.

I became frustrated with my inability to write anything that I could consider "of merit" about the poetry community. Now, when I sat at my computer, I would invariably drift from WordPerfect to Duke Nukem while attempting to figure out whether I was a perfectionist or a procrastinator, and cursing myself for being the latter as Dr. Proton beat a hasty retreat to the moon.

My frustration caused me to dwell on other less-than-successful aspects of my life, which only made me feel worse. I wasn't exactly enamored with my job. I wasn't happy with my car (the moment I had everything wrong with it fixed, I was involved in an accident). I certainly wasn't happy with dating — it seemed that every time I had made a connection with someone, something went wrong. This "something" always eluded me… did I come on too strong? Did I reveal too much about myself? Did I say something that offended, without realizing it? This coveted "connection" became my own personal Holy Grail, and often times looked less of a possibility to me than folly.

"Connection."

I woke up with this word in my mind, ate, worked out, rode the bus, went to sleep with this word, and wondered why such a simple, basic concept was so hard for me to grasp — why I felt as if I was always standing outside the window of a great party, able only to watch the fun, but never participate.

"Connection."

As the second week of January came around and the bones of Christmas were set by the curb, the word morphed from a vexing riddle to an intellectual yoke about my neck. Why has this word staked a claim in each fold and crease of grey matter? What purpose is served in holding on so tightly to a word whose meaning is so obviously to be denied me?

It was January 13th. I lay awake the night before as even sleep had escaped me. I called my office and reported sick, I was in no condition to work. It was about 11 in the morning when I finally fell asleep.

I didn't dream that day so much as remember. A story that Amelie Frank had told me of an afternoon with Nicole Harvey and Nelson Gary. The after-Christmas party at Mona Jean's and my first sampling of Absinthe, just two days after Kennon Raines's party and closing out both with bowerbird. The midnight run to the Hollywood Tommy's with Jayleen Sun. My interview with Ellyn Maybe where she repeatedly mentioned the term: "Kindred spirits."

"Connection." I woke… knowing.

The poetry community is all about connection. I have seen this connection in a quiet, child-sized Latina who spoke of passions and emotions larger than life, and a loud, boisterous party animal who attacked me with her feather boa on Election Night. The connection that exists in two women who share one broken heart, or a broken man who has used poetry to glue himself back together.

The laughing hyena… the horny octogenarian… the drunken cowboy and the man cursed by the shadow of his father. This is all poetry.

The 6'4" Venus… the hemp-smoker in Republican County… the teen who cuts himself, the New York Giant, the slam-master, the sexy Croatian with the intimate piercing and the angry man with leopard-spotted hair… It is all poetry. It is all community.

It is all… connection.

It was about 10:15 p.m. when I called Murray and asked him how much time I had to turn in my article. He told me January 15th. I said "No problem."

I hung up the phone and remembered it all: Yvonne De La Vega's poem on the left shoulder of my L.A. Spoken t-shirt… the precise moment at Java Joint when I understood life from Dafydd MacKharay's perspective… the poem that Tony Goldstone asked me to read the night of my birthday at Highland Grounds and the enthralling charm behind Scott Wannberg's smile… the actress who shook excitedly after her first reading, her joy virtually leaping from her eyes to mine.

I cried with the realization that this is my connection. I have waxed not Hemingway, but L. Frank Baum, off in search of a home I stupidly failed to realize had surrounded me all this time, replete with scarecrows, lions, good witches, bad witches, tin men and poetry dogs.

Thank God for Poetry.

Thank God… I'm home.

(2/97)

Illustration by Brian Hagen

LET'S GO TRIPPING

By G. Murray Thomas

During January, I had the pleasure of playing host to Clebo Rainey and Garland Thompson on the SoCal legs of their poetry tour. They slept on my sofas, smoked me out, and entertained me with tales of the road. I also saw at least half of their SoCal performances. By the time they left, I was ready to pack up my Honda and hit the poetry circuit myself.

It wasn't just the thrill of the road, the scenery, the encounters with new people, the casual lifestyle of performing at night, and playing tourist all day. The possibility of a new audience every night was definitely part of it; the chance to do the same old stuff to new ears has a powerful appeal. So does the notion of actually making some money from poetry — in the first leg of their trip, Clebo and Garland were actually selling enough books to meet touring expenses (though it must be admitted they ended the tour in the hole). It wasn't even the amount of poetry they were writing every day, inspired by the road.

The main inspiration came from watching them perform every night. What might seem to some an exercise in tedium, I found quite enlightening. Garland varied his set every night, playing off the audience and his own moods, just like the jazz musicians he admires and writes about. Some nights he hit a connection with the crowd which was almost magical, which was the sort of connection I aspire to.

Clebo, on the other hand, performed essentially the same selection of poems each night, but was no less interesting for it. He demonstrated the talents of a true showman, making the material fresh every night, and playing with the audience, pulling them into his work through his presence on stage. His performance did vary, in tone and emphasis, depending on the audiences responses. Most important, I saw him rediscovering for himself the meaning in his poems.

For myself, this opportunity to rediscover and reconnect with my own words through many audiences is the ultimate appeal of a poetry tour. Sure, I like all the rest of it, and I am a travel junkie, but I find the meaning in my poetry through interaction with an audience. Yes, I am firmly in the performance camp, but this is something more than that. I believe the essence of all art lies in a communication between artist and audience via the artwork (I know there is an entire article lurking in that statement). In poetry, performance is the most direct interaction you can get with your audience (readership, whatever). Therefore, give me performance opportunities. Give me a tour.

I'm not the only one. Plenty of poets are discovering the joys of touring. Quite a few have hit, or will be hitting SoCal this spring. I have even received an interesting video of Japanese poet Kei Kunihiro performing his poetry at the Jack Kerouac Festival in Massachusetts.

Different poets have different motivations for touring. Says Lisa Martinovic, from the Ozarks, "I absolutely love touring! It's like being a kid — free and w/o responsibility. All I have to do is what I love to do! What a life! One of the most rewarding things about my involvement in the whole poetry scene is that I have discovered my 'tribe.' I've never been an antisocial loner by any stretch, but for the first time in my life I feel fully a part of a community."

Martinovic's touring partner Brenda Moossy agrees. "I love performing. I love giving the characters in my poems their voice… it's sort of like being possessed or channeling." On the benefits of touring, she adds, "The more experience, the better your performance… Also, putting your work out there is sort of like 'chumming' the water. You never know what opportunities might come your way."

Cowboy poet John Kulm, who is coming down from Washington for the Santa Clarita Cowboy Poetry Festival in early April, simply says, "When I'm in town, I'll work some local poetry venues. I won't be reading and running either. I look forward to hanging out, meeting people, and learning about your poetry scene."

All of us at *Next…* encourage you to take your own poetry on the road. The weather's turning warm, the passes out of town are melting, start planning your own tour now. And attend some of the readings by touring poets this month. Hear some new voices. And say hi to them; all touring poets said they like meeting other poets in their travels.

Happy trails to all of you.

(3/97)

ALLEN GINSBERG 1926-1997

By Mindy Nettifee

Allen Ginsberg was born on June 3, 1926. He died on April 5, 1997, amongst good friends, old lovers, and, if my imagination serves me right, several hundred candles. I'm not sure, but I think he had a smile on his face.

The prerequisite events leading up to the meeting are of little importance, much like the colors you see behind your eyes just before the dawning of a great vision. Nevertheless, somehow I found myself mingling amidst hipsters and cocktail intellectuals at a gathering in Greenwich Village, just after the election night events of The Talking Book Festival, when I suddenly noticed that there, standing a mere ten feet away, was Allen Ginsberg.

Now, Allen Ginsberg is a hero of mine, right up there with Auntie Mame and Noam Chomsky. When I was eleven or twelve years old, I found a copy of his poem "America" shuffled away in a box in my grandparents' basement. I picked it up, brushed off decades of dust, and began to read. In reverie, I say, without doubt or hesitation, that my entire universe was altered irrevocably from that moment on. This man spoke to me in my own language. He wove words together with a seamless and natural beauty I had never experienced. He pandered to the betrayal I was already beginning to sense and fed fuel to the first sparks of rebellion and artistic abandon within me. I remember thinking, now this, this is poetry. I remember thinking, I could write like this. I was enchanted, and without further prompting, picked up the pen and paper that would bring a new magic into my life, the magic that led me here.

Perhaps I'd had a little too much to drink (god only knows what were in those cocktails, maybe magic?), or perhaps it was all so surreal that I merely responded as naturally as anyone would to the absurdity of a dream, but I somehow mustered up the gumption to seize what I recognized as a golden opportunity by the scruff of its neck — I walked up, was shortly introduced, and shook my hero's hand.

The next hour is not much more than a happy blur. At first I tried desperately to mentally record every word he spoke, but then I realized I was missing the cosmic point, so to speak, and relaxed into the joy of the moment. I remember words and phrases, a general thematic bend here and there, but mostly I recall his obsessive but passionate rantings on the international media conspiracy (or something to that tune), and how lovely the expression was on his face, an odd combination of his crazed eyes and that serene buddha smile.

I walked away quite elated, a healthy dose of stardust in my eyes, and yet somehow disturbed. I couldn't put my finger on what exactly had so struck me about him. A few hours later, lingering at some blues bar with Dali-esque canines painted on the walls, it hit me.

Once I had made that first discovery in the basement, I threw myself into studying 1950s Americana and the Beats, finding it all to be completely irresistible. And once I'd picked up their rhythm, I avidly followed the current that swept me through the sixties (with Ginsberg's buddhist "be ins," frenzied political activity, and travels into psychedelia), the seventies (more of the same), and all the way through to the nineties and his last project, "Ballad of the Skeletons." What had so struck me was what I had always known, but never really grasped until I met him — how relevant Allen Ginsberg still was. Where many of the others of his ilk had either drowned or taken to the shore for a little rest and repast, Ginsberg had stayed with the current, using his influence to expand minds, advance the cause of freedom of expression, and give the finger to the likes of Newt Gingrich. He championed the essential liberation of the individual where conformity and mediocrity remained the status quo, invoking the spirits of Whitman and Thoreau through his writing. He sang his own tune amidst the existential hum, reveling in the passion and joy of life, carving out his own unique version of the American dream, and passing on the magic.

The news of Allen Ginsberg's rather sudden death did not hit me as hard as I thought it would (mind you, I still break out into a cold sweat whenever the inevitable death of Reverend Burroughs is mentioned). Perhaps it is because his death does not carry with it that sense of finality that most do, for I cannot help but feel that Ginsberg and the work he leaves behind are definitively immortal, giving off the unmistakable scent of the timeless and the heavenly. That I am writing this at all is proof of that. (That "Ballad of the Skeletons" now airs on MTV is proof of that as well, although probably more proof than any of us needed.)

America owes something to Allen Ginsberg and the rest of his tribe, a tribe of warriors that has struggled to emerge and re-emerge over the centuries and a tribe that struggles still. Because the struggle is worth it. Because poetry, beauty, and magic are worth it. And because maybe somewhere, as I write this, a little kid is shuffling through a box of old books in the basement, unaware of what is about to transpire.

Here's to you, Al.

(5/97)

POETRY VS. GUESS INC.

By Julia Stein

On September 18, 1997, Guess Inc. filed a libel/slander suit against the literary reading I had organized. The reading was in support of the garment workers' union, UNITE, organizing this manufacturer. How did my literary reading wind up getting sued by this corporation?

My involvement started when my grandmother sewed shirts at the Bennett, Hollander and Louis pants factory in Pittsburgh, Pennsylvania. A Russian Jewish immigrant teenager in 1906, her family sent her into the garment shop; her wages supported the family, letting her younger brothers and sisters go to school. My grandmother read Yiddish writers such as Sholem Aleichem as well as Russians like Tolstoy — both were forces in their culture, and both had huge literary funerals in which 100,000 people showed up.

Reading Yiddish sweatshop poets and also Pablo Neruda showed me that poetry can talk about labor. During the 1980s I wrote two books of poetry, *Under the Ladder to Heaven* and *Desert Soldiers*; in both books I had a number of poems about my grandmother's garment work, the heroic strikes of immigrant women garment workers from 1909-1915, and the Triangle factory fire in which 146 women lost their lives. I included a line from Yiddish poet Rosenzweig's poem on the Triangle Fire in my poem "The Flame." During the 1980s I discovered that a number of other contemporary poets also were writing about the Triangle Fire: Mary Fell, Zoe Angelsey, Chris Llewellyn, Safiya Henderson-Holmes, Carol Tarlen, and Hilton Obenzinger. Janet Zandy, an English professor, anthologist and critic, delivered a critical talk about this "fire poetry," including my own work, at the 1991 American Studies Association Conference.

San Francisco poet Carol Tarlen showcased this "fire poetry" in a reading commemorating the Triangle Fire in March, 1996, in which I read. At the reading, Tarlen announced there was a small storefront sweatshop three blocks away in Chinatown. Listening to her, I felt I could no longer just write about the past as a poet or a critic. I felt I needed to act in the present. Returning to Los Angeles, I joined Common Threads, a women's group trying to eradicate sweatshops. UNITE, the garment workers' union, was beginning to organize Guess Inc., the largest garment manufacturer in Los Angeles.

During August, 1996, over a hundred garment workers lost their jobs for trying to organize a union at Guess Inc. and its contractors. I produced the first Justice for Garment Workers reading on September 8, 1996, at Midnight Special bookstore in Santa Monica as an act of support of UNITE's organizing efforts. My event was modeled after Carol Tarlen's March reading in San Francisco. The co-sponsors of the Los Angeles reading were the L.A. local/National Writers Union/U.A.W. and Common Threads.

Guess Inc. filed its libel/slander lawsuit against the literary reading on September 18; Daniel Petrocelli, their lead lawyer, was also the lawyer for the Goldman family in the O.J. Simpson civil trial. In the Guess Inc. lawsuit , their lawyers had called my literary event a "so-called literary reading." The participants and audience thought it was a real reading. I read poetry and was the MC. Mary Helen Ponce read from her autobiography *Hoyt Street*; Carol Schwalberg read a short story about a seamstress and spoke about the L.A. local/National Writers Union. Edna Bonacich, a sociology professor at UC Riverside and co-author of a book on the apparel industry, spoke about the UNITE campaign. And Enrique Flores, a garment worker who used to work for Kelly, one of Guess's contractors, told us about doing illegal homework, lack of minimum wage and losing his job at Kelly. About thirty-five people attended, including a spy from Guess Inc. named Joe Vargas.

The Guess lawsuit said that the organizers of the reading had conspired with UNITE in an attack campaign against the corporation. Most of the year, I hadn't been conspiring at all but writing literary criticism. In June 1995, while visiting the National Historic Park in Lowell, Massachusetts, I saw the first textile mills in this country. In the gift shop I picked up Nancy Zaroulis's novel about a Lowell mill girl, *Call the Darkness Light*. Inspired by this wonderful novel, I researched and wrote a long essay, "Tangled Threads," about American fiction and poetry on garment work from 1810 to the present day. Besides Janet Zandy, I discovered two other literary critics had, in their books, written brilliantly about this literature: Paula Rabinowtiz's *Labor and Desire: Women's Revolutionary Fiction in Depression America* and Laura Hapke's *Daughters of the Great Depression: Women, Work and Fiction in the American 1930s*. I was also inspired by Elizabeth Wayland Barber's *Women's Work The First 20,000 Years: Women, Cloth, and Society in Early Times* who looked at textile work in Greek (Homer's *Odyssey*) and other ancient literatures.

The Guess lawsuit disrupted my writing criticism. After I heard about the lawsuit, I consulted with Harry Youtt, lawyer, fiction writer, and member of the L.A. local/National Writers Union. He called the Guess Inc. suit a Strategic Lawsuit Against Public Participation (S.L.A.P.P. Suit), which many corporations file these days to harass and silence critics. So many of these lawsuits have been filed that California recently passed an anti-S.L.A.P.P. statute.

In October, 1996, I decided on a press campaign. If my efforts gave Guess Inc. enough negative publicity, I predicted they would drop the lawsuit. There is a two-hundred-year-old tradition of writers helping to support workers. Shelly and Byron both supported English workers— Byron's first speech in the House of Lords was on behalf of the British weavers who were starving at the time. Both Melville and Whitman wrote about the suffering of workers. Alongside these writers, working class movements fought for and won free speech both in England and the United States during the last two hundred years; in Los Angeles the International Workers of the World (Wobblies) waged a free speech fight in 1922 in which writer Upton Sinclair participated that won free expression in the Los Angeles area. More recently, I had participated in successful PEN U.S.A. campaigns to free writers imprisoned abroad. Though some think poetry is weak

and marginalized in the United States, I believed that poetry can be a force in our lives. If poets and novelists can be powerful in France and Russia, why not here?

After I sent off the first press releases and press packets, the first newspaper articles appeared in November and early December. Some West Coast poets were very supportive of my efforts to fight the lawsuit — Uncle Don Fanning, Carol Kent Ireland, Alexis Krasilovsky, and Luis Campos. Uncle Don helped me in doing Internet research on S.L.A.P.P. suits as well as in setting up a email list of poets to help publicize our efforts. At a December 14th Common Threads demonstration against Guess Inc., I got to meet my alleged co-conspirator, David Young, who was then Director of Organizing for UNITE. It was three months after we were sued, but we'd never met before.

Before the court hearing on December 23, Common Threads held a press conference which resulted in us being on Channel 9 TV, Korean TV, and more newspaper articles. At the December hearing our lawyers invoked the anti-S.L.A.P.P. statute, asking the judge to dismiss the lawsuit, but the judge postponed her decision. During this period some of the women in Common Threads experienced mental anguish over this lawsuit during this time-consuming fightback.

Mid-January Guess Inc. announced it was moving production to Mexico, Chile and Peru. Then, on January 31, the federal Department of Labor (DOL) indefinitely extended Guess Inc.'s probation from the Trendsetter's list, which lists companies that adequately avoid sweatshops; the DOL's action was in part a reaction to Guess's announcement that they were moving jobs out of the United States. I produced Justice for Garment Workers II at Midnight Special on February 2, 1997. The women in Common Threads and the poets refused to be silenced. With hundreds of jobs on the line, we felt we needed to speak out.

At Justice for Garment Workers II, Common Threads again held a press conference which resulted in more newspaper articles in Los Angeles as well as radio coverage. After the plaintiffs won in the O.J. Simpson civil trial, their lawyer Petrocelli was on the cover of *Time Magazine* and on Larry King Live. But we continued to get press, too. By March we were getting favorable articles in the Bay Area and the New York press. On March 9, I read poetry in honor of garment workers at the luncheon of Women's International League for Peace and Freedom.

On March 23, 1997, I heard that lawyers for Guess Inc. had, on their own, dismissed the lawsuit. One can speculate on motives of the Guess Inc. executives, but if the lawsuit tried to silence the poets and Common Threads, it hadn't worked. Instead, Common Threads battling the lawsuit had generated months of negative publicity for the corporation. There was a way, I knew, that poets could become both central to the culture and powerful.

(6/97)

WILLIAM S. BURROUGHS 1914-1997

Burroughs, along with his contemporary Allen Ginsberg, were forces that represented monumental changes in American thought and language. Burroughs's passing, unfortunately, will only bring notice on how such little creativity exists today. In a world filled with complacency, where daily we tolerate cookie-cutter poets, writers, artists, and philosophers, Burroughs broke out of the mold and gave us originality. He not only colored outside of the lines; he took the coloring book, ripped it up and painted his own visions of the way the world really looks. There is no one now who could take his place. This is the sadness of his passing.

— Lawrence Schulz, Poet/ Writer, Huntington Beach

Burroughs was the first Beat writer I read, his work being fashionable among rock'n'roll kids not too into literature (in the same way Bukowski's work was). But Burroughs never appealed to me as much as his compatriots — Kerouac, Ginsberg, etc. When I read *Junky* and *Naked Lunch*, the nihilism put me off. Maybe I just couldn't relate to his particular sense of humor, his satiric sensibility. But his cutup technique influenced countless writers, myself included.

— Gwynne Garfinkle, poet, writer, Los Angeles

The last of the big three Beat writers has beat it out of this earthly existence. Burroughs was older than

Kerouac or Ginsberg. He influenced them in the '40s and provided safe havens for them to visit in Mexico City and Tangier. They believed in each other and their mutual faith served as the foundation for the appearance of their howling originality.

No one expected him to live so long. In recent years his connection with the living seemed tenuous. I do not feel sad at his passing because he had written himself out and was biding his time, waiting for the appropriate moment to break through to the next realm. "The water we live in is Time," he wrote. "That alien medium we glimpse beyond time is space. And that is where we are going."

William was a wild boy. His writing was a test site for literary explosions. I feel sure that his vision has transported him to the western lands. Burroughs is looking back at life askance, cheek by jowl with the pharaohs in the Valley of the Kings.

— Joe Speer, Speer Presents, Nashville, TN

Burroughs was an amazing individual and a powerful magickian. We were really blessed to have him involved with our debut CD release, it gave it the essence of magick we needed to make us believe... that I guess was the core of what Burroughs was about... he could make you believe...

— Lob, Instagon, Huntington Beach

The last pillar of the Triumvirate has fallen, but shall remain forever indelibly etched in the recesses of our memories.

William Burroughs created for his readers a surrealistic junket into an insane world where his images constructed a new meter to logic. His perverse sense of humor intruded sharply into our senses where his cynical narratives laid bare concepts we didn't want to know existed. His natural inclination was to smash every rule imaginable... giving new definition to "cause and effect," and in his sometimes compassionate portrayals of the desperation of madness and drugs, he never failed to surprise us... right up to the last word... of the final chapter... his death....

— Circe, poet, Montrose

(9/97)

CONTROVERSY AT THE NATIONAL POETRY SLAM

August 1997 • Middletown, Connecticut
By Victor D. Infante

When the last poem was finished and the scores tallied, the air was filled with both resounding applause and bitter jeers. The team sponsored by Mouth Almighty records, a New York-based Spoken Word record label affiliated with Mercury Records, had won, beating out strong showings by Chicago, Cleveland, and Worcester.

It's not a stretch to say that this was probably the most controversial victory in the eight year-history of the National Slams. The Mouth Almighty team consisted of Taylor Mali, a school teacher and member of last year's champion Providence team; Beau Sia, a young poet of Chinese-American Nationality who competed on last year's New York Team, which had made the finals; Regie Cabico, a gay Phillipino poet who made the individual finals in 1993 and who appears on the *Grand Slam* CD (Mouth Almighty Records); and Evert Eden, a South African poet and playwright who placed second as an individual last year while competing for the Winston-Salem team.

In addition, Da Boogieman, a poet from Cleveland, won the Individual finals.

The major issue surrounding the team was that it represented a corporation instead of a geographic area, causing many to believe that it represented an unwanted intrusion of business interests in poetry. "Had we called ourselves Hell's Kitchen, where our slam was held,"

says Mali, "I think we might have been able to stave off the majority of the controversy." In addition, there were accusations that the Mouth Almighty Team was handpicked. According to him, the team was chosen from a pool of nine poets, all of whom had competed at Nationals before, in a series of three invitational slams.

"The rule says that, although handpicked teams are discouraged, they are allowed (at the discretion of the host city)," says Mali, who wrote the National Slams rulebook that was approved in Chicago in April of this year. "The structure of the competition that picks the team is up to the individual venue and slam master. If how we were chosen is disobeying the spirit of the rule, then I would have to rewrite that rule."

The controversy surrounding the Mouth Almighty team became apparent at the Saturday Morning Slam Masters' meeting, when earlier allegations of use of a prop – Mali's belt being used to symbolize a penis — were discussed. The belt was undone by Cabico during a team piece. Whether this was intentional or accidental is still open to debate. Host Jim Nave, who has taught workshops in the past with Julia Cameron, author of the best-selling *The Artist's Way*, postponed a decision until more concrete definitions and penalties could be decided. The team was not penalized at this time, and a makeshift rule was developed, to be expounded upon in Chicago at the March 1998 Slam Master's meeting.

Mali, who is renowned for his precision in performance, later told the *Connecticut Times* that he did not expect the other slammers to believe his innocence.

Illustration by Walt Hopmans

Despite these and other related controversies, there were several remarkable instances of camaraderie over the course of the weekend. One instance is the dreaded "Head to Head Limerick Slam," wherein a woman named Margaret, who is not a poet but has attended every National Championship but one, defeated several experienced poets with clean limericks. Near the end of this slam, poets had begun to run out of material, resulting in raucous audience laughter and impromptu opening lines like Beau Sia's "True Stories of The Highway Patrol."

Another was the success of the Swedish National Slam Team, who said that they were made to feel extremely welcome, and were not treated as foreigners. Says team member Bob Hensen, "I feel as though we have a family in America. I hope that someday we will be able to return your hospitality in my country."

Perhaps most remarkable was the fact that Henry Taylor, a Professor of Literature at American University, competed this year, as an individual.

"I want to be fair about my own performance, how I felt about it," says Taylor, who won the Pulitzer Prize for Poetry in 1986 for his book *The Flying Change*. "My work is a little different, I'm a print poet. My main reasons for competing were, first of all, that it's a hell of a lot of fun. Another is that I'm involved in the teaching of poetry and contemporary literature, and I don't feel that it's wise to ignore this, and I don't think that you can find out about it by only going to different local slams."

While Taylor, who placed 75th overall, remains delighted with the slams, he admits that it's not for everybody. "I think it's a matter purely of temperament, whether you'd be willing to deal with this. I have plenty of friends, who are fantastic poets whose personalities and performance styles are doomed in these circumstances, and I don't see any point in encouraging them to humiliate themselves in what would be, for them, artificial circumstances. On the other hand, there are plenty of poets for whom this environment works… I found out in the semi-finals that I don't have any work that I'd like to take into the realm of performance poetry, although I admire the work of many of the poets I saw, including D.J. Renegade and Glynnis Scheer. Just because I don't want to doesn't mean other people shouldn't."

While the final rounds were tinged with controversy, there were still moments that made it clear that there is more to this than the scores. "If [Da Boogieman] hadn't held me upright after I got offstage at the finals, I would have collapsed sobbing onto the floor," says Worcester slammer Dawn Gabriel, discussing the aftermath of her extremely emotional poem "Frayed." "Instead, I collapsed sobbing into his arms. That he was on one of the teams we competed against, and still offered me the love and support I needed was amazing. At that point, it was no longer about winning. It was about poetry." (9/97)

A BRIEF HISTORY OF LAGUNA POETS

By Daniel McGinn

The Laguna Poets have come full circle. The group emerged from a small neighborhood reading to become the most visible poetry reading in Orange County. Once again, under the direction of Pat Cohee, the Laguna Poets is a neighborhood reading. As director of the Laguna Poets from the mid-seventies to the late eighties, Marta Mitrovitch was the host of a series of large poetry festivals that attracted major poets, such as Gary Snyder, Diane Wakowski, Galway Kinnell, Gregory Corso, and Charles Bukowski, to come and read in Laguna Beach. On the afternoon following Marta's eighty-seventh birthday, Pat Cohee and I visited her and her son-in-law, Gene Harrington, at her Laguna Canyon home. Marta's back room is decorated with flyers — advertisements from previous shows that featured Lawrence Ferlinghetti ("the nice Italian fellow. He had a bookstore."), Philip Levine, Allen Ginsberg, Lynn Lifshin and others.

Marta was smiling when she told me, "We used to put them up, sometimes, for the night, you know? Poets." She looks to Pat for verification. "We found places for them, didn't we?" She takes my hand and points out the sliding glass door. "Allen Ginsberg sat right there, in the garden."

Pat Cohee remembers meeting Ginsberg, "a great individual, very independent, and a very good reader. When he left the high school auditorium, he reminded the Laguna poets to go get laid."

Gene Harrington tells this story about Charles Bukowski: "He was the first one they had here. He's on the stage; he's got a twelve-pack with him. He was great. Some people left — he got a little dirty as he went on, he got pretty loaded up there… He wasn't famous then, he was just – you know, Bukowski. But he did have a following."

Originally, the readings were held in living rooms. Pat remembers attending hootenannies at a neighbor's house with his mother, Alice Jackson, and seeing poets congregate in a corner reciting verse. Two of those poets, Sue Blevin and Nancy Wing, were already meeting and sharing their poetry with each other. Eventually that circle of two began to expand, and a poetry group began to take form. In the beginning the poets of Laguna had no need for an official name or a public place for readings. Average attendance at the poetry workshops was somewhere between ten and twelve writers. Neighborhood musicians and artists who dropped by formed the audience. They began meeting weekly at each other's homes and they printed their poetry on an 1876 printing press that belonged to Peter Carr. Peter was the host of the hootenannies and a professor of comparative literature at Long Beach State University. Over the course of time the lives of these Laguna poets became intertwined. Their shared passion for poetry and a strong sense of community formed the strong foundation that the Laguna Poets stands on today.

Marta Mitrovitch, who attended these homegrown poetry workshops, eventually became the navigator when the group went public. She has been the host to thousands of poets in several locations. The Laguna Poets have met in homes, at the beach, in church meeting halls, bookstores, and the public library. For seventeen years it was Marta Mitrovitch who got the flyers made and posted. She set up the chairs, encouraged the writers, and kept the reading alive. Why did she do

this? "We were interested in each other's thoughts and feelings. We were, honestly."

John Gardiner, a Laguna poet who occasionally teaches performance poetry classes at the University of California in Irvine, remembers Marta, "She got me my first reading… She made you feel so important. I mean everyone. Before you stood up to read your poems it was as if she had a little gemstone in her hand that she was sharing with everybody. And she kind of held it out and pointed at all the glitter that came off of it and then said, 'But why am I talking about him or her? Here they are in person!' When you came up you were overwhelmed, you almost went, 'Oh great! Now I've got to read.' She made you feel like everybody was the most mystical magical saint on the planet just to be doing this act. She really did. And in the library it was a pretty dreadful setting, but not with Marta there. It was washed with color."

Today, the Laguna Poets meet in the courtyard just outside of the Upchurch-Brown Booksellers. Pat Cohee has been the host and director of the Laguna Poets since 1987. Victor Infante, Laguna Poet-in-exile, attended these readings for years. He had this to say about the Cohees: "Pat and Marcia run a wonderful reading. They are wonderful people. They are two people who make everybody feel comfortable. At points, it's like

Photo of Marcia, Devin & Pat Cohee by G. Murray Thomas

hanging out at your favorite aunt and uncle's house and reading your poetry in their living room."

In addition to its incredible longevity, what makes the Laguna Poets different from every other poetry reading in the county is that the current host, Pat Cohee, produces an original chapbook for every featured poet who wants one. The chapbooks in the Laguna Poets series usually contain six or seven poems and are between sixteen to twenty pages in length. The books Pat Cohee produces are both professional-looking and inexpensive. The Inevitable Press has published several established local poets who are prolific writers and experienced public readers. But, according to Pat, "The people who come to Laguna poets are, by and large, not established poets and they don't even have a chapbook. A lot of them can't figure out how they would possibly get one." So on the first three Fridays of any given month, the Laguna Poets release another chapbook in the series.

I asked Pat why he does this. He said, "This makes poets smile. It's a great way of getting them to organize part of the material that they are going to read in a reading. To get them to think about, 'What would I put in a chapbook?' and 'How would I write a chapbook?' It's hard for anybody to write a book that short. You have to be selective, see what fits and then throw out the crap… Some of them say, `Here's a bunch of poems, you pick them.' They haven't thought in those terms before, of actually getting their work out. Poetry is an oral art. It needs to be performed as well as seen on the page. Why do I do it? I enjoy it. It needs to be done because the job was given to me, really. (He laughs.) Marta said, `You take over, I must find somebody trustworthy to take over.'"

The poetry readings are held in or just outside of the Upchurch-Brown Booksellers. Admission is free. The average cost of a chapbook in the Laguna Poets Series is only $3. There are over sixty chapbooks in the series. Bring some poetry to the Cohee's outdoor living room; everyone is welcome to join in the open reading.

(10/97)

NEWS CLIPS AND EGO TRIPS
By G. Murray Thomas & Lizzie Wann

The February 18th episode of *Home Improvement* featured a poetry reading (neighbor Wilson gave a performance piece based on his life story). Pasted on the walls of the coffeehouse set were several copies of *Next…* Maybe we can get a speaking role next time…

–GMT

(3/97)

The Tuesday after William Burroughs died, it was hot downtown. Barefoot, sluggish, as few clothes as possible kind of weather that you pull in with every breath. A small group was gathered at El Campo Ruse after some hasty phone calls from organizing wonder woman, Janis Jordan, to pay tribute to Burroughs. Jimmy Jazz hosted the evening and kicked it all off by announcing (beautifully) he was glad Burroughs was dead. How else are new things going to get heard until the Beats are dead? Jimmy read something he'd written about looking for Burroughs' house once when he was in Lawrence, Kansas that will be part of a new book he's working on. He read excerpts from *Naked Lunch* and showed a scene with Burroughs from *Drugstore Cowboy*. Jimmy invited people up to read, including Elyse, Mary Leary, and the ever-present Chris Vannoy, who all read pieces inspired from or devoted to the Beats, Burroughs, and other related subjects. I left the Ruse, slightly more educated about Burroughs, and still very hot.

–LW

Poetry-music collaborations seemed to be the theme this month, at least in the handful of readings I managed to catch in my rare forays out of the office (and in a couple of high-profile readings I missed).

It started with the Last Poets visit to SoCal in late July. On Thursday, July 24, they gave a low-key performance/talk at Sam's Book City, laying out the history of the group in an informal, tag-team discussion between Umar Bin Hassan and Abiodun Oyewole. Then everyone rushed over to Beyond Baroque, where they performed with the "Onyx house band" (you'll have to excuse my ignorance in not listing the members by name, but they were the musicians who often back up the poets at Projector 97). Although they (the musicians and the poets) had never performed together before, they jammed hard, turning in a dynamic evening of words and rhythms. I missed their House of Blues show the next night (with Watts Prophets and Third Rail), but the reports I got made me believe it didn't come close to what I saw at Beyond Baroque.

Speaking of poets and musicians who had never performed together, the next Wednesday brought an interesting mix of just that at Liz Belile's Body of Words show at Spaceland. I found the various pairings of poets and musicians always interesting, and usually successful. Highlights for me were Steve Abee's and Jack Brewer's sets — both cooked with full band (which included Joe Baiza of Saccharine Trust and Stew of The Negro Problem, among others). Steve Salardino provided an intriguing sonic background for Rick Lupert's quips, and El Rivera barely needed musicians at all to power her own vocal music. Unluckily, as great as the individual parts were, they never quite cohered, or built any momentum. Much of the fault for that probably lay with the audience, who mostly conversed at the bar throughout the show.

A few weeks later (Thurs. Aug. 14, to be exact), we caught John Sinclair and his Blues Scholars at the House of Blues. This was a case of poet and musicians tight together. The band, featuring Wayne Kramer on guitar, played a fascinating atonal version of the blues, while Sinclair related his stories of blues history and tribute in perfect rhythm. Don't miss them the next time they're in town.

–GMT

(9/97)

BAD YEAR FOR POETRY?

1997 in Review
By Victor D. Infante

In late December of 1996 — I was on the East Coast and learning how to use this dang mechanical contraption that I'm writing on now — I received an e-mail from my friend R. Eirik Ott. It was just a personal note, updating me on his life and goings-on in Chico (and written somewhat before the happenings detailed in his depressingly funny chapbook, *Eirik Goes To Jail*). He ended with the sentence, "I have a feeling that 1997 is going to be a banner year for poetry."

I suppose 1997 being a "banner" year is one way of looking at it. I suspect most people will think of 1997 as "the year all those writers died." The list of casualties this year is enormous: Allen Ginsberg, Michael Dorris, William S. Burroughs, novelist Kathy Acker (not a poet herself, but her fiction has had a tremendous impact on several emerging poets — check out the poem "Kathy Acker Kathy Acker," by Mike Mollett in the Carma Bums' *Twisted Cadillac*).

Perhaps the most striking loss of the year, at least in the context of Southern Californian poetry, was that of Bob Challman. Fittingly, he was memorialized with a madcap open reading in Laguna Beach — his life celebrated by his friends, family and peers — as well as with a keg of beer. Ironically, this may have been the first time ever that the majority of people who've run readings in Orange County over the years were all in one place.

One of the more important functions of a poet in a society or culture is to see that important things are memorialized and remembered. I can think of no better way to memorialize these writers than to go back and read their works. The tough one is Challman, but you can find his last book, *Sunsets in a Sandcastle Between Tides*, at some independent bookstores in Laguna Beach.

It's difficult to conceive of the significance of the loss of nearly a generation of poets in such a short span. Oh, others are kicking around — Ferllinghetti, Snyder, Pinsky — but even here we're beginning to see preparations being made for new generations of poets to take the fore. One is forced to wonder if the emerging poetry "scene," on either a national or local level, is prepared to take up the mantle.

On the SoCal level, despite the decimation of venues the past year seems to have brought, there seems to be a certain feeling of... shifting. There seems to be very little agreement on a communal direction, although I would suspect the growth in influence of the Valley Contemporary Poets is proving to bridge that gap a bit. I've made no secret of my high regard for these poets, and the work that they've done to promote the most literary of Southern California's emerging poets

has gone a long way towards stabilizing what is, at the moment at least, a rather volatile time of transition.

Outside of Southern California, however, the general emphasis remains on "competitive poetry," a concept which has been heatedly debated here (although I wonder if the great success of this year's L.A. Slam Team will go a long way towards mending THAT gap, too — or has no one taken note of what a wonderful job these poets did, and how highly regarded they were by a national audience? Perhaps it's too early to say.) This year proved to hold some of the biggest challenges to the concept, as the two foremost venues of competitive poetry, The World Championship Heavyweight Bout held annually at the Taos Poetry Circus, and the National Poetry Slam Finals, held this year in Middletown, Connecticut, were rocked by protests and controversial victories.

Interestingly enough, the splits and discontent in the competitive poetry communities can really be seen as an echo of what's happening here. This is made all the more fascinating by the fact that this seems to be the year when the poetry "establishment" seems to have taken a greater interest in the goings on of the slam community — the reports of "major" poets mingling with slam poets have been trickling in a constant stream all year — Ginsberg's last reading was at a slam at NYU, Gary Snyder judged a slam in Arkansas, Pulitzer Prize winning poet Henry Taylor competed as an individual at this year's Nationals. Yet nowhere was the fireworks of the inevitable — if still somewhat uncomfortable — intermingling of the "establishment" and the slam more evident than at the Taos Poetry Circus.

In Taos, the long-awaited ten-poem competition between defending World Heavyweight champ Jimmy Santiago Baca and four-time National Poetry Slam champ Patricia Smith, ended in a tie — the result being that Baca kept his title. The audience was stunned, with several on-goers openly booing the judges and the referee.

Illustration by Brian Hagen

126

Considering the participants, this bout was seen by many to be a metaphor for the long-standing rivalry between the Bout and the Slam — a rivalry which has poked its head up in the past in the *Next... Magazine* letter column (but then, what controversy hasn't?). Several viewers, particularly those actively involved in the Slam, felt that the cavalier finish was intended as a slight at Smith, although that result is indeed the way the rules are written, and, in fact, there is a precedent for it.

As an audience member there myself, though, I recall the empty feeling the end result left me with, particularly considering that, from where I was sitting, Smith clobbered him. It disturbed me that I had gotten myself so invested in the event, as I know that, quite frankly, the results of these things mean very little. I think what got to me is that the cheap ending was a bad finish to a good show. If competitive poetry is about building audiences and making poetry more exciting for Joe Average, this poor ending did little towards that goal. Another round would have made the event more enjoyable, and would have made the loss more palatable for either poet.

More of competitive poetry's dark side emerged in Middletown, with the highly controversial victory of a team sponsored by Mouth Almighty Records. Consisting of New York poets Evert Eden, Beau Sia, Taylor Mali, and Reggie Cabico, the team edged out a victory over Chicago, Cleveland, and Worcester in the final round, but not before being forced to weather several controversies, including questions regarding the authorship of one poem, the alleged use of a prop during the third round, and general concerns about the intrusion of corporate interests into poetry and the over-dramatizing and sterilizing of poetry to suit a general audience.

As has been noted in earlier issues of *Next...*, the more practical of these matters will be resolved at the next Slam Masters' meeting, scheduled for March of 1998 in Chicago. Perhaps they are issues that all of us need to think long and hard about, as on a general level they affect us all. It's interesting that the general discontent at this year's Nationals somewhat mirrors the general criticism that has been (often unfairly) aimed at the Slam over the years.

I've heard it said, repeatedly, that "Slam" is the movement in poetry that is replacing "Beat." I'm not sure that I hold much stock in that opinion, although I will admit that Slam has done more to create a general notice and appreciation for poetry (for better or for worse) than any other single approach being used today. What IS evident is that, nationally, newer poets (newer than, say, the reading at Six Gallery where Ginsberg unveiled "Howl"), particularly in the Slam, seem to be trying to ascertain their place in today's poetry world, and let's face it, these are not simple times.

One question we are faced with is, "Has competitive poetry served its purpose, and if so, is it time to move on to the next thing?" What the heck is "the next thing?"

If something positive has come out of the controversies at these twin events (and although the organizers of either would disagree, they are more similar than not), it is that many poets seem to be reconsidering their attitudes about competitive poetry and the impact it's had on their own poetry. Some have stated that Slam has no place for them anymore, while others seem to be embracing it again with a new conviction, ready to continue on while refusing to relinquish whatever personal artistic standards they hold for what is, in truth, a rather arbitrary score.

Perhaps now should be a time of reflection for all of us who attempt to create poetry — a time to reconsider our inspirations and predecessors, to re-examine the institutions that form the borders of contemporary poetry across the U.S. and beyond. We, as poets, do not exist as singular occurrences, but are in fact connected to a greater heritage of language that predates us by centuries, and in that common root, we are indeed connected to the poets of other communities — whether we acknowledge this or not.

It would seem that, if anything, this has been a year of questions. On some very real levels, we — nationally and locally — have lost more this year than any of us seem willing to admit, and yet we seem unable to quite fill that void. We have no "next thing" to move to. Yet it is also true that nature abhors a vacuum, and poetry is, if anything, a force of nature, somewhat greater than all of us who claim to be poets. If I were to predict anything for 1998, I would predict change — but what changes and where, I have no idea. I only know I can feel the storm brewing.

(1/98)

WHAT IS BEYOND BAROQUE?

An overview by Victor D. Infante

It's difficult to find a poetry venue or institution in Southern California that evokes such varied and intense emotions as Beyond Baroque. Depending on whom you ask, it's just another poetry venue, a vital resource for all writers, the last Bastion of The Literary Arts in L.A., a den of snobbery, the centerpoint of the poetry community, an excellent bookstore and literary archive, and so much more. Are any of these points of view true? Perhaps. Quite possibly all of them.

But what is Beyond Baroque?

Beyond Baroque Literary Arts Center was founded in 1967, "to advance public understanding and involvement in the practices and the issues of contemporary writing and encourage the creation of new literary art."

"The walls are impregnated with the souls of poets who came before," says HyperPoets co-director Richard Beban, who first began attending workshops and events at Beyond Baroque in 1994. "Even so small an event as my Sunday afternoon featured in the black room made me feel like I was contributing a bit to that history myself. That black room is like a black hole in reverse, a gravitational center in the poetry universe that throws out light instead of consuming it."

In an informal survey, several members of the SoCal poetry community — as well as a few out-of-town poets who've read at Beyond Baroque — were asked which particular events held by BB stood out as significant. The responses were as varied as the poets themselves. Among the favorites were the Carma Bums' movie, *Luxurious Tigers*, the "Nearly Fatal Women" reading, Ellyn Maybe's birthday readings, and the vast numbers of non-local poets who've appeared there, including the likes of Bob Holman and Sean Thomas Dougherty.

For many people, BB is significant because it's where they discovered such Los Angeles luminaries as Jeff McDaniels, Laurel Ann Bogen, Suzanne Lummis, Holly Prado, Ellyn Maybe, and Pam Ward.

The event that seemed to strike most respondent's imaginations was the recent Small Press Conference put together by director Fred Dewey and poet S.A. Griffin. The event, which included readings and workshops on issues concerning small press publishers, such as distribution, cost, working with (sometimes difficult) talent, compensation for the writers, production, sales, how the presses differ, how much they have in common, etc., was greatly praised and considered a success by attendees.

"Such an event created an unprecedented forum for publishers in this particular community to sell our books, learn from the mistakes and successes of our fellows, and establish contacts we might not have made otherwise," says Sacred Beverage Press co-publisher Amelie Frank, "Beyond Baroque managed to take an area of the creative/literary arts and turn it into a small business seminar. What we all learned can only make us better at what we do, and what's good for small business is good for the economy and community at large."

Perhaps even more significant than the events, however, are the Wednesday Night Workshops, which are currently run by Jessica Pompei, and have been run in the recent past by Bill Mohr and renowned performance artist and writer Bob Flanagan. Known most widely as the place where Exene Cervenkova and John Doe first met — before going on to form the band X and securing BB with a place in music history — the workshop has served as a starting point for several SoCal poets.

Still, Beyond Baroque is an emotional mixed bag for many poets. One poet, when asked, says she supports BB "half from default." Other poets have changed their opinions, such as Matthew Niblock, who says, "A few years ago I didn't give a shit about Beyond Baroque. Certainly I understood the significance of the John Doe/ Exene meeting, certainly I was a fan of Bob Flanagan's work (even more so than his performance work — which was pretty fucking stunning — I really appreciated his written work, his poetry) and even attended his famed Wednesday night workshop a time or two — but good Christ, if I thought I was an elitist, I had nothing on the Beyond Baroque folk. Honestly, Fred Dewey has turned that all around. What a fantastic job he has done. First of all, by expanding the programming to include avant garde film and musical performance, secondly, by opening his ears to more local performers (myself included), thirdly, by his tireless phone-calling and scrounging and obvious dedication to the place. And of course, for Christ's sakes, this is the dude who gave

Ellyn Maybe a job. What better criteria for sainthood is there?"

For many poets, it's a matter of symbolism (and what isn't for most poets?). Beyond Baroque represents a metaphor for "Greater L.A. Literature" itself — with all the good and bad that entails. "I think the thing that makes Beyond Baroque most important is its presence," says Robert Wynne, co-director of the Valley Contemporary Poets. "The fact that it has weathered all that it has and continues to exist. The fact that it still provides a venue for local artists and national artists. The bookstore. The archive. The free workshops. The small press fair."

Whether they see Beyond Baroque as a bastion of an elitist clique — as many do, or as a vital and necessary part of the community, the thought of any compromise of the space's integrity is fraught with metaphoric repercussions that even its most ardent critics would rather not wish to see come to pass. As S.A. Griffin says, "It is really up to the community, (who or whatever that or they might be) to see to it that it continues to exist. That it is maintained and respected. These things, most especially the archive, make this place not only a source of real history, but it also makes it a living thing, something that needs attention and there are too few people doing this. Like with most things of this nature, there are few that are willing to bake that bread and many willing to partake…"

(2/98)

REMEMBERING MICHELINE

By Alan Kaufman

As you enter this funky little church in Jack's beloved Mission District, his green monkey grinder hat is prominently displayed. It is a night for characters in hats to pay tribute to the greatest character of them all: San Francisco Beat poet Jack Micheline. The sheer crush of colorful folks gathering has forced some of us to sit to the side of the scuffed old stage. Here is bearded old poet George Tsongas in a black Bart cowboy hat on my left, and Beat chronicler and Bukowski biographer Neeli Cherkovski in a smart tam o' shanter on my right. Now, in a stingy brim fedora, comes Alfonso Texidor, that dapper down-at-the-heels cafe poet of frayed renown, limping up to pinch my cheek and park his skinny ass in the last available crack of space.

We're all here, all the self-suiciding maniacs of the San Francisco poetry scene, with bitten off bits of each other's ears still stuck between our wolfish teeth: Jack Hirschman, Harold Norse, Q.R.Hand, Gerald Nicosia, Bruce Isaacson just in from Nevada and now, for crying out loud, Michael McClure, who wouldn't give Micheline the time of day when he was alive, has just walked in, humbly lowered himself to the floor and immediately sent several signals to Kush, tonight's organizer, to jump his name ahead of the peons on the sign-up list.

In the downstairs reception area, growling videos of Jack wailing verse to a screeching sax entertains the moochers and hanger-ons who really don't give a shit about some croaked old Beat poet: they're here for a free nosh on bagels and wine. Somehow one feels that Jack would have liked these folks best. At least they're more real than the famous phonies showing up, folks who once walked right past him when he was alive, broke, hungry and hawking his three-buck chapbooks out in the rain under the marquee of the Roxie cinema, around the corner on Sixteenth Street. By now, about three hundred people

Illustration by Charles Ellik

have filled the upstairs hall. Jack could have sold a lot of books tonight.

As cameras roll, Kush kicks off with a convocational chant that wrings the heart. The wind has Jack, it goes. A lot of eyes in the place tear up, mine included, for the poetry of death. Then Jack's old sax man mounts the stage, axe in hand. In the thirty years he'd played behind Micheline, he says, "Micheline would growl: 'Sax man, when my hand goes up you play.' So let's imagine Jack's up here with me now, and his hand is raised for me to blow this one last time for him." The grieving memories of his horn turn the room into all the little jazz spots and dives where Jack broke indifferent hearts with the truth burning in his guts.

Now Neeli jumps up and delivers generous poetic praise of Micheline's raw power with words. This is followed by a message from Ken Kesey (e-mailed from Oregon where he is laid up ill with a minor stroke), in which he recalls all the word orgies they gigged together, the wild times. Then a balding Ferlinghetti eunuch emissary in a sweater vest reads the City Lights publisher's typical Imperial apology for his usual failure to appear for something as insignificant as the death of a poet, followed by a few brief words of begrudging admiration and ending with how much he'll miss running into Jack on his evening walks. Whereupon George Tsongas leans close to my ear and rasps: "When was the last time that piece of shit went out at night?"

Now a procession of yawn-crafters have their turn, McClure the chief Sandman among them. Soon it will be the turn of us lesser proles, who actually knew, performed with, and published alongside Jack, to restore the dozing crowd. It is Jack Hirschman, that uncompromising street activist poet who brings down the house with one of the most magnificent eulogies I have ever heard. Refusing the mike and detesting the camera, he steps to the edge of the stage, leans out into space and, in his overbearing Bronx accent, hurls a Molotov verse cocktail of elegiac raging love that brings the crowd cheering to its feet. At that moment I glance over at the famous phonies, to register their reactions to one of life's unfailing truths, something that Micheline knew and Bukowski lived by: in the end, the American democratic mob, just like every other audience throughout time, doesn't give a fuck about your fame, your craft, your hyper-deconstructionist French poodle theories. They want bloody truth and awful beauty. I looked at McClure and wondered: "Who's gonna care about your words when you're dust? I mean, really care?"

Just one more recollection of the fierce street poet Jack Micheline. A few years back, I had an invite to read for no pay in a few Chicago music clubs, and so went working temp downtown in San Francisco for a soulless lawyer, trying to earn scratch to catch that Greyhound bus and put up in some cheap Northside hotel. I was busting my ass for the right to perform, cutting through greedy gray flannel crowds on an errand to buy the shyster prick hand lotion or some such crap when there's Jack old beat street poet Micheline rushing along with a wine-stained scowl. Upon seeing me, his face brightened like a little Bronx urchin weaned on Eddie Cantor and Legs Diamond, a pure poet three sewer hitter Blakean mug of open road and tenement. He said "Wot the fock you doin' here?" I stammered and laughed, ashamed, because his sea-blue eyes were so innocently pure. He showed me a letter he'd just got from John Martin of Black Sparrow Press that read: "Dear Jack, Thanks for your work. But I have decided not to publish any of Bukowski's friends" and other hurtful bullshit and as we both stood there riveted amidst the pyramids of our oppression, Micheline said, sadly, "I'm going back east for a while, getting out of California. They're killing me here." So we were both leaving in the night on that poetry exodus bus and Jack raised his arm as one who had been to the mountain top, he swept his cracked old hand over the heads of the minions of greed scurrying by and he shouted: "You know wot's wrong with Martin!? And you know wot's wrong wit dese people down here? Dey are afraid of the light! Dey fear! Dey are afraid of da fucking light!"

And so you have left Jack Micheline, on the last bus into the light, with poetry and honor, poverty, unleavened dreams, unafraid of your terror, with the chariots at your back and the sea before you, waiting to part.

(4/98)

MOUTH ALMIGHTY POETS

Bob Holman, Sekou Sundiata, Maggie Estep, Last Poets
Thursday, April 30, 1998 • Barnsdall Gallery Theater
Reviewed by G. Murray Thomas

Okay, what's wrong with SoCal poetry audiences? What does it take to get them into a theater? Is $15 really too much for a dynamite poetry show? Or did you start giggling as soon as I said "poetry audience?"

These are the sort of questions I pondered after watching four of the country's top performance poetry acts — Bob Holman, Sekou Sundiata, Maggie Estep and the Last Poets — put on a dynamite show to a nearly empty theater this past month. Whatever the reasons for the lack of audience — poor publicity, ticket prices, an uninterested public — the poets still rose to the occasion.

The evening was kicked off by Holman, the impresario behind Mouth Almighty, the primary spoken word record label in the country (a division of Mercury Records) and the sponsor of the evening. Holman is one of the most explosive, high-energy performers in poetry today; it was actually nice to see him tone down the hyperness for a change, and read some of his quieter, more "poetic" works. Not to take anything away from his ability to word-whip an audience into a frenzy, but this gave him a chance to demonstrate the strength and craft of the words beneath the delivery.

Sekou Sundiata's reading was intimate, friendly and beautiful. The serene flow of his words fit filling the space. He did the best job of relaxing into the situation, interrupting a poem about Nelson Mandela's visit to New York to explain a line about "the disseminating Monkey" with a quick, rappified retelling of the folk tale, and then sliding back into the original poem without missing a beat.

Maggie Estep did not tone her performance down any, delivering her tales with a rapid-fire, speed freak style, which fit nicely with her absurd, almost surreal take on urban life. The centerpiece of her set started with a man thinking about flossing hair from between his teeth and took him through an incident of sexual harassment/attempted rape without ever losing its internal logic.

Unfortunately, the Last Poets suffered the most from the nearly empty room. While they gave their all, and did not let their spirits flag, their high energy, call-and-response style really requires a crowd to bounce off of. Still, they accomplished their usual blend of entertainment and message-bringing.

So all I can say to all of you who weren't there (which is certainly the vast majority of those who might be reading this) is that you missed an evening of powerful and entertaining word art. If you have a chance to see any of these four again, don't blow it a second time.
(6/98)

TAOS POETRY CIRCUS

Reviewed by Victor D. Infante

By the end of the third round and, effectively, seventh hour of the poetry slam, it was less amazing that the packed crowd at the Alley Cantina was still as enthusiastic as ever than it was that they were upright at all. As poet after poet fell out of the competition — including slam heavy-hitters like Albuquerque, NM's Danny Solis and Worcester, MA's Bill MacMillan — the pressure of competition lifted from their shoulders and their cheers rang in with the rest of the crowd's, until finally Albuquerque's Eirean Bradley stood victorious. Smiling ear to ear, he accepted his prize: $100, a pass to the festival, and a T-shirt, and was promptly engulfed in an onslaught of congratulatory hugs from the poets whom he'd just defeated.

It's moments like these that are the true strength of the Taos Poetry Circus — when poets from across the U.S. can relax and bask in the company and camaraderie of their peers. With the controversy of last year's World Heavyweight Poetry Bout still looming in the air – four-time National Poetry Slam Champion Patricia Smith tied World Heavyweight Bout Champion Jimmy Santiago Baca, resulting in Baca retaining his title, resulting in raucous audience disapproval — it's fortunate that the festival began on such a positive note.

Although the Heavyweight Bout is generally considered to be the festival's big draw — with this year's pairing of Baca against Native American poet, novelist and screenwriter Sherman Alexie drawing in excess of 700 people — it was Wednesday's experimental "tag team bout" that drew the lion's share of critical attention. In an eight-round competition, Smith, teamed with Worcester poet, slammer, small press publisher, and novelist Sou MacMillan; and Baca, paired with prominent poet and former Heavyweight champ Ntzoake Shange, alternated reading. The poets were scored on a "binary system," the four judges giving a one to the group who supposedly won each round, and a zero to the one who didn't. It must be noted that judges are given no parameters to determine who won.

MacMillan and Smith were solid from beginning to end, every syllable of their hard-hitting, intensely powerful poetry enunciated and easily heard. In addition, they had worked out and rehearsed several dual voice versions of their poems. Personally, I've always felt that the majority of group/dual voice work muddies a poem, but here, the added layer of interpretation and inflection brought out new depths in each writer's work, nowhere more strikingly than in MacMillan's poem "Sex in the Age of the Automobile." Although a less famous voice than the others, MacMillan's poetry shone with an unparalleled brilliance, proving beyond a shadow of a doubt that she belonged on that stage.

Shange and Baca were less prepared, very obviously arranging their sets as they went, and showed less finesse on stage. While Shange's poetry was absolutely gorgeous, and she at the very least showed presence, her diction made her difficult to understand. A shame really. Being familiar with her earlier work, including the immensely powerful *For Colored Girls Who Have Considered Suicide/ When the Rainbow is Enuf*, I was aware of just how powerful that work was.

Baca, for his part, is a bit too prone to abstractions and melodrama for my tastes. Perhaps I shouldn't have been surprised by the Shange/Baca team victory, but I found a cry of disbelief rising from my throat as the results were announced. It always amazes me how wrapped up I get in this stuff. Still, Baca was far more gracious in both winning and losing this year than last, and for that at least, he deserves some respect.

Of the single readings, my nod for the strongest performances goes to Patricia Smith and Jim Carroll. I've seen Smith read numerous times, and she's never failed to be anything less than stellar, but here were sides of her that you rarely get to see in a slam situation. Her poem about losing her husband to Diana Ross was hysterical, the excerpts from her forthcoming novel were chilling, and her next-to-last poem about being a journalist hit me right where I lived. The woman is nothing less than phenomenal.

Carroll I was apprehensive about. I've heard tapes where the poetry was great, but the delivery was flawed. Whatever's happened in the time since then has agreed with him. He read with a poise and presence like few I've ever seen, each piece settling into the audience with resounding energy. After a few minutes, I had lost the urge to shout out "People Who've Died!" This wasn't a rock star. This was a poet.

Of course, the Bout is the big draw, and I won't deny that I was solidly rooting for Alexie. He's a brilliant writer. Little did I know that he was a polished and professional reader, also. I'd put Alexie on a slam team in a heartbeat. His was not only one of the strongest readings of the week, it was one of the strongest I have ever seen. To my delight, he read my favorite poem of his, "How to Write the Great American Indian Novel." Alexie is a master of poetically setting up his audience with laughter, then knocking them down with a truly chilling idea or image. His improvisational poem, "Chaos," resulting in a beautiful poem about the horrid things he's lived through, balanced against the birth of his son, was amazing, and the skill with which he prompted the audience to chant along with him on the poem "1000 Ponies" was amazing to behold. This man is an absolute treasure of a poet, and I cannot recommend him highly enough. His victory in the Bout was not just well-earned, it was a vindication of the best a poet can aspire to be.

If I have one disappointment in the week's festivities, it's not that I once again saw the ill-ease with which emerging poets co-exist with the established ones, it's the realization that this ill-ease will continue for years to come. Clearly, a new "generation" of poets — heralded by the likes of Patricia Smith and epitomized by the likes of Sou MacMillan — is beginning to come into its own, especially now that the Beat Generation begins to fade. It's through poets like her that I get a glimpse of poetry's future. It's to the credit of festival directors Annie McNaughton and Peter Rabbit that they've begun to realize this.

And even if there was an air of tension between groups, I consider the camaraderie of that first slam.

Recall the relaxed air of sharing at the daily open readings. Most of all, I recall the intensity with which Shange was listening to MacMillan — how obviously her words were sinking in. It's here that I see hope — the simple act of sharing, and above all else, listening.

(7/98)

TWENTY-FIVE YEARS AGO

The Span of Poetry
By Joan Jobe Smith

Twenty-five years ago, nearly to the day, I saw my first poetry reading at California State University Long Beach, featuring Charles Bukowski, and tonight, March 19, 1998, I go to see my twelfth million, Yusef Komunyakaa, the 1994 Pulitzer prizer for his poetry collection Neon Vernacular. At least 100 poetry lovers are there at the CSULB Center for Faculty Development (a nomer that makes you think you might get yourself an eye exam while there — or maybe a Rorschach test). A small gathering compared to the 300 at Bukowski's in 1973, packed standing room only in the auditorium. The crowd tonight, however, is quiet, and listen respectfully as Komunyakaa reads his dancing with tall grass poetry with the grace of a feeding swan, his aura a midnight magnolia musk compared to Bukowski's chartreuse of sunburned beer. After the reading, Komunyakaa is asked the usual cordial questions most gently: how does he write ("in long hand"), who are his favorite Vietnam War writers (he's noncommittal), which of his own poems is his favorite ("The one I'm working on," he says slyly, getting one of his few laughs, for he is a very serious poet), and finally someone asks him what he thinks of Bukowski's poetry, and Yusef says, with the sane sobriety of a fine father: "I thought his early work was too formalistic. I prefer his middle work. Next question—"

Yusef Komunyakaa and I attended the University of California Irvine MFA Program at the same time — he the poetry writing segment, I the fiction. Prior to his reading, at the wine-and-cheese reception (except they're sparse with the wine these days), he vaguely remembered me, for the poets and fiction writers did not hobnob in those days, each group considered their group superior to the other (which, in this case, shows how right the poets were, for they cranked out the likes of Yusef and Garrett Hongo those years and from my cronies emerged the surf-writer Kem Nunn). Bukowski did not approve of me when I bragged to him about being accepted at UCI, then the #2-rated MFA Program in the U.S. "My main criticism of you, Joan," he said to me, "is that you have plugged in too much to the college scene. That's a bigger mirage than love. The most vicious people that I have known, those furthest away from reality and compassion are the college profs. And these teach. Be careful, Joan. Feed your brain on me."

What Bukowski would have thought of Yusef Komunyakaa, an academic/prof, a Vietnam War vet, and a black man with Messiah eyes that can read your soul because he can, I don't know. But I do know how very, very different it all is tonight, all this poetry business with which I've been incorporated all these twenty-five years: Komunyakaa sipping good bottled water from a plastic cup, twenty-five years ago Bukowski sucking vodka from a bottle wrapped in a brown paper bag, the feminists in the audience heckling him with sharpened we're-ready-for-you-pig harpy barbs: "Who's your favorite whore this week?" one yelled at him. "I don't know any whores," he answered. "Why are all your poems about yourself?" yelled another. "Who do you write about?" he asked her. "I don't write," she replied. Yelled another: "Would you come to hear Bukowski read?" Bukowski lit a cigarette, slowly, and finally answered: "I wouldn't waste my time." "Why do you use dirty words?" another asked him. "Give me an example of a dirty word." "Why don't you write poems about your mother?" another asked, and Bukowski quickly answered, as if he'd rehearsed it, "My mother died before I was born." Silence. "Any more questions?" Silence. "Good, then I gotta take a piss," he said and staggered off the stage with pages from *Factotum*, his novel-in-progress, falling from his hands. The young men cheered, whistled, and stamped their feet. The feminists got up and got out of there. When Bukowski returned, zipping up his fly, he continued to read, smoke, and suck vodka, and a good time was had by all.

People at Komunyakaa's reading tonight whistled too, several times, especially after he read about a dead soldier in Nam: "When I got to him, a blue halo of flies had already claimed him." But no one got up and got out of there.

Poetry is poetry, but never the same.

(7/98)

POET BEGETS POET BEGETS POET

A Search for the Influences of Contemporary Poetry
By Victor D. Infante

I suppose it all starts somewhere. You're minding your own business, stumbling out of the rain into a coffeehouse or bar for something to warm your bones, and *blam*, you're confronted with some weirdo up behind the mic ranting at you. It's kind of scary… it's kind of annoying… and what makes it worse is that some of it makes sense. You go home to try and write it down, because something inside of you has shifted.

You barely recognize that the words are yours.

I suppose I might as well start with myself. One day, when I was younger, I was languishing in my stereotypical adolescent angst while reading the newspaper, when I came across a poem in the Anne Landers section. It wasn't very good. I don't even remember the title or author, but it was from a mother to her daughter, who seemed to be going through the same junk I was.

I sat down and wrote a poem for the first time since second grade. Oh, it was even bigger trash than the one in Anne Landers, but it was mine. And I couldn't stop. As Ellyn Maybe once put it, "There was now a healthy way to vent rage/ it made me sick/ I couldn't justify throwing things."

Now it's more than ten years later. I'm still scribbling, just more people read it now. Thinking back on the poets who influenced me, I've become curious to see what my peers had to say on the subject… are there any common threads. What pushes someone to make that transition from private scribbler to public?

Greg Paye's (Boston, MA) story is probably the most typical introduction people have to poetry. Says Paye:

"During my freshman year of college I developed this severe crush on this young woman. We had little in common, she was a hippie-poet and I was an angst-ridden-punk-rock-refugee. She told me her favorite poet was Anne Sexton. I'd never heard of the woman, and had never read poetry outside of classroom before, but decided to check it out. I wound up falling in love with Anne after reading her poetry. I consumed one book, then another. I started to look at poetry in a whole new light."

Paye is not alone in this. While Sexton (who was often mentioned alongside Sylvia Plath) was probably the least considered of her Confessional-Poet contemporaries, her vivid imagery, lyric sensuality, and brazen honesty seem to have struck a chord with several contemporary poets. Indeed, in the informal poll conducted for this article (which can in no way be considered scientific), she scored amongst the five most seemingly influential poets on the "live" poetry scene, along with T.S. Eliot, Walt Whitman, Charles Bukowski, and Jello Biafra (who, admittedly, was often mentioned in the same breath as Henry Rollins. While neither are traditionally "poets," their influence on contemporary poets cannot be denied.) While disparate, it's interesting that these writers represent five specific schools of artistic thought: Confessional Poetry, the Modernists, Classic American, Recent American and Punk Rock.

Says Robert Wynne, co-director of The Valley Contemporary Poets in Glendale, CA:

"Poetry can teach and delight. That's why all of our influences tend to be so disparate, I think. All of these things come together in our heads and there aren't any lines between them anymore, and soon you've got Schoolhouse Rock's version of *The Wasteland*, or animated characters singing 'I grow old I grow old I shall wear my trousers rolled.' And that's cool, because then someone else gets influenced and who knows what they'll come up with because of it."

By looking at these five representative writers and their immediate peers, you can get an idea of where recent trends in poetry are coming from. There are several qualities of their work that have heavily influenced a number of poets on today's "live" poetry circuit… the ability to transcend the personal into the universal, such as with Sexton and Plath. An ability to transcend the page and to push the limits of form and structure… to create original work from a constantly rehashed world, such as Eliot did. Honesty and an ability to echo one's own personal alienation, such as Bukowski held for many. Musicality like Whitman's. An ability to tell a story or lay a perspective on the line, like Biafra or Rollins. While there are probably as many influences on today's poetry scene as there are poets, these qualities held true for most.

For many, the ignition of inspiration begins with an exploration of one's own heritage or community. Merilene Murphy, director of Telepoetics, cites African-American poet and playwright Ntzoake Shange. Brent Long, a poet from Arkansas, notes the influence of Southern writer Frank Stanford on his own work. NoCal poet Aaron Yamaguchi relates the influence of his grandmother, a prominent Japanese "Shijin" poet. Liz Gonzalez cites Sandra Cisneros and I would be remiss as an Irish-American to not mention Seamus Heaney. I have long believed that a poet serves as an extension of his or her community, so it is natural that each community within the greater one would develop its own voices, somewhat different than the others but none-the-less related.

We see several factors influencing a developing poet… a historical tradition, a powerful oral component, and the direct influence of another poet. In today's world, where nearly every area has at least one or two established readings, this is a common experience. Lisa Martinovic, an Ozarks based poet, relates this story:

"I wandered into this dank and dirty bar, squeezed past dozens of strange looking people to get into the back room — a cramped, smoky hole covered by a corrugated tin roof. Bleachers were the seating accommodations. Peanut shells littered the floor, heckling and raucous audience participation were *de riguer*. And if your poem was really bad, someone might throw beer on you. I was in heaven! I sat, completely mesmerized, for three hours. Walking out into the Mission afterwards, I marveled: Why in the world would anyone go see a movie when they could instead experience the thrill of live, unfettered creative expression? I was gone. I didn't know that you could yell, swear, be nasty, and do this stream of consciousness thing — and get away with it. My writing changed immediately and irrevocably. I was emboldened to speak my mind fully and also, to be funny – another quality I hadn't heretofore associated with poetry."

In a world where culture seems emaciated, where the onslaught of media has deprived nearly everything of meaning, it is remarkable that so many voices have reached out to ignite a flame within others, and that these others have gone on to ignite that flame elsewhere. From Whitman to Bukowski, Shange to "Shijin," it seems that today's poets represent the fusion of disparate inspirations and perspectives, all seeking that same elusive "truth."

Perhaps no true conclusion can be drawn from this information, or perhaps the disparity of it all IS the conclusion. I think Huntington Beach, CA, based poet Charles Ardinger best summed it up:

"I think part of being a good poet (to the extent that I can talk about being a good poet; please excuse me) is keeping oneself relatively susceptible to influence. Nearly everything I read is a potential reformation; I sometimes wonder about my own voice, how I have one, what is my individual talent."

(A longer version of this article originally appeared in *Omnivore Magazine*, and appears here courtesy of editor Sou MacMillan. Gracias.)

(7/98)

Illustration by Walt Hopmans

THE QUALITY OF MERCY

(A Question of Ethics)
By Victor D. Infante

Shakespeare wrote "the quality of mercy is not strained," but more often than not the daily news disproves that. The quality of "mercy" seems an alien concept to the American people. We don't want icons, we want to see our leaders, our celebrities, our idols, torn down. We sit in rapt anticipation for the next issue of the *Enquirer* to be released. For far too many, life is little more than an episode of *American Gladiators*, and we wanna see blood.

That being so, I shouldn't have been so surprised at how quickly the pack of media jackals jumped into the feeding frenzy when *Boston Globe* columnist Patricia Smith was dismissed for fabricating persons and quotations in four of her Metro columns.

"From time to time in my metro column," said Smith, in her parting column, "to create the desired impact or slam home a salient point, I attributed quotes to people who didn't exist. I could give them names, even occupations, but I couldn't give them what they needed most — a heartbeat. As anyone who's ever touched a newspaper knows, that's one of the cardinal sins of journalism: Thou shall not fabricate. No exceptions. No excuses."

She's right. There are no excuses. In fact, she should be summarily executed right now, on pay-per-view, so the defiled, blood-thirsty American public can get the satisfaction it so readily deserves. Hey, why stop there? Let's set up The Execution Channel so we can sit googly-eyed to the TV as they line up all the senior citizens, cancer patients, and AIDS victims that bought medicinal marijuana from Cannabis Buyers Clubs in California. We can watch 'em puff their last joint before sending 'em off to see Jerry in that Grateful Jam in the sky.

More and more, Adam Smith's *Invisible Hand of Capitalism* swats away any vestige of mercy in today's society, leaving us with a Darwinian nightmare where the small indiscretions are punished mercilessly, while the greater ones — the gargantuan lies, the explicit racism, are ignored, forgiven and forgotten. This is a competition. Only the strong survive.

I first encountered Patricia Smith in 1994, when she and her husband, poet Michael Brown, came to the now-defunct Living Planet, in Long Beach, to perform their poetry. I've found it fascinating how few of the newspaper articles about the incident that I've read have noted that she's also a widely published and respected poet — one who's won the National Poetry Slam performance poetry competition a record four times and has published three books, including the recent *Close To Death*.

While I've always admired her as a journalist, it's always been Smith's poetry that's most moved me. Even four years later, I can still feel the impact of that performance. The frightening energy that radiated from her tense body as she spoke her poem, "Undertaker," a brutally graphic and honest depiction of a gunshot murder, and of a mother's deterioration at the sight of the body. The chilling sound of the mother pleading, "fix my boy," has long resounded in my head.

By accounts given in the *New York Times*, as well as by Smith herself in the *Boston Globe*, it seems the fictionalized "characters" of her column were created to facilitate an "everyman's" reaction, to allow the reader to associate with the news. At this writing, I do not know which persons in the column were fiction. Was the cab driver responding to a radio report of two kids opening fire on a classroom real?

Yes. Regardless of whether or not that person existed — whether or not Smith happened to be in that New York cab at that particular moment — his musings were the ones we were all thinking at that time — fear for and of our own children.

Does this make the act of fraudulent reporting any less wrong? No, not really. But how can a sentence of journalistic exile fit the crime when newspapers daily use more innocent methods to commit far greater atrocities? By all accounts, Smith judiciously used fiction to illustrate greater truths — most often to speak to the best of human nature. This is what a poetry professor of mine once referred to as "the big lie."

How does that compare with, say, the burying of Gary Webb's "Dark Alliance," the story originally published in the *San Jose Mercury News* which detailed the connections between the CIA and cocaine entering the United States, despite critics' inability to disprove Webb's evidence? Or with the *LA Times/OC's* nonsensical support of former U.S. Congressman Bob Dornan's unsubstantiated allegations of a great Latino Conspiracy to remove him from office? Or with the *Rhode Island Journal*'s refusal to cover an Independent Candidate's run for Lt. Governor, dropping the candidate overnight from being a close second in the polls to being effectively out of the race?

No, the sins of cowardice, special interest and omission are sanctioned evils, and allowed to continue as a matter of course. It's only when someone falters in the attempt of speaking for the common good that we crucify them.

"Ashes, ashes, we all fall down." Everybody does, sooner or later. The rabid dogs of journalism nationwide had best remember that, because sooner or later, it'll be their time, too. And who's gonna speak up for them?

(8/98)

LETTER FROM TIM BROWN

Dear *Next…*

The August issue of *Next…* contained two articles about scandal surrounding Patricia Smith's forced resignation from the *Boston Globe* in late June. Curiously, both articles seemed to lay responsibility for the unfortunate situation at the feet of the newspaper rather than where it belongs — at the feet of Smith herself. Moreover, neither article addressed the situation's implications for Smith's credibility as a poet. I personally will have trouble respecting Smith's work in the future on account of her actions at the *Globe*.

Let me begin by stating that I was a fan of Smith's ever since she exploded onto the Chicago poetry scene in the late 1980s. She added a much-needed dose of dignity to a scene dominated by performance poets trying to pass off dirty jokes as poetry. Her readings were electrifying. What's more, her work stood up on the printed page, as I found when I bought an autographed copy of her first book, *Life According to Motown*, when it was first published. Like many Chicagoans, I was sorry to see her move away to Boston. But I was glad to hear that she was meeting with success in her new life, both as a poet and as a journalist.

Then came the shocking news of June 19. At first I was saddened to learn of Smith's situation. Very quickly, sadness gave way to a sense of betrayal. Without a doubt, Smith's employers at the *Globe* felt betrayed, albeit for a different reason than I did (which I'll turn to in a moment). Simply put, betraying the trust of her employer and readers was the reason Smith had to resign.

Neither Mr. Infante nor Mr. McCarthy discussed the journalistic climate surrounding Smith's departure, which came on the heels of two high-profile cases where news was falsified. Stephen Glass had recently been exposed for writing totally fictitious articles for several national news magazines. To fool fact checkers, he falsified notes and went so far as to create a website for a fictitious company about which he wrote an expose. Even a trusted institution like CNN was not immune from this disturbing trend. The network had just fired two producers for airing an untrue story claiming that nerve gas was used by the U.S. army during the Vietnam War. Disgustingly, CNN's star reporter, Peter Arnett, who reported the story, was let off the hook, despite his admission that he didn't research the story and put his name on a follow-up article in *Time* that he didn't write.

Given events like these, it's no surprise that when Smith was found out, the *Globe* gave her the boot, because any hint of impropriety creates doubt about the paper's credibility. Credibility, a very fragile commodity in this era of sleazy journalism, is the only thing that separates a respectable newspaper from the supermarket tabloids, which do in fact falsify the news. Acting as Smith's apologists, Messrs. Infante and McCarthy excuse her actions, apparently believing that telling little lies is okay compared to the big lies told constantly by the mass media. What they fail to realize is that the little lies inexorably lead to the big lies to which they rightly object.

"What does all this have to do with poetry?" you ask. After all, Smith was called on the carpet for an offense occurring in the nonfiction world. And, anyhow, even if she inserted an occasional untruth in her nonfiction, she was writing opinion pieces, where such liberties can be taken.

The answer to this question has to do with the aims and purposes of nonfiction and poetry and how the genres are different but also similar. Yes, nonfiction differs greatly from poetry. The former is based on fact, the latter on fancy. Nonfiction is created by accumulating real-life examples that are presented as evidence to support a main idea. True, opinion is different from hard reportage in that the author's viewpoint is inserted. However, basic rhetorical rules still apply, requiring you to use facts, not fiction, as support. These rules are strictly enforced in journalistic settings.

Poetry has no such restrictions. Poetry is based on imagination and word play. In poetry, the poet's subjective take on reality is paramount. A distinctive voice, original ideas, and verbal dexterity make a poet successful. Yet, though different from nonfiction, poetry is similar in a crucial way: both genres present the Truth, with a capital "T." Both demand emotional, intellectual and spiritual honesty to lay claim to the reader's trust. I distrust a nonfiction writer who draws conclusions based on evidence manipulated dishonestly. Likewise, I distrust a poet who dazzles with verbal fireworks but imparts a hollow message.

There is a definite stylistic line between nonfiction and poetry. But honesty is a trait that crosses all lines and should be present in every style of writing. When it's absent in one genre an author practices, you begin to wonder if it's absent in another genre, too. This, then, is why I feel betrayed by Smith's actions: I feel I was manipulated to put trust in her words when quite possibly there was no honest expression contained within them.

To her credit, Smith owned up to her misdeeds in her final *Globe* column. This indicates that she has begun the process of looking inside herself to determine what went wrong. Smith is a talented writer, so I anticipate she will eventually apply her fictionalizing skills in producing honest, penetrating writing. I look forward to the time when her words have earned back my trust.

Tim Brown, Chicago, IL

(9/98)

SOCAL SLAM TEAMS

By Daniel McGinn

Here's a little game you can play at home. Did you know that all of Emily Dickinson's poems were written to the tune of "The Yellow Rose of Texas?" Try singing along with them, it's fun. I'm sure Emily Dickinson would do just fine at an open mic reading. Open readings are a Sunday drive, a stroll through the park, with plenty of time to stop and smell the yellow roses. Slams, on the other hand, are a sprint through the hood on judgment day — with the hounds of hell snapping at your heels — and there are exactly three minutes between you and the next chain link fence.

"Are You Ready Judges?"

"Woof Woof"

"OK. GO!!!"

Slams are what you get when you cross a drag race with a demolition derby. Slamming is live poetry — not dead poets — and if Dickinson shows up in Austin, Texas, for the 1998 national slam competition she won't even survive the first round! She's gonna get her pasty little white butt kicked! It's gonna be hot and it's gonna be sweaty and it ain't gonna be pretty. Win or lose, for the slam poet slamming is an adrenaline rush that pushes poetry into other realms: stand-up comedy, dance moves, melodramatics, politically correct diatribes, smut, drug induced cosmic messages, angry declarations of sexual orientation (angry is good, so is bitter), and repetitive use of the seven words you can't say on television (fuck is good, very good). Maybe it's just a backlash to cookie-cutter MFA programs and post-modernism, maybe this is poetry of the people, attempting subversive communication to a visual — not a literary — culture. Like it or not, this gathering of the spoken word tribe is growing and slams are becoming an institution.

There are forty-five teams converging in Austin for the 1998 national slam competition. Four of those teams are from Southern California. Five teams applied but only four teams were accepted. (More on that later.) Interest in slams keep growing. Derrick Brown of the Laguna Beach team just e-mailed to inform me that "Denny's has a grand slam and I'm the fourth alternate for the team." Slam teams are springing up so quickly (no pun intended) that I can't keep up.

What follows is a consensus of the teams that are leaving SoCal for Austin: Los Angeles, Long Beach, Laguna Beach, and Venice. (Remember that this information is for entertainment purposes only. *Next…* does not post odds. It is illegal to bet on slam teams.)

LOS ANGELES

(Jerry Quickley, Poetri, Deborah Edler Brown, Thea Iberall)

Los Angeles has two veteran Slam Masters, Robert Carroll and Mark Pomeroy. Los Angeles has done well in the semi-finals both years it has

attended, winding up a percentage of a point behind the final four. This is Jerry Quickley's third time around for L.A. team — he never seems to lose a slam. Last year he made it to the finals. Jerry and teammate Monica Copeland were among the ten highest scoring individual poets. As a slammer he is currently ranked 5th in the nation. This is Deborah Edler Brown's third visit to the nationals; she attended last year as an alternate for the L.A. team and won the National Haiku Slam. The poet named Poetri is a man who loves to perform. This is his first time attending the nationals. Thea Iberall is also going to the nationals for the first time. "I'm preparing myself mentally for what it's going to be like," Thea said, "it's not like anything I've ever been in, although I've been in clown competitions, that's sort of similar."

LONG BEACH

(Jim Bolt, Mack Dennis, Crystal J. Waterford, William McLain)

Long Beach (the team formerly known as SlamTasTic) is "the quieter, gentler alternative slam," according to Slam Master Patricia Bowser, who quickly added, "this team is going to kick butt!!" This is the second year that

her slam has tried to send a team to the nationals. The application SlamTasTic submitted last year was the 34th and final application received by the slam committee. It takes three teams to make a bout at the national level; if two more teams had applied, the application would have been accepted. That SlamTasTic team, which included current Long Beach team members Mack Dennis and Jim Bolt, was not allowed to compete. Jim Bolt did compete in the nationals last year as an individual; he combines verse, dramatics and dance in a Jungian search for keys. Mack Dennis was sitting in the audience in Connecticut last year, taking notes. Since that time he has been seen slamming at every venue from here to San Francisco. William McLain is a local treasure. This octogenarian rocked an erotic poetry reading at the Nationals in 1996 with his rendition of "I'm a Dirty Old Man." You shoulda been there, it was a Kodak moment. Crystal J. Waterford is the team's best kept secret.

LAGUNA BEACH

(Chris Tannahill, Derrick Brown, Mindy Nettifee, Victor Infante)

This is the first time that Orange County has sent a team to the big show. The community support has

Photo of John Gardiner, Mindy Nettifee, Victor D. Infante, Derrick Brown and Chris Tanahill by G. Murray Thomas been astonishing. Laguna Beach finals happened before a packed house at the F.A.C.T. gallery. Lee "scary poet mode" Mallory hosted the show and he kept having telethon moments, announcing "I'm a whore, I'm a poetry addict, now show me the money." People were writing fifty and one hundred-dollar checks and passing them to the front. I've never seen anything like it before.

I "did lunch" with the Laguna Beach team on a Sunday afternoon about two weeks after the finals. Before rehearsal they were having cherries, caviar ($2 from Trader Joe's), and paté on cute little biscuits, followed by baklava and coffee. It was all so very Laguna — except there weren't any Wyland paintings on the wall — this team has a youthful rebellious spirit. Lea Deschenes, their Slam Master, is a pro. She has slammed with and Slam Mastered east coast teams for years. The Left Coast has never won a National Slam, perhaps it's a good idea to import coaches.

Chris Tannahill slammed with the 1995 Colorado Team and the 1997 Silverlake team. His poetry is dark, smart, and says something about a gun. Victor Infante was a member of the '96 Long Beach team, and also attended the '97 slams. This is Derrick Brown's first time attending the nationals. He's a jolly chap who says, "Slams are the Star Search for nerds and I'm just here to pick up chicks." Mindy Nettifee is new to slams. She was a *Next… Magazine* cover girl at sweet sixteen. Mindy is a natural phenomenon: blonde and literate.

These three teams are products of existing monthly slams taking place at Caffe Luna, Saint Mary's Episcopal Church and Fahrenheit 451. In the past it has not been unusual to see teams attending the nationals that are not connected to an existing slam. Southern California has been sending handpicked teams: the '96 Long Beach team was handpicked and in 1997 we sent P.O.T. (Pacific Ocean team) and Silverlake/Los Feliz. Once again, this year two teams representing local venues without existing slams applied: Hollywood/Los Feliz, and Venice.

The Venice team, after jumping through a few hoops, was accepted. A Hollywood/Los Feliz team featuring Ben Porter Lewis, Milo Martin, Josh Millican and Nathan Green was not. They paid the entry fee and sent a letter explaining their position. They gathered and sent a petition. After long deliberation their application was rejected by the national slam committee. According to organizer, Phil West, "Their team did not meet the criteria established by the poetry slam community… although necessary, given our role as hosts and arbiters of the team eligibility verdicts, [it] was not an easy decision for us." There are two sides to this story. According to Milo Martin "The slam guidelines were made out to be gray matter; after the fact it became very black and white." This decision was made just as this issue of *Next…* was being put to bed; I suspect it will be a topic of discussion at the Slam Masters meeting in Austin and beyond. It seems to me that slams, by their very nature, should be as UN-serious as possible. One thing seems certain: the rules will no longer be as loose as they have been in the past.

VENICE

(Jeff McDaniel, Ellyn Maybe, June Melby, Matthew Niblock)

The Venice team is the surprise of the year. Jeff McDaniel tells how it came about, "The first time I thought of going I wanted to go with Justin Chin, Beth Lisick, and maybe Matt Cook or Ellyn Maybe. Phil (West) said that wouldn't be a good idea because they live in San Francisco and we live in L.A.. It also would have been a bad scene after the Mouth Almighty thing." Following the advice of the slam committee, Jeff posted flyers and organized a slam which turned out to be "a disaster, the weather was really really nice. We thought it was going to be this mellow thing, poetry in the sand. People couldn't find a place to park, couldn't even find each other." So the slam was held on audio tape, producing a team featuring Jeff McDaniel, who was on the Washington DC team from 1993 to 1995, and three poets who, as a general rule, don't slam: June Melby, the other half of the Constantine/Lupert world tour, Ellyn Maybe, the "giggling goddess" who everybody loves, and Matthew Niblock, a serious student of things both sacred and profane.

One last thought for you slammers out there — a comment about slams from Jeff McDaniel — a battle-scarred veteran of the slam wars. "On one level it's so obvious that slams are a joke. If you're picking judges from the audience to say if something is good or bad and a good qualification could be: 'I failed English, I'm drunk, I got dumped last night or I drive a truck and I just don't give a shit!' It's making fun of the idea of literary mandarins or literary experts. But when you're in competition you take it seriously, because it hurts your feelings. As corny as it sounds, I think that there should be some sort of group hug between all of the teams. We oughta foster love between everybody. The real objective of the teams going there should be to put on a good show and make it entertaining for the audience and themselves."

(8/98)

1998 NATIONALS A SUCCESS

SoCal Rocked Austin, but NYC takes the prize
By Victor D. Infante

Great. Back to Sports Writing again....

Drove twenty-four hours straight to get from Austin, Texas to Southern California – exhausted, with my head still spinning from a week filled with great parties, good friends and words, words WORDS!!!!!

This year's National Poetry Slam Finals was the biggest one to date. Forty-five teams, plus ten individuals, competed for a $2,000 grand prize and a chance to perform in front of well over a thousand people at Austin's gorgeous Paramount Theatre. When it all fell down, New York City, based out of the world-famous Nuyorican Poets Café, was the champion, with Belwood, IL, slammer Regie Gibson slamming his way to first place as an individual.

Although the year was plagued with small disputes left and right, the only one that seems to have survived the week is a question of nudity and "clothing removal." The question began when Dallas poet Clebo Rainey removed his shirt during the poem "Rarified in Arkansas," an action which he cleared in advance with the Slam's grievance committee. The action has spurred a debate between the idea of artistic freedom and the recognition that clothing removal is not necessarily an option for female poets. There is furious discussion of the matter on the internet, and will probably be at least somewhat resolved at the Slam Masters meeting in Chicago next March.

On the home front, Southern California teams acquitted themselves well. Here's a team by team breakdown:

Los Angeles: If L.A. holds their pattern, they'll be slam champs next year. The team was ranked 7th in 1996, 5th in 1997, and this year they finally broke the final round, ending with a ranking of third. (See the pattern?) Veteran slammer Jerry Quickley powerfully read a poem for the death of his cousin, while Deborah Edler Brown nailed home a poem about her Jewish heritage. (Which prompted anti-Semitic comments from some assholes a few rows behind me, but I understand they were spoken to by someone with a clue.) For the first year ever, L.A. broke out a team piece — used in Thea Iberall's space — and it kicked serious butt!!! Buy them beers.

Laguna Beach: I'm biased, since I was on this team, but OC's first ever slam team did extremely well. As a team, the Laguna made it all the way to semi-finals, losing to Cleveland (who ended as a team finalist) the first round, but defeating Dallas (also a finalist) in the second, before being beaten by New York and Knoxville, TN, in the last round. Team member Derrick Brown progressed as an individual to the finals, finishing 2nd overall, a remarkable accomplishment for a first-year slammer. Buy him a beer.

Venice Beach: Likewise, the Venice team made it to semi-finals, and gave L.A. a run for their money in a heated match at the Electric Lounge. The team, which featured veteran slammer Jeff McDaniel and "giggling goddess" Ellyn Maybe, won several hearts over the week.

Los Feliz/ Hollywood: Hollywood, admitted at absolutely last minute due to the cancellation of a team from Outer Cape Cod, MA, did well despite tough draws. Defeated by the champion New York team on the first night, and the finalist Los Angeles the second, Hollywood refused to let down the pace and fought to the bitter end. Team member Sister Yo was particularly well-received, and won the "props slam" during the day-time events.

Long Beach: Never had an opportunity to see Long Beach this year, but "dirty old man" William McLain and return slammer Jim Bolt informed me that the team bounced back from losing their first bout to win their second. It wasn't enough to progress them to semi-finals, but at least they went down fighting.

(9/98)

MAKING A LIVING

Thoughts on Jewel
By Lizzie Wann

Sitting at Java Joe's on a beautiful Sunday afternoon in Ocean Beach, CA, I look at the stage that has held up some of this city's greatest singer/songwriters, some of whom have gone on to "bigger and better things," as they say. For example, Joy Eden Harrison, a bluesy gal, moved to Chicago and had a couple tunes in movies, Lisa Sanders is also having some scripts thrown her way to contribute songs to films, Gregory Page's second record was produced by John Doe of X fame and is currently seeking a label to distribute it, Elizabeth Hummel was on the bill at Lilith Fair when it came through San Diego this year, Steve Poltz's face and music are making themselves known around the world, and who can forget Jewel, who, although from Alaska originally, did the gigs in San Diego that led to her global familiarity.

Most of these artists would admit to writing poetry on the side or keeping a journal along with being a songwriter, but with the release of her book and spoken word CD, *A Night Without Armor*, Jewel adds her name to a list of musicians turned poet, although she feels it should be the other way around. In a recent interview with CNN that I checked out online, Jewel said she was a poet first, that poetry isn't an option for her, and that it's something she needs to feel complete. You'd think completeness might involve knowing how to correctly spell Bukowski, who she lists among her influences (look it up: the books all have it spelled with a "y"). Jewel is aware that it was easier for her to get her poetry published, although, because of her fame, her writing "has to be that much better" or else she'll "get torn apart." She mentioned that she considered publishing the book anonymously or under a pen name; however, the powers that be at HarperCollins must have changed her mind since the book, the CD, and all promotional material have her face plastered across it making sure no one forgets that Jewel is now also the poet.

So what? Will this impact poetry? Perhaps. Will it impact the spoken word scene of SoCal or the nation? I don't think so. So she tapes some spots reading her work that will air on MTV, she does a promotional book tour stopping in to Virgin megastores and Tower Records to do readings. This idea of musicians admitting their true "passions" after they've created their fame through music is not new. Henry Rollins, Exene Cervenkova, Dave Alvin — music to spoken word; Janet Jackson, Cher, Harry Connick Jr. — music to acting; John Mellencamp, Ringo Starr — music to painting. What these people do through their obscure and somewhat haphazard lives as someone "famous" is expand their

creative visions, and some do it better than others. Jewel will get torn apart by critics but she'll also be heralded by some. She'll open up the world of poetry to many people who might not know Walt Whitman from Slim Whitman and maybe when her movie or her new record comes out, this whole poetry business will be forgotten.

But sitting here in Ocean Beach, the world goes by and someone asks me if it's poetry Sunday at Java Joe's, and I say yes.

(7/98)

A NIGHT WITHOUT ARMOR

Book by Jewel Kilcher (Harper Collins)
Reviewed by G. Murray Thomas

Jewel has been taking her licks for this book (a particularly hilarious review appeared in the July issue

Illustration by Walt Hopmans

of Spin), and not totally without reason. There is no doubt the book was published on the strength of Jewel's fame, not the merits of her words. Much of these poems are exactly the sort of bland, generalized mush which gives open readings a bad name.

But, if I heard Jewel read these poems (as an unknown) at an open, I would probably encourage her. For glittering in murk of obvious ideas and flat statements are hints of poetic talent. A few carefully selected lines: "The clear bottle/ of vodka in her hand/ lighting up/ like a watery lantern." "Vincent said she was like screwing a corpse,/ but a 16 year old corpse with young tits/ so it wasn't bad…" "…to face things as they came/ so they wouldn't… become/ like huge ships, impossible to turn around."

Publication came too easily to Jewel. Yes, I know, she lived in a van, played coffee houses, and worked hard until she hit big. But those were music dues, not poetry dues, and yes, it makes a difference. Easy is a word which applies to these poems. In many, it seems, she got halfway to a good poem, and then moved on.

Take the poem "Dionne & I":

We looked in the fridge only to see moldy Kraft singles and some eye cream. That eye cream was our pride and joy, so extravagant and luxurious, it made us feel rich. The cracked walls of the bathroom fading away into the small lights of her tiny vanity mirror.

We may have had no food, but we knew the eye cream was all we needed — we were both young, with pretty faces and a lot of faith in the system.

Some men would take us out.

Now imagine a new ending line, something which makes the same point, but poetically, and see the potential of that poem to be something, maybe still not great, but decent and amusing. I'm sure you can come up with one. I would bet that if Jewel had spent another hour on this poem, hell, another ten minutes, she could have too.

That is the crime of this book. Not that Jewel (or Harper Collins, or whoever) is attempting to make a few more bucks over her probably fleeting fame. It is that it came too soon, before her talent had a chance to develop and ripen. Now she may never be motivated to turn into the real poet she has lurking inside her.

(Widely available. It was on the *New York Times* bestseller list, after all.)

(8/98)

ATTACK! ATTACK! GO!
CD by Beau Sia (Mouth Almighty)
A Night Without Armor II: The Revenge
Book by Beau Sia
Reviewed by G. Murray Thomas

A friend of mine used to rant about poems which "begin with the word 'I' and end with the word 'me'" This is exactly the kind of poem Beau Sia writes. The very first line on his CD, *Attack! Attack! Go!* is "I wake up every day/ and tell myself how great I am." The amazing thing is that he has the wit to pull it off. This is a funny CD, and I laughed all the way through, despite the relentless "I, I, I." With lines such as, "When I get the money/ I'm going to publish 382 page books with nothing but my name on the cover/ and people will buy them!" how could I help it?

But Sia has tapped into a deeper truth, which is that we perceive the world and its various topics through ourselves. His poems really are about celebrity, love, and high school, through the prism of his ego. This point is best realized on the cut "Death." When we truly think about death, we don't do it in the abstract, we think about "What does it mean for me to die?"

Still, the ego only lets up on the final cut, a tribute to Allen Ginsberg, which is so thoughtful and sensitive that I almost thought my CD player had moved on to the next CD in the chamber.

This same ego and audacity enables Sia to pull off *A Night Without Armor II: The Revenge*, a parody/response to Jewel's best-selling book of poetry. I have no doubt a certain amount of professional envy inspired Sia ("How can she have the best selling book of poetry in America, when I am the real poet here?") to write a book of poems with the same titles as those in Jewel's book. (The packaging of the book — cover, typefaces, etc. — is a direct copy as well.) The poems themselves are hilarious, and are even funnier when compared with their counterparts. Part of Jewel's poem "Paramount, NY, 9:34 A.M." reads:

I am unwoven
    the rich yoke of slumber
    unraveled thread by thread
until I am naked and glistening
standing before the newness
of another day

Sia's poem, merely titled "Paramount, NY," is, in its entirety:

right now
I'm trying
to astral project myself
to this place
and time
so that
I can
catch
the naked jewel
mentioned in the
same titled poem
as this.

I am unsuccessful.

It does not
matter.

I am not sure how successful these poems would be on their own, without the object of their parody. Some would surely be funny in any context, but much of the humor derives from Sia using a similar diction as Jewel's to discuss decidedly non-cosmic thoughts. If you are appalled by the success of Jewel's book, or even if you enjoy it, you should pick up *The Revenge*. Otherwise, you might be better borrowing a copy, or reading it in one of those comfy chairs at Barnes & Noble (assuming they ever stock it).

(10/98)

NEWS CLIPS AND EGO TRIPS

By G. Murray Thomas, Jaimes Palacio & Monica Lee Copeland

Adding to the list of 1997 losses, I was recently informed that James Laughlin, founder and editor of New Directions press, also died last year. Through New Directions, Laughlin immensely influenced 20th century poetry, publishing such notables as…, well, just go look at the spines on your bookshelf, you'll see what I mean. Less known was the fact that he was a talented poet himself, writing with a strength of imagery and clarity of style which rivaled the "star" of his publishing house, William Carlos Williams.

–GMT

(3/98)

Generously taking time out from promoting his book *Soul of the Game*, Jerry Quickly was the featured reader on the 17th at the Cobalt. I was the surrogate host (replacing Rick Lupert who was sick), but unfortunately, I just lacked enough Lupertness. Luckily June Melby dropped by for a most welcome cameo and provided her own brand of delicious lunacy. Unluckily, a rude individual bearing a really pretentious self-imposed name decided he was special and didn't have to stay within the seven minute allotted time limit. After some argument he lifted his royal chin and proclaimed stoically, "In another time, in another place, I could be a feature!" and left.

–JP

(4/98)

Many of SoCal's finest poets showed up at Beyond Baroque on April 24, not to read, but to listen to and honor one of their own — Ellyn Maybe, whose new book, *The Cowardice of Amnesia*, is now available on 2.13.61. The main room was packed, and Maybe read with a wonderful giddiness (at one point remarking, "I've never seen so many of my poems typed before!"). If there was any flaw in the evening, it was only that she didn't read enough; the audience clearly would have loved an hour or more, instead of the mere twenty minutes she gave. But there were friends to hug and books to sign (if that evening is any sign, Maybe could have a best-seller).

That same weekend found us wandering the UCLA Campus, enjoying the *LA Times Book Fair*. While we were disappointed to find out we just missed Mayor Riordian reading Shel Silverstein, we did catch D Knowledge entertaining and educating a growing crowd that afternoon. And it was wonderful just to see so many Angelenos enjoying the world of books.

At the Book Fair, we discovered that Eric Idle would be reading a new Dr. Seuss story at Storyopolis (a children's book store near the Beverly Center) on May 16. We marked that date in red on our calendar. The reading was everything we might have imagined (including some Monty Python voices making guest appearances), made even more enjoyable by the audience, a huge crowd of rapt children.

–GMT

(6/98)

It always seems that I am writing the L.A. Scene Report from every place but L.A. I was in Phoenix last week, attended my sister's wedding in Ann Arbor, and am now seated in my hotel room in Albuquerque. Flickering the remote, I catch a glimpse of Malcolm Jamal Warner on Magic Johnson's show, and he is spewing a bit of spoken word. This causes me to reminisce about Saturday nights last summer at Checca Lounge. Warner was featured at Josh Millican's Dorothy Parker Hour, along with a host of other L.A. wordsmiths. It was one of the few spots where you could have a little party with your poetry. Cocktails and dinner a la carte. It failed, however, because the management did not support the poetry hour. What does this have to do with this August, you may ask? The answer begins and ends with Aaron Spears of Big Mouth Entertainment.

Spears has succeeded in creating a well-attended poetry venue in a nightclub setting. Arriving in Los Angeles in 1994, Spears started up a small printing business called Big Mouth Design. Wandering in and out of local establishments to develop his business, he came across "a lot of poets with papers in their hands reading to melancholy audiences." A spoken word artist himself, Spears was disappointed. Hence the creation of Big Mouth Entertainment (BME), proof, according

to Spears, that "spoken word can be mixed with any type of entertainment and get a crowd." On July 3rd, Casa Blanca Lounge (the home of BME) had to turn people away. The capacity of 300 had been reached. Malcolm Jamal Warner was featured that evening, but Spears regularly gets audiences over 200, and they pay a ten-dollar cover to listen to a feature only performance.

This is a full time gig for Spears, so he is determined to make it work. "I promised to pay my poets from the beginning. At first it was only three or four dollars, but now performers can make up to $50 each." Unlike other local spoken word venues, Spears maintains the integrity of the feature list. "I honor my guests by not squeezing people in." Having featured at the first show of this year, I was impressed upon receipt of a thank you letter on BME stationery and my very own BME T-shirt. Poets, this is a shirt you want to own. BME's logo is a great big mouth with a wagging tongue and a huge afro.

–MLC

(8/98)

SURREAL MEDIA MOMENTS

A Sampling of Poetry on Television
By G. Murray Thomas

It's three in the morning, and I'm channel-surfing, looking for something that will either make still being awake worthwhile, or put me to sleep for good. I hit a Maggie Estep video, a new version of "I'm An Emotional Idiot" (featured in *United States of Poetry*). Cool, I think, one of the late-night variety shows has actually picked up on poetry videos. But no, it's a show about websites. They quickly segue into talking about some Jack Kerouac site where you can "write your own Beat poem."

Welcome to the surreal world of poetry on television.

Recently (perhaps in "honor" of National Poetry Month) an episode of *Suddenly Susan* featured star Brooke Shields taking a poetry class. Pretty scary, huh? Even scarier was that she was the character into poetry (proved by her ability to recite not only Keats's "Ode on a Grecian Urn," but his entire biography as well); the plot revolved around her co-worker joining the class to pick up women. The joke was that her co-worker (of course) wrote better poetry, coming up with a moving ode to lunch meat rotting in the back of his refrigerator. But I must give points for the secondary lesson of the show (the primary lesson being, apparently, that, yes, poetry is a great way to pick up women), which was that when it comes to reciting poetry, long poems are bad, bad, BAD!!!

But leave it to the Olympics for my most surreal poetry moment. It was the last night of the games, and I watching CBS's wrap-up coverage. They had MTV VJ Kennedy on, providing "color." Surreal enough, in itself. She chose to summarize the games in a series of haiku! First she gave a quick lesson in the haiku form (at least the 5-7-5 part), and then rattled off ten haiku inspired by the Games. The most amazing part was that some of them were pretty good, ranging from meditative Japanese-style to American-style punchline haiku. Maybe we should be on the lookout for the book.

This is the point where I launch into some endless rant about how out of touch TV is with the culture we poets live in, but somehow I think that would be superfluous. Just watch a little yourself (but only a little, it is a very dangerous narcotic).

And I'm not even going to mention the commercial in which a cute white car recites poetry from a curtained stage, and all the other cars in the audience snap their car doors.

(5/98)

NEW MOVIES *SLAM* POETRY INTO THE PUBLIC EYE

By Victor D. Infante

Dozens of poets, poetry aficionados, and even a few curiosity seekers jammed into Austin, Texas's Alamo Drafthouse the day before the 1998 National Poetry Slam Finals caught a glimpse of the films that will undoubtedly have a tremendous impact on the perception of contemporary poetry: *Slam* and *Slam Nation*.

Slam, directed by Marc Levin and starring New York poet Saul Williams, is an odd choice to be a crowd-pleaser, but it works. The story of Ray Joshua (Williams), a street poet from Washington, D.C., who is arrested on petty drug charges and finds redemption and survival through poetry, has an uplifting feel to it that belays the fact that it is, essentially, a musical with poetry. (A poetical?)

In a lot of ways, though, the film is more about the oppressiveness of the prison system than it is about poetry. Early on, a rich Asian kid (played by New York poet Beau Sia) is dragged out of the room and beaten by cops for his ethnicity. Ironically, the poet-dominated crowd in Austin laughed at this — Sia was in the room and well-known to most in attendance — but the scene's not funny. Indeed, it's one of the most disturbing scenes in a somewhat disturbing movie.

Throughout the exploration of prison violence and inter-inmate politics, Williams's character uses poetry to get through — once even halting an assault by reciting a poem at his would-be-attackers. Realistic? I don't know (although Williams told *The Guardian* that a similar scene had occurred during filming.) Cinematically powerful? Oh yes. I think, for me at least, the highest bit of private amusement was seeing cameos by a large number of East Coast poets. Most, like Bob Holman and Taylor Mali, were merely anonymous faces reading snippets of their poetry. Amusingly enough, Washington, D.C.'s D.J. Renegade is the only poet shown and identified by his real name.

Slam Nation, Paul Devlin's documentary of the 1996 National Poetry Slam Finals in Portland, Oregon, in many ways takes a similar tact toward presenting poetry on screen. Like *Slam*, the poems are not the star so much as the poets — although a plethora of "slam stars" are portrayed performing excerpts from their work. The fast-paced and engaging documentary shows some background on the evolution of the poetry slam, but centers solidly on the New York team (Saul Williams, Beau Sia, Mums the Schemer, and Jessica Care Moore), whom Devlin follows from their final slam at New York's Nuyorican Cafe, all the way to the final night of the competition. The documentary has encountered some criticism that it centers far too much on New York, particularly considering that Providence, Rhode Island (Bill MacMillan, Taylor Mali, Sean Shea and Corey Cokes) won, but it's somewhat understandable. It makes much more sense to follow one team and see where it goes, to give the non-initiated viewer a feel for what goes into the process. On the other hand, Devlin's damn lucky that New York made it to finals. One wonders what would have happened if they hadn't.

While there's a definite attempt to capture a wide variety of the poetry performed that year — the clip of Vancouver's Alexandra Oliver is wonderful — the documentary's a bit frustrating in that it centers more heavily on the competition and some of the behind the scenes politics than it does on the camaraderie that develops between poets — the camaraderie that actually brings many poets back year after year. (Although it is fun to see "perpetual slam villain" Taylor Mali being taken to task by slam founder Marc Smith for wearing a suit and tie for the camera.) Still, this film is breath-taking and intriguing for those not heavily involved in the slams — and will certainly provide incentive for non-poets to seek out the film's subject.

Throughout the '98 Nationals, there was a soft grumbling that, perhaps, the films were influencing public opinion too much. *Slam* centers on one talented rap-based poet — Williams — while *Slam Nation* truly focused on the more "spectacular" performance pieces. Taken together, one can see where a fear would arise that the public would develop a very limited sense of what poetry is "supposed" to be. I don't suspect that will be the case, however. The vast majority of the public already has a solid opinion as to what poetry is supposed to be — it's supposed to be "Beat." It's supposed to be Emily Dickinson. It's supposed to be so dull and abstract that no one remotely normal could relate to it at all. If these films go at all toward rejecting that belief from the collective consciousness — if they even get a handful of people to take a look at "poetry" and say, "Hey. That's not what I thought it was!" Then the movies will be, if not necessarily a success, then certainly a start.

(10/98)

ADVICE AND COMMENTARY

Illustration by Charles Ellik

TIPS FOR OPEN READERS: WHAT TO READ WHERE

By Charles Ellik

At initial glance, "What to Read Where" might not seem to be a wise choice for the first column of open reader tips, and some friends suggested a discussion of mic-handling or how to overcome nerves instead. With a little thought however, one realizes that we start with the "What" before the "How." I will leave the "Why" to you. (Or a different column.)

Before giving advice on what or where in concrete terms, I'd like to clarify my feelings about "where" you are going to be reading in deeper terms. What is a poetry reading? When you read a poem before an audience, this is no longer a "literary" or written art form. This is a performance, a ceremony, a ritual. This is an *exchange*! Care for your audience because they are your other half. This is why a good audience is so critical and so much more rare than a "good" poet. They must care as well. Myself, I'd rather be part of (or create) an active audience that brings out the best in a performer than be a tragic genius reading to dead space. A reading is a place where people share.

Now that you are at a poetry reading, how do you decide what to read? Whether it is your first time there, or your hundredth, it is always wise to ask yourself the Four Ws" Who, What, Where, When? (and the 'fifth W': How).

Who is here? Who is reading? Who do I know? Have they heard this poem a dozen times before?

What is the time limit, or average length of the work? What is being read? What do I want to read? What is the overall feel? Do I want to join in, rebel against, or ignore the other readers? What makes me interesting? What do I want to communicate beyond my poem?

Where is the reading held at? Where is the space I will be reading from? Where am I now? Where are the people I want to reach?

When am I reading? Before or after the feature? Early, when people are fresh, or later, when I have to work for their attention?

How will I read? How big is the room? Is there a microphone? How are the other poets reading? How long/how many poems will I read? How can I BE my poem as well as just read it?

Ultimately, it comes down to the first 'W'. Who *you* are. Sometimes, it is best not to ask any questions, and just trust your intuition! Avoid over-compensating for your audience (though this is rare indeed), as poetry is best when it comes from the heart. Poetry, and all the arts, is communication. Sharing oneself. There is *nothing* you can do that does not reflect you. So when you do decide to read, go up confident that you cannot fail to be yourself. Though audience and artists are equal in the exchange, none of it is meaningful if you don't feel it in the first place.

(3/94)

Illustration of Charles Ellik by Charles Ellik

WHAT IS PERFORMANCE?

By Charles Ellik

What is it about our culture that seeks definition? As if by placing meaning in a box we could control it. When I was asked to do the lead editorial for this issue, my knee-jerk response was to write a definition of what we believe performance poetry to be. Yet with introspection, I realized this type of separation into specific genres is destructive to our creative freedom. Instead, let me describe our views of performance as they relate to poetry.

Here at *Next...* we have received criticism for focusing on just "performance" poetry. So much so that we decided to devote an entire issue to the subject. Let us make it clear, however, that when we use a label like "performance," it is an inclusive, rather than exclusive, tool. In other words, it is for clarification, not definition. After all, aren't we all performers?

Is the academic poet in suit and bifocals behind a podium any less a performer than some kid juggling silly rhymes for his mate? Certainly there is a difference in delivery, but I would argue that it is degree rather than genre. To say that "performing" is less true or less genuine than simply "reading" is to miss the whole point. All communication is performed.

Whether it is a prehistoric shaman describing a hunt, an astronaut on the moon, or a post-historic shaman on electric modem, all stories are performed as communication, as communion, as a unifying tool. Only when "telling" is separated from "story" and used as a tool of the ego do we get readings as dull and lifeless as a jaded screw. There is no respect. Yet, when performance is approached as an act of love and communion, it can be as exciting and refreshing as any conception. This is how we are un-alone.

We do not make a distinction between "poetries" here at *Next...* In truth, none exists. This magazine serves all performers of every stripe. We hope that it will inform, and, perhaps, inspire people to explore. With it, they may go themselves into our community and tell stories without any labels narrowing their horizons.

(7/94)

PROMOTE YOURSELF!

By Charles Ellik

Your reading is good. There is a body of interested people who will enjoy it. In other words, you have a product and you have consumers. This is an honest relationship, and does not diminish the artistic value of your effort. There are many reasons why a reading will succeed or fail, both spiritual and mechanical, but here we will focus on the second alone. How do you tell people about your event?

The first step in promoting a reading is the same as creating one. Attract a core group. This is the hardest step, and the most personal. Any method can be used, but meeting people face-to-face is best. Choose wisely. Ask for their input. Listen. They are your bread and water. If you have a happy following, you may have no further work to do. You are the foundation, they are the house.

Second, what kind of reading do you have? It is essential to know, in order to communicate it to others. What kind of person are you, and what is the personality of your core group? Focus on strengths, even if they aren't exactly what you'd like them to be yet. If you are honest and hard working, your event will eventually reflect the best in you. We all start at the bottom.

Third, decide what kind of people you want to show up at your event. Ask poets you like to come read, they'll bring friends. Put yourself in the shoes of the type of person you'd like to show up. Where do they hang out? What do they look at? Where do they work? What do they buy and where? Here is where you will place your information for them to *find*, as I have found that demanding attention does not work. A billboard may be ignored by ten thousand people, but a flyer in the right hands may bring in a hundred.

This brings us to our last element: Media. How do we communicate the most for the least? There is a huge industry willing to meet your needs, but I am going to assume you are on a small budget, which is where my experience lies. There are three main avenues for your ideas — flyers, free listings, and paid advertising.

FLYERS are the staple. Did I say necessity? Have them on you at all times, as opportunities spring up when you least expect them, that is their nature.

Pressing an object into a person's hand is always most memorable. Be succinct and neat. This is important in all your promotions. It pays to spend the extra time to make your work clever and visually pleasing. Put them everywhere, but focus on maximum exposure. A flyer given to the host of another reading sees ten times as many people as one to your mother. Record stores, museums, coffeehouses, and even hip restaurants often have a special place for flyers. University instructors of arts and literature have personal mailboxes. Many make it a requirement to go to a reading, so be sure to leave extra. Remember to be polite!

FREE LISTINGS. Here is where you put in the time on letters and the money on postage, but it is well worth it. Local papers, TV, and radio stations often promote arts events free. Specialty publications like *Next...*, *Poetry Flash*, and *Caffeine* all go begging for information. Be sure to address your letter to a specific arts or calendar editor. Be polite, neat, and to the point. Include the name of the venue host and feature talent. List addresses, charges, dates, phones and times. Remember to say "Thank you!"

PAID ADVERTISING is a good idea, even on a tight budget. A small ad in a local magazine can be had for thirty dollars. That's a lot cheaper than flyers, folks. Even newspapers are reasonable. Be creative, and you'd be surprised what can be had for cheap.

WORK HARD. Perseverance always pays no matter what media you use. My own reading has been going on for three years and has been promoted in all these avenues, yet still hovers around thirty to forty people each week. You may never need or want to advertise and list. Each event is unique, and builds in its own way, but covering ground, working hard, and presenting your event to the most people cannot fail to help.

(8/94)

EDIT!
By Noah Dziobecki

I swear, if I am subjected to another long-winded poem about nothing of consequence, I just might snap. Readings had better start checking me for automatic weapons at the door....

I really don't understand this longer-is-better attitude. Even at readings that have time limits, people seem to feel the need to "impress" us with the sheer volume of words they can write. Oftentimes, otherwise good poems are more or less ruined by rambling monotony.

If these people would bother to spend time on editing their poems, they would have much more powerful work to present. Too many of the words in too many poems are "dead" words: they serve absolutely no purpose in expressing the poems themes and ideas. To get rid of these words can only improve the poem.

Editing, I admit can be hard work — I sometimes spend over a week on just one poem — but the end product is much more potent. When you edit, don't just throw away a couple of words here and there — whole lines need to go, stanzas need to be rearranged, punctuation needs to be seriously considered. The question you must always ask yourself when editing is *"Do I really need this?"* Sometimes an idea that seemed genius in its conception will turn out to be useless, nothing more than a cool idea.

It is also important not to go overboard in your editing. While you don't want your poem to be too long, you don't want it to be too short either. You want the reader or listener to do some work in interpreting your poetry, but you want to retain enough clarity so you don't become cryptic. If no one can understand what you are saying, then you have failed as a poet. You have not expressed yourself.

Probably every one of your poems could use some editing, even the shorter ones. Don't be afraid of changing your earlier work; it is a misconception that changing it will devalue your previous words. If you can say the same things with less words, you will greatly increase the impact of your work. And if you have toiled for days on end and your poem still takes up three typed pages, that is okay. As long as the language is as compact as possible with no needless garbage, then it will truly be impressive, not monotonous.

(3/95)

ONE FOR LEE FLICK

By David Madgalene

My friend, Lee, could publish a poem of mine in his zine and it would be solid. Lee could shoot a video or promote me in some other way and I would owe him. Or Lee could write a poem and perform one night down at the club and touch us all where we live and breathe.

As the performance poetry scene blossoms, all of us have to be on guard that we don't urinate away our creative energy behind the promo and the package.

A poem is hard copy or soft copy. A poem stands on its own amid others in any given 'zine. A poem, if nothing else, is a gift enclosed in a letter to a friend or sent across the net. A poem is a performance in town. A poem may become an appearance on public access or a popular song. A poem may become a cog in a cycle. A cycle is a chapbook. A chapbook is a CD and an audio cassette. A chapbook is a long-play video. A chapbook is a one-person show.

All of these avenues are easily accessible to each of us and vital in terms of promulgating our work. But we must never forget that they are the means and vehicles of self-expression and not to be coveted and cherished in and of themselves.

How many well-packaged chapbooks and zines have we read where, immediately after reading, we find we can't remember one line? Too many trees are being chopped down to print poems which aren't worth the paper they're printed on. Many desktop publishers would be doing us all a favor if they stopped printing lousy poems and wrote some good ones. Please appreciate that my intent is not accusatory! Just bear in mind that everything done and every step taken down the paths of packaging and promoting, takes one further and further away from the beloved muse. Or are the advertising copywriters the true poets of our age?

I know of one self-aggrandizing poet who calls himself the "poet of the '90s" and in an ironic sense which he doesn't intend, it's true – because he's all hype!

I used to stay at home all the time, with no social life, writing incessantly. Then I became involved in "this little thing of ours." I wrote less and less as I performed more and more. Then I got into publishing and promoting. It got to the point where I was M.C.'ing events at which I didn't read and publishing a 'zine to which I did not contribute. Finally, I had to ask myself, and I challenge you to ask yourself this question, "What about me?" If you're editing the 'zine this article is in or if you're reading it, then I dare you to put this down right now and write a poem, if you call yourself a poet.

If you want a video for personal use, by all means, go and get a camera and shoot it. But if you're hoping to share with a larger audience, I'd advise you to cut back on your alcohol intake for a week or two and take your video concept to a pro. An audio cassette to share with friends? Sure, burn a few copies on ye olde home dual cassette deck (what's a little third-generation hiss among friends?), but if you seek a wider audience, take your business to a studio. Chapbook or 'zine? Ask yourself: "Truly, have I ever seen a poem as lovely as a tree?" Be tree-friendly. A fool prints one hundred chapbooks that nobody reads. A wise man prints ten which are read.

Now I'm back at home and writing. I no longer print my 'zine and the world is a better place. This is not self-depreciation — it was a sturdy little yeoman-like effort. Yet, with thousands and thousands of zines crushing the collective subconscious like the Blob, how could anyone dispute that one less 'zine, regardless of literary merit, is not a relief? As far as promoting, I'm out. Since my "retirement" from promoting and publishing, I have found out who my friends were and weren't. We don't need big high-power promoters, we don't need public-access television celebrity poets, we don't need famous guest M.C.'s. What we need are more good soldiers who are willing to pitch in and help carry the load, with or without a plug. What we need are more poets who are working up their poetry and leaving all this other mess to those who do it best.

Print my poem? Make my day. Shoot my video? I owe you one. But read a poem that you wrote down at the club some night that breaks my heart? You I'm gonna love.

(5/95)

POETRY WORKSHOPS

By Gwynne Garfinkle

Probably all you need to do to learn to write poetry is write a lot, read a lot, and find some poet friends you trust to exchange work with. Nonetheless, I have found myself in various workshops over the years. Some were worth their weight in gold, while others were more hindrance than help.

My first poetry workshop at UCLA was taught by a witty, erudite man known more as a scholar and teacher than a poet (years later he would win a prize for his first poetry book). He liked strict forms but was equally tolerant of free verse, and the workshop was characterized by openness to various kinds of poetry. I made several lasting poet friends, the first I ever had. That was the best thing about the workshop, aside from the professor's careful criticism and exciting praise — meeting poets whose work I could relate to and vice versa. Though there were poets whose work I did not care for, I always looked forward to Sylvia's poems, and Elise's, as well as their response to mine.

Next, I took a workshop taught by a prestigious visiting poet. She was the first "famous" writer I ever studied with, and I am sure I expected too much — some ideal Woman Poet, life-saving and heroic — but

what I got was a cranky woman who seemed bent on squashing my poems to fit her idea of what a poem should be. In private consultation, she took a five-section poem of mine (which had been the hit of my previous workshop) and cut out its middle because she liked the juxtaposition of two images, one at the beginning of the poem, one at the end. Then she told me the poem did not make sense! I was bewildered and discouraged — she was a famous poet, I thought, she must know what she was talking about. From this experience I learned that a good poet might not necessarily be a good teacher.

Some years later, no longer in school, I took a workshop at the home of a local poet. These were exciting sessions. I always left wanting to write, to read. Sometimes the teacher tore my work to bits. Sometimes the criticism was truly helpful, while sometimes the criticized poems lost their luster and I never touched them again.

The trouble was, I found myself thinking of the workshop when I sat down to write. The teacher preferred a certain type of representational poem, so when I wrote more experimental work, I thought: he will not like this. I did not feel free to write whatever I pleased. So I quit the workshop.

Twice I went to summer sessions at the Jack Kerouac School of Disembodied Poetics at the Naropa Institute in Boulder. The first year, I was fresh from doing

Illustration by Brian Hagen

readings in L.A., San Francisco, and New Mexico with the Los Angeles Poetry Ensemble. I felt like a success. But at Naropa, my reading style was criticized as too dramatic, artificial. This shook my confidence, but I think my reading style did become more conversational, more natural. It was inspiring to be in the presence of so many wonderful poets (Eileen Myles, Anne Waldman, Diane di Prima, Lee Ann Brown, etc.) talking about writing, performing, and publishing. I learned new poetic forms and was excited by poetic comradery and tradition.

My advice about poetry workshops is, learn all you can, but do not let anyone undermine your confidence. You have to choose what criticism to take, and figure out the spirit in which it was given. The buck stops with you, the poet.

(9/95)

HOW TO PUT TOGETHER A PRESS KIT

Basic Promotional Tips for Performing Poets
By Pleasant Gehman

Okay, you've got some good material, and you've done some time at open readings. You got some good reviews, and are ready for feature readings. You've done a fair amount of work, and you need a professional way to prove this to the people who could provide you with a gig. What you need is a press kit.

It doesn't have to be elaborate — a million pages long, bound with high-tech graphics and cover stories from magazines. A nice photo, a concise to-the-point bio, and maybe a couple of notices are all you need. Simple.

PHOTOS

Professional headshots (like the 8x10 glossies actors use) are nice, but not really necessary. If you want to spend the money, though, they usually run somewhere in the $50 - $200 range. What you'll get is a few rolls of B&W photos of yourself, close-up head-shots, or from the chest up in a studio setting. I would advise getting a friend to snap some pix on B&W 35 millimeter film, saving you some money. Or maybe you know a photographer who'd like to barter with you or do you a favor. Many photographers need models for their own portfolios and will take pictures of you for the cost of film. The next step is to take your pictures to a photo duplication lab. You can get multiples made in increments of 25, 50, 75, etc. Most labs will put your name right on (or under) the photo in a nice font for a nominal charge, or even for free. This adds a nice, professional touch.

THE BIO

Your biography tells people who you are. It doesn't have to be — and actually never should be — long-winded. People don't usually care where you were born, or went to school, unless perhaps you studied with a particularly known writer or poet, or did some impressive kind of workshop, or have a degree. Facts to include: any books, chapbooks, or major articles you may have published; awards won; television, film or radio appearances; interesting artistic collaborations. Also good to include are information on upcoming projects, artistic influences, maybe even a very short personal anecdote. Remember, your bio doesn't have to be long, just a simple reflection of who you are.

RESUME

You may want to include this on a separate page — a simple listing of publications you've been featured in, or major gigs you've done. This isn't really necessary, and you *don't* have to list *every* reading you've done at *every* coffeehouse, okay?

PRESS CLIPPINGS

If you've got any reviews, you want to make a page, or pages, featuring them — but only if they say positive things about you! In a press kit, you really don't need to put mediocre or bad reviews; after all, a press kit's purpose is to show you off in a flattering way. Take your reviews, cut them out (unless you were featured on an entire page, then just Xerox the whole thing) and put them under the cut-out logo of the paper the review came from. If you don't have the paper's logo, just type it in: *BUMF★CK, IOWA NEWS AND REVIEW,* May 1999, or whatever. This simply lets the reader know you've been reviewed; your work has been taken seriously enough for some paper to assign a writer to cover your show.

GETTING COVERAGE

If you don't have press, it's not that hard to get. Next time you book a reading, make a little notice, featuring the name of the venue, time, date, admission (if any), address, and, if you want, other people who are reading with you. Send this to the entertainment editor of your local paper, along with a note asking to be listed. The best time to do this is usually about three weeks before the show. If you wait until the last minute, you'll probably miss the deadline. If you have a picture, send it along, and be sure to label the back with your name, and the photographer's name (after all, if your friend took the picture, they should get credit for it, huh?). Send out these notices to dailies, weeklies, school papers, music magazines, fanzines, even glossy monthlies. Most papers have space to fill and will use your resume if they get it in time. Also, most publications will use your press release verbatim, so… you're a writer, make it fun and creative! If you've got a particularly hot show, try to get a picture of everyone who's involved and boldly ask if the paper would consider your show for a performance pick or recommended date. What have you got to lose? Also, if you have any books or other product out, send one along to the writer or editor, so they can see your work and judge it for themselves. You may make a new fan — or at least somebody will begin to know your name and your work. Send these same notices to radio stations too, especially college stations. They often read entertainment listings over the air, and some even feature spoken word shows.

Get your name out there! Writing is only three-fourths of the work. You want to have readers and listeners too. And that will only happen if people know who you are. Go for it!

(3/96)

BEYOND THE FIRST DRAFT
By Thea Iberall

There was a time thirty years ago when I was in college, emotions bubbled up and came out poetically.

I thought, this is fabulous stuff. Natural-born writer. Who needs to know anything? I mean, this was raw stuff. The real thing

Well, twenty-five years later I picked up the poetic pen again, but this time, I joined a poetry workshop. And I discovered there is a big difference between raw poetry and crafted poetry.

Raw poetry is a first draft. It's like the marble block of Michelangelo. Since a poetic marble block can't be bought at your local Galleria, we as poets have to create it ourselves. Some people just stop there and call it a poem. In some rare instances it is. But more likely, it is the raw materials where one can find the poem; as Steve Kowit says in his book *In the Palm of Your Hand*.

Once a poem is "complete," it is hard to rewrite such a fabulous golden gem. Writing teachers suggest that we put the work aside awhile, to help us detach a bit, and then come back to it to look at the work critically. My latest poem was an absolute masterpiece when I first wrote it last November (ask the writers in my writing group or anyone who is still my friend). But, by putting it aside and coming back to it again and again over the last eight months, I managed to make it a lot better.

With examples and exercises, Kowit outlines a variety of ways you can fine-tune your first draft. He suggests looking for generalized phrases and replacing them with details. I remember my writing teacher Terry Wolverton saying, "Thea, don't tell us you feel sad. Show us! Use vivid details we can relate to." Details can be provided through specifics. This color can be further enhanced through imagery which can be accomplished using metaphor, simile, figurative language, foreshadowing, allusion, and personification. Decisions can be made in terms of the best point of view, the theme, the scene, and the conflict. And Kowit says, lie! The essence can be real, but the details don't have to be. Some things I write about didn't actually happen to me, but I put it in the first person to make it more real.

Another decision a crafting poet can make is on structure. Besides making poetic terms understandable, Su Soref gives a simple explanation of meter, foot type, line length, and classic forms in her book *The Mechanics of Poetry*. Each choice gives a certain tone to one's work. Most of my poetry is free verse, which I feel helps make it real and accessible. But recently I wanted to write a silly poem, so I used anapestic quatrains. The anapestic lilt ("in-my-WORK") gave me a fun space to play in and a way to clue in my audience that I am not trying to be serious.

The step that was new to me in reading Kowit's book was the texture of sound. Sure, I had heard about rhythmic verse. I knew Elizabeth Barrett Browning created magnificent poems, a mastery I could only drool over without ever hope of achieving. But Kowit opened my eyes to a dimension of sound beyond just the use of end-rhyming. Poetry consists of words and words have sounds. The sound of the words you choose can affect the mood you are trying to convey. Make each word sing. Interior music can be created with assonance, repetition, alliteration, consonance, anaphora, sentence grace, internal rhyme, and onomatopoeia. Go look these concepts up. Memorable poems use them.

Kowit suggests that awful poems contain trite language, have rhymes at any cost, use archaic words, or are trying to sound poetic. In addition, bad poetry suffers from sentimentality, too much honesty, adjectivitis, inappropriate imagery, and the misuse of allusions. He suggests that the poet try to be clear, simple, direct, and keep the ego out of the way.

Whether you read any one of numerous books or join a workshop or take a class, you will get insights in how to improve on your first draft. Kowit's book is subtitled *A Portable Writer's Workshop* for a reason. There are free (or almost free) workshops around town, such as at the Midnight Special Bookstore, Beyond Baroque, the Christian Writer's Guild, the Perspectives in Writing Program at the Gay and Lesbian Center, or others. Take a class at the UCLA Extension Program or at a community college. Form your own writer's group with other poets who know critique. I belong to two different writer's groups on the Internet, which is all my schedule affords me at the moment.

Mark Strand says, in his introduction to *Best American Poetry of 1991*, that in poetry "the power of language is most palpably felt." Find your poem. Find the slave struggling to break free from your marble block. Add color, clarity, imagery, interior music. Make it soar. Make it memorable. Make it well-crafted.

(11/97)

REJECTION
By Ed Jamieson

For a few years now I've been submitting poetry to magazines, some small press and some big circulation magazines. In my experience, there are four types of rejection letters: generic, don't bother your poetry sucks, no thanks try again, and out of business.

The generic rejection letter usually is from a big circulation magazine like the *New Yorker* or *Harper's*. The words "unfortunately" and "regrettably" often appear in the letter which is never signed. In the small magazines the letters run longer with an explanation like, "We read with interest, but did not select it for publication." The only difference being small magazines include a subscription offer or advertisement, "Don't miss Volume One at local book stores." The major magazines know better or they just don't care.

The "don't bother your poetry sucks" rejection letter is the most amusing. I'll admit in the beginning I would tear up the letter and throw it in the garbage, now I file the letter with all my other letters. Editors like to re-write the poems or accuse the writer of plagiarism: "…'Contemplating Suicide' inspired by Dorothy Parker's verse??" Who's Dorothy Parker? I asked myself; I know now. "If you can make it a point to dedicate some of your time to writing poetry as well as mailing your poetry to publications, you're headed in the right direction" is a favorite. My favorite of all time "don't bother your poetry sucks," is not a letter but a poem:

"Hello. Hello.
Do you like my poems?
I do not. Good-bye.
Good-bye."

Sometimes the editor likes the writing but not the poems, "I like the sensibility behind the poems but not the incidents you choose to express your ideas." Submitting in this case is a no-win situation.

The third is the "no thanks try again" rejection letter, or the polite way of saying, "don't bother your poetry sucks." The poem is read and the criticism is mostly positive. However, some are borderline, "Though we appreciated your economy of language… looking for more interesting work." Some are better, "Don't get discouraged; keep writing and sending. Who knows? Maybe next issue." And "You've got a good sense for detail and description." But still, rejection is rejection.

The last type of rejection letter is not really a rejection letter, but a feeling of dissatisfaction. The "out of business" letter doesn't happen too often, but when it does there's a feeling of, "I could've been published if the magazine didn't go out of business." "Due to circumstances concerning funds... there will be no magazine at this time." At the same time, the magazine could've rejected the poems. My last "out of business" rejection letter started as a "no thanks try again" letter, "Please try again in six months." I tried again, then it came in the mail, "With much sorrow I regret to inform you that we're closed…"

Writers must accept rejection letters not as a personal attack, but as a motivation tool to enhance their writing. Remember, for every rejection there's an acceptance for publication; if you don't believe that, at least they're sending your poems back and not keeping the extra stamp.

(11/97)

POET WITH
REJECTION SLIPS

Walt Hopman

LETTER FROM MICHELLE BEN-HUR

Dear *Next*…

Okay, you set the bait, so I have to respond.

First, rejection letters (as an editor and submitter, as well as a professional legal writer, I'm more qualified than most to comment on this): If the rejection comments on your writing, that means something. It means the editors cared enough about your poems or poem to think about what would make it work better. Don't dismiss it. Too often we writers know what we're saying; it's the reader/editor who brings to our attention the fact that it's not clear to everyone else. Sometimes, that's all an editorial comment is saying: You write beautifully, but I don't understand it. Or, you write clearly, but it needs to be more "beautiful/poetic." Listen to those comments. They're worth their weight in fonts.

Second, getting published. Mr. Magdalene has one valid point, send to people who you know like your work, i.e. have published you already. If you're serious about becoming a "Poet," publishing credits are important. They help build a resume and prove to other editors that someone else liked your work. But, unless you're getting accepted in *Ploughshares* or *Poetry* or the *New Yorker* or various university journals on a regular basis, being published by the same rag/mag/journal over and over again doesn't mean anything to another editor except "that one other editor likes her/his work." Take risks; send to someplace in the Midwest that has never seen you perform your signature poem at its signature best. Send to journals that you know your work isn't

Illustration by Walt Hopmans

ready for but which you feel will like what you're striving for (see comments re: rejections above). Get out there. I guess that's the key, the willingness to be rejected. Once that hurdle is overcome, acceptance is a simple gift.

On a related note, there's a reason why great poets are considered great. Eliot had Ezra Pound. On a more local note, Niblock has Frank. Edit! And let someone you respect for her or his poetic ear and eye edit for you. Not every word that rolls off the pen or keyboard is worthy of an audience. I don't care how clever or beautiful it is. It must mean something and resonate to others. Let someone you trust help you be the judge of that. I speak from experience: My editors are my best friends and worst enemies!

Michelle Ben-Hur, Costa Mesa

(12/97)

POETRY DOES NOT COME IN AN INSTANT

By James Maverick

Poetry is an endangered art. Endangered, because poetry demands from its audience. Endangered, because the very notion of going to a poetry reading bespeaks of an enormous intellectual and emotional commitment in very transitory times. We get our fix of information in five-second sound bites or, if we have twenty-two minutes, we'll take the world, thank you. Our newspapers now encapsulate the state of the world today in two-inch margins on the left-hand side of the page, further rewarding us for our unwillingness to become involved. Commercials now bombard you with hundreds of images in a thirty-second span to saturate your mind with subliminal lust for their product. Even the top two television drama series, *NYPD Blue* and *E.R.*, move the camera so frenetically that the eye never has a chance to rest, for fear it might miss something. The viewer isn't drawn in by a good plot or compelling characterization, but a high-tech shell game. Somewhere along the line, America was told that it is entirely possible to get a maximum benefit for minimal effort or commitment. Somewhere along the line, we believed it.

When other media are willing to relay culture to you at the speed of light, where is poetry? When all we need to do is sit back and let the twitch of an index finger play to our dictates for entertainment, where is poetry? When we refuse to become involved in the future of our community or our very country because we are unwilling to look beyond two bickering losers berating each other to see past the moment, then where is poetry?

Poetry is germinating somewhere in the back of a bookstore or coffee shop, or in a restaurant on a slow night. Poetry, despite it's wonderful, colorful and often tawdry heritage, is still a seedling in a vast garden of art.

This is not right. It goes against the very nature, the very meaning, of the art. According to *Grolier's Encyclopedia*, poetry is derived from the Greek word *poiein*, "to make," and the poet is therefore one who invents, or makes things up. By this definition, poetry is the most powerful artform in existence, now or ever. To be able to create something is far and away the most positive, empowering and life affirming act any one person can do. That being said, everyone ought to commit pen to paper, and convey our innermost desires and frustrations to posterity.

1997, if it must be given a title, should be known as the year of instant gratification. Society has been downsized to operate faster, leaner, meaner, almost anorexic. Dieters have pursued remedies such as Fen-Phen like the Holy Grail for its efficacy without heed to its consequences. Our judicial system is second-guessed, harangued and ridiculed because the verdict does not agree with the 11 o'clock News. Computers have become ever faster, operating just short of tachyon speed, and even that is not fast enough for some. Some computers have had most of their fat trimmed away in the form of little boxes on televisions, allowing you to surf the internet with only a remote control. How Special.

When I am asked what is remarkable about poetry this year, I say it's that poetry survived, and not because of a gimmick or slick promotion or prizes awarded to decibel delivery. Poetry survived because it has been true to its roots.

Poetry… is. It has always been that. All that. This past year, more artists and aspirant poets have focused less on the instant gratification offered by certain venues and show formats, and more on the need for personal expression. Some poets have criticized much of the scene today as having too many poseurs on the Los Angeles poetry landscape. I find such a criticism unfortunate. It's like oaks putting down acorns for their lack of shade.

Poetry readings in and around Los Angeles have been more about self-discovery and less about clique-ism, which abounded cancer-esque just two years ago. Today's aspiring artists are reading more, studying more, and in so doing, have rediscovered the school of poetry. The poets born of this year are not simply writing indiscriminately and going to readings to listen to their voice as opposed to their words. The poets born of this year are taking time to learn of those that came before, and searching themselves diligently to find the next creative step. The poets born of this year have realized that poetry does not come in an instant, and that it takes more than rantings about monthly seasons and underused male appendages to craft a poem. More people are taking the time to become poets. I look toward the coming year as an opportunity to experience the acorns as well as the oaks.

I think we have found our direction.

(1/98)

HOW TO GET A NAME IN THE POETRY UNDERGROUND

By EA Lynch

Ok, so I've been lurking in the shadows, watching poets, event organizers, and editors from here and there, and I've made a couple of observations which will help me alienate my peers, and be despised by one and all. Oh well, antisocial behavior was the high point on the 'ole fifth grade report card, and I see no reason to stop now. To soften the blow, I will add this one amendment: My criticisms apply only to those who find my diatribe to be offensive.

Low blow? You betcha.

Poets these days seem to have several priorities, the foremost of which is name recognition, as if our identities were a new brand of snack food or toilet paper. It doesn't matter whether we affiliate with the intelligentsia or the so-called underground, as long as our name is mentioned with reverence at the coffeehouse or in a classroom during a discussion of something like, "new directions in poetry." The marketing of our names seems to take a higher priority than fearless public scrutiny of our work. People rarely seem to become poets because they enjoy the process of writing. It seems that we write poetry as if it were a check cut for our personal bid in the high stakes lottery of immortality. Mostly we lose, but we host events and rallies to our tribes, stand screaming behind a microphone, attend slams, and promote our names above our work, all in the off chance that we will be remembered for more than our allotted fifteen minutes.

We have mastered the art of networking. We seem to have become so expert in the skills required for schmoozing, that we easily could form a consultation firm for corporate types who need a gentle reminder that when they think someone's work sucks, instead of firing them, they should *lie* and tell 'em they simply love it. One never does know who will become important down the line, so it's best to make everyone our friend. Allies are everything, especially allies who will drop names. Preferably, of course, our names.

As an editor of a highly unimportant e-zine, I have learned that poets who don't know me tend to either be obsequious, or they spend an inordinate amount of time

Illustration by Walt Hopmans

telling me how much of a somebody they are. My theory on this is that if they must convince me that their work is good, then it, more likely than not, balls. Oftentimes, it seems that more attention is placed on the bio than on the poetry, as can be illustrated in volumes like *Best American Poetry*. Now, I may be a bit misguided, but I don't really see it as relevant to the verse whether or not someone has graduated with an MFA, or has failed the high school equivalency exam. Certainly the person with the MFA probably has a better grasp of theory and terminology, but it does not guarantee that they can write anything of substance.

I digress. This rant was supposed to be about how to gain name recognition in the poetry underground, thus I return to the topic at hand. Getting a name is quite simple, really. The first rule of this game is to offend no one. Be friendly, but as distant as possible. The goal is to appear as if one is terribly busy with book signings, fun filled appearances in suburban coffee shops, and traveling around the countryside terrorizing small towns. One must maintain the appearance at all times that one simply has no time to develop any real relationships with those not considered well known.

The second rule is that if someone is willing to publish something of yours, make them sweat a little. Send your work either moments before their deadline, or, even better, miss it altogether. (It's always a plus to look like you are irresponsible — it's an artist thing.) Try to avoid doing that which you have promised to do; it keeps the editors on their toes, and they will certainly remember your name for all eternity when they are scrambling to fill your blank hole. Granted, the savvy editor always has a back-up plan, but it's good to play with their minds.

Next, if you have a project for which you want money, be a pest. It does not matter if the people you are contacting have just been evicted for non-payment of rent, or if their lover has suddenly developed a nasty drug habit and drained the bank account. Accept no excuses. Hound them ceaselessly, because art, after all, is more valuable than anything. Treat them as if they are a traitor to the gods if they will not give you the twenty bucks, and tell your friends that this person is unsupportive.

Publish everywhere. It doesn't matter if it's on the restroom wall of the bus station, as long as your name is on it. If this does not produce the required level of recognition, write five or six poems a day, and assault the publishing industry both in print and on the web. It does not matter if you are pleased with your work, just make sure that you have a long, long, extra specially long, list of credits. If you are on the web, make sure your name is prominently listed on as many sites as possible, and maintain a home site which has at least twenty pictures of yourself looking either windblown and sexy, or as if you're in the throes of withdrawal. Better yet, show pictures of yourself looking as if you are having an orgasmically good time at the most recent poets' party. For a special touch on the web, list the year of your birth with a dash afterwards, so no one mistakes you for dead. Also, be sure to make it difficult to find the poetry on your home site, as the poetry, after all, is secondary. The goal here is to be recognized while out sipping coffee with your eccentric and deliciously stylized cronies.

Finally, and most importantly, attend every open mike within 1,500 miles of your base of operations. Make sure your name is listed in bold print in every magazine possible, preferably as having done something bizarre like hiding small mammals in highly uncomfortable-sounding places. The squeamish may want to avoid actually doing this, so writing a particularly graphic piece, and then rubbing oneself suggestively while reading will have to substitute. If that doesn't work, go Dada.

Well, that's about it for now. I have to load the kids in the car, and terrorize the countryside in search of a name. I hope this has been a helpful guide to anyone currently in need of an identity. Next time: How to avoid listening to other poets while still looking interested.

(3/98)

HOW TO SELL YOUR POETRY BOOKS

By Lawrence Schulz

It's every writer's dream: you write your book, turn it over to a publisher who does very little editing, it is released to the public, and you get a whooping big check and asked to go back and write again.

Now wake up! It's the '90s and you're a poet trying to sell your chapbook or book at a poetry reading filled predominantly by poets who also have their own book or chapbook they would like to sell too. It's like trying to sell Slurpees to Eskimos.

Face it! It's a rough task. You've put your heart, soul, and thoughts into the creation of your book. Maybe you've put some graphic creative efforts into it and decided to self-publish it. It doesn't matter. You've created a product and now you've got to sell it and the road looks mean.

Now the good news! There is an audience out there and they are interested in buying (as in cash and checks) your poetry book. According to the November issue of *Poets and Writers*, sales of poetry books have increased as much as 100% over last year and are expected to be strong this year.

This means that, while you probably won't be able to buy a house in Palos Verdes from the revenue from your poetry book, you can get at least enough gas and beer money from the night's sales and maybe have some money left over.

In my twenty years in the sales profession and also as a sales instructor, I have sold other people's products and a few of my own that I produced. Nothing is ever as psychologically mean and hard as selling poetry. There was a point that if I did a reading and brought twenty books and sold nineteen, I beat myself up for days, wondering why I didn't sell everything. I felt like Sally Field in reverse saying, "why don't you really, really like me."

While your poetry is a creative expression of what exists inside your soul, to the audience it is one more product for sale. And while there is no formal rule for selling your books, there are some simple "Do's" and "Do Not Do's" while you are trying to sell your books.

1) DO bring enough books to sell. Never do a reading, or attend a reading without having at least five of your books with you. It always amazes me how many poets do an outstanding reading and have an audience willing to buy anything from the writer and they fail to have books with them. Carry your books everywhere. You never know when someone wants to buy them.

2) DO NOT rip off the audience by giving them an inferior product. When someone buys your book it may be the only book of poetry they have in their house. Take the time to have it edited, inspected, and be graphically creative. Don't short-change yourself and short-change your audience by being in too much of a hurry to get a product out.

3) DO be smart when pricing your books. Here is a simple rule: in every wallet and purse you will probably find a dollar bill, five dollar bill, or ten dollar bill. Price your books either under five or five or ten. This is the simplest way to get sales for your books.

4) DO NOT hype your book... too much. Remember, you are a creative person and not a used car salesman. There is a very subtle difference between the

Illustration by Walt Hopmans

two when it comes to selling your book. For some crazy misconception, poets are looked upon as being sensitive souls, so stuff like sending your kids out in the audience to help sell your books is not going to be looked upon as being… cool. Also the Cal Worthington approach to selling books is not too hip either. "If you liked tonight's reading you will find some of my poems in…. and it costs…" is a good way get the audience warmed up to the fact that you have books for sale.

5) DO be entertaining. I'm not talking about Robin Williams funny but try to make an entertaining impression on the audience. It goes a long way towards helping to sell your poetry books. Does that mean you have to write/be funny when you do a reading?

No, entertaining at this point means memorable. What impression do you want your audience to have of you five minutes, five days, and five months after you've given the reading? Think about that before you recite your first poem and try to sell your books.

"I sold 1,000 poetry books last year and you know why… 1,000 people liked me and my poetry," one jazz-poet from Chicago said in 1997. It is the element of three: They like you, they like your poetry, they like your book. When you reach that concept selling your poetry books will be an easier road to take.

(3/98)

PATTERNS OF PERCEPTION

By Robert Arroyo, Jr.

To say Southern California is a melting pot of poetic style would be an understatement, and any attempt to codify it under one banner would be fruitless. So, what I propose to do in this column is to speak of only one facet of the poetry community. For the lack of a better term I call it traditional contemporary poetry and define it by what it is not. It is not performance poetry, spoken word, or slam poetry. Those styles have their own champions who are better able to speak for, and about, them than I.

But even traditional contemporary poetry (hereafter referred to as poetry) comes in many styles. These different styles include narrative, lyrical, digressive, discursive, meditative, or any combination of the aforementioned techniques. So what is the common link between the various styles? The link is not based on theme, but motion. That motion is perception.

I remember once when I was in a lecture, the professor asked us to write down the first thing that came to mind when he cued us with a word of his own. He wanted an immediate reaction, not a thoughtful one. His word was "corpse" and mine was "mother." The subconscious motion between those two words is perception. He then asked us to track the thinking process of how we came to our word. I tracked mine thusly: corpse-death-loss-mother. This is not poetry, but the logical underpinnings of my perception. This is the work that passes for poetry in a lot of the local venues.

The passages that state the logical underpinnings of a poem are what poets need to learn to weed out. Poetry is not about thinking, but about feeling, and feelings are more authentically rendered before they have passed through the cognitive center of the brain. At the moment of perception, our intellectual guard is down and thus we are vulnerable to our base emotions; we are more vulnerable for something surprising and unexpected to pass through us. By the time the moment of perception has passed and the poet has come to ponder what it is that he/she was moved by, the perception has been tainted by intellectual prejudice. Subsequently, what comes out on the page is summary, complete with what it means to the poet, and not the experience. It should be left to the listener/reader to validate the emotions, not the poet to prove they have worth.

Of course all I've said is theory. Nobody really writes at the moment of perception. Poetry is truly what William Wordsworth said it is: "strong emotions recalled in moments of tranquility." Inspiration is little more than the conscious mind realizing something is going on and sparking the poet's ego into thinking it's the milk of paradise being spilt onto the page. More likely than not, that milk is curdled. The challenge for writers is to create the illusion of spontaneity and that takes training.

There I go, I've said it. The "T" word. To a lot a people that's a bad word. They believe that somehow training pollutes the artistic process. I hate to be the one to break the news, but training shows us how we're our own worst enemies when it comes to creation. But that's a topic for another column.

(4/98)

STOP THE PRESSES!

Tips by Patrice Wirth

Ed. Note: As many of our readers know, Lob and Victor were running readings in Orange County prior to their becoming heavily involved with **Next…** *At about that time,* **The OC Weekly** *emerged, bringing with it one of the coolest Calendar assistants we've had the pleasure of working with, Patrice Wirth. From day one, Patrice was interested in and supportive of OC poetry, and while she's moved on to being the* **Weekly**'s *copy editor, we here at* **Next…** *are pleased to present her tips for us poet types dealing with the print media.*

I know you poet types hate us media types, but I want to help. I want you to get your events publicized. I want you to get the word out.

I want you to quit bugging us when some event doesn't get the attention you feel it deserves. Oops. Did I say that out loud?

Okay, here's the deal: you want to get your events listed in some papers' — maybe, for argument's sake, the *OC Weekly*'s — listings. And you want people to read that little listing and show up. I'm going to give you some helpful hints here. And I expect you to follow them. Just don't tell anyone I helped you (I would hate to ruin the "all media people are Satan's Mouthpieces" illusion for everyone).

First off, send press releases. When I was the *Weekly*'s Calendar assistant, I compiled the Readings listings. I loved nice, pretty, informative press releases. If you're hosting a readings series, send out a list of dates and readers. Include where you're hosting the series, that venue's address, what phone number to call for information, and any other pertinent facts. (Whether there is a beverage minimum counts as a pertinent fact. Trust me.) And for Pete's sake, please, please, please put your phone number on there. If you're reading at some venues, and you want to get the word out, include all that other stuff, too. Especially your phone number.

Step two is really important — so pay attention! Tell us something about the poets! (Or yourself, as the case may be.) "May 5: Bill Jones. Gypsy Den, 8 p.m." tells me nothing. Except that some guy named Bill Jones will be at the Gypsy Den at 8. *But who is Bill Jones?!?* Once upon a time, I attended poetry readings regularly. I got to recognize certain people; I knew their poetry. I knew

what they were like. I could describe something about them. At first, I went to readings because I believed it was part of my job. Not everyone who compiles listings thinks that way. As sad as you feel about that fact, you must push on. You must continue to send press releases anyway. And you must tell us about the poets. Victor Infante was wonderful at this. He always included where the poet was from, what their general style was, maybe some fascinating tidbit. And he did so to get me to pass it on to the readers. And maybe it intrigued them. "May 5: Bill Jones is an amazing poet from Visalia who likes to write prose while white-water rafting. He likes to eat marshmallows while reading. Gypsy Den, 8 p.m." Oh, so *that's* who Bill Jones is! Now, I'm interested.

Get those press releases ready early. Most publications have a standard amount of time they want — and, most often, need — to receive information by. One man who I remember being so very helpful in this manner was Lob. Nice guy. Always sent those press releases to me months in advance. And he'd update them! It was April, and I knew who'd be reading on June 25. Ah, the good old days. He, too, remembered to write a little something about the poets. Very helpful. And he also put his phone number on there. Nice guy.

Now that you've got all of that down, you're ready to fax and mail your releases off. But wait! Do you know who to send them to? Most publications feature a little line that names who compiled the listings. At the *Weekly*, the Readings listings are done by a really cool woman named Annalise Winkle. So you'd want to send information to her. Or Anna Barr, the Calendar editor. The editor-in-chief, quite frankly, will simply pass it on to Anna when he finally gets to looking through his mail. At which point, he leaves a large stack of papers on Anna's desk. Then she has to sort through it all. And then it goes to Annalise. What do you say we cut out the middle man here? If you can't find a tag line of some sort in the publication, call up their reception desk and ask. Receptionists are incredibly resourceful people; they almost always can track down the right person for you to talk to.

An important aside to remember: make sure the publication actually prints readings listings. Some papers don't, but you can get around that by asking them to include your information with their coffeehouse/cafe listings — provided they print those. You'll also want to double-check what area that publication covers. Sure, you'll find listings for poetry events in Whittier (which is technically in L.A. County) in the OC Weekly, but chances are you won't see a Brea-based event in the *LA Weekly*.

You do not — I repeat: you *do not* — have to call the recipient three million times to make sure they got the release and that they know how important it is. (Special note to Lee Mallory: They know. Trust me. Please don't call three million times. If you stop, we'll stop having those "Lee Mallory Alerts" you read about. I promise. Deal?) Say this is your first time faxing out a press release: call the recipient to make sure they got it, that you want to make sure you faxed it to the right number. Offer to add any information if they so require it. Tell them they can call you anytime. Then stop calling. Your job here is done. And your name won't cause anyone to fear picking up the phone.

Exception to the rule: If something changes, and you need to update that press release after you've sent it, call the person you sent it to. Tell them you'll be sending them a new one as soon as possible. Then do so. It's that easy and painless.

Exception to the rule, No. 2: If an upcoming reader is just so cool, so good, so wonderful, so out-of-this-world unbelievable, then you can call the listings person. Tell them this person is worthy of extra mention and offer to send them a little bio with more information and the poet's phone number. Ask who it would be best to send that info to. Then thank them and do your job. Do *not* call an hour later and ask if they're going to write something on that poet. If they want to, they will. That's all there is to it.

Well, now, that wasn't so bad. See, it's all so easy. I'll tell Annalise to start looking for those fabulous releases. But I won't tell her what prompted the change. She thinks you're all wonderful — and you all are — so let's not tell her I said anything. I can live with her believing the planets aligned perfectly to divine this knowledge to you all, making you all more wonderful than you were before. We'll just keep this guide our little secret.

(5/98)

WHAT WE WRITE ABOUT
By Robert Arroyo, Jr.

In the August issue of *Next*…a letter writer took exception to a review of a chapbook of poetry. His complaint was that the reviewer wasn't so much critiquing the poetry, as he was the "things" and subjects that inhabited the poet's work. A week later I was talking with a friend and he was wondering why poets still insist on invoking Greek mythology in their poems. These two issues are related because they both speak to how we, as poets, utilize the world in which we live in order to create an authentic voice. Authenticity is the goal because it begets empathy, which allows the reader to come in close contact with the poem. In addition, it demonstrates the poet's right to the subject matter he is exploring. In an era when it is almost always assumed that the "I" of the poem is the poet himself, what we write about should be personal enough to not only be important, but crucial. Even when the "I" of the poem is not the poet, that illusion must be maintained in order for a reader to be empathic, to feel they have a stake in the emotion being exposed. What we populate our poetry with speaks volumes about our connection to the work and the life being depicted therein.

I'm of two minds when it comes to the contemporary poet's use of Greek mythology. Many of the stories are archetypal, and thus timeless. Even though the myths deal mostly with gods, the psychology embedded in them still has relevance in contemporary society. But does that mean we need to cling to them as a child does to his mother? After all this time, the stories have become an emotional crutch; their paths so rote that no amount of re-visioning can expand the psychological foundations that at one time made them necessary. Yet, time and again, we're lured back to them. The lure (and the problem) lies in the fact that since they are so familiar, they are safe, and this is counter to what poetry, what art, is about. Art is about exploration, be it your psyche or imagination. Art is about freedom, about letting go of the conscious mind in order to chart the subconscious, and it's difficult, to say the least, to chart the murkier areas of the subconscious if the path is already known.

The conventional wisdom of critiquing poetry these days is "What did the poet risk?" Although at times this mindset sickens me because "risk" is such a subjective term, it is at the core of art. When we utilize any sort of mythology system we are writing toward distraction, not revelation. Wake up and smell the allusion. What does Persephone really know about your life? If Dionysus could, do you really think he'd give a damn about the fact you can't put down the bottle? Using myth romanticizes experience until the poet can't tell the difference between reality and the cocoon he's constructed in order to deal with his experience. It would be too sweeping a statement to say nothing new can be created using myth, but it would take more than just a good writer to accomplish that task.

We live in a time when the stuff of poetry has been brought so low as to be almost debased. When the Confessional poets began airing their dirty laundry in order to gain perspective, they broke the rules on what was thought to be acceptable as "good" poetry. If nothing else, go back and hear what they did to the diction level. Surely this lowering of diction goes back to the Modernist William Carlos Williams, but poets like Robert Lowell, Sylvia Plath, Anne Sexton, W.D. Snodgrass, took it one step further by moving away from what had traditionally been "proper" topics for poetry and bringing it into the home. Former poet laureate Robert Hass takes it one step further: "Shame: An Aria" evolves from the initial image of the speaker caught picking his nose in an elevator. Hass brings the private into the public in two ways: first by writing about a private activity, and second by writing about performing that activity in public. This sort of layered revealing ups the ante on the speaker's vulnerability and so deepens the emotional/psychological/ imaginative depths Hass can explore.

Earlier I made mention of having the right to write about any particular topic. I don't mean to say certain topics should be forbidden; that's a decision every writer must make with his own conscience. What I mean is that the right to a subject is borne out in how well the poet honors that subject, how well he inhabits it through relevant detail. A little goes a long way. If a speaker owns a subject and that subject owns (or possesses) him, then that ownership is embedded in every word through nuances of language, not only images, and invites the reader to engage. It demands that the reader engage.

What we write about, what ugly, everyday things enter our poems should never be a question up for debate with regards to how mundane or disgusting those things may be. The question for consideration should only be how we write what we write about. Is what we're writing about merely a good idea, will it shock or garner interest because of its subject matter, or does it have some relevance to how existence filters through our centers of perception? I'd opt for the last latter. What good is art, what good is the poem you're working on, if it doesn't challenge the assumptions you wake with every day?

(10/98)

REDISCOVERING WORDS
(Why We Love Open Mics)
By Michael Elton Crye

We fear conversation is dead. Lost on some wavelength, bouncing between the satellites, never reaching the ground. Its extinction a tragic myth, spread by a culture too occupied with speed. We invert communication devices that throw our voices and faces across the globe, but information isn't interaction.

Conversation cannot be expected to thrive in the mouth of white noise. It doesn't somehow merge formed out of a fax machine's buzz, or deepen resounding on talk shows. The art of conversation lies in intimacy. A long pause for the air to gather, then the inhale and exhale as we speak and listen.

Build an atmosphere, someone said, for talk. Put it indoors, paint the walls, stuff it with chairs and couches.

Illustration by Taylor Mali

Reduce the light sources to lamps and single soft bulbs. Crack the door on hot nights or keep warm with all the bodies huddled close together over coffee. Every week put an open mic in the center and watch the creatures we thought so long quiet and unaffected sneak up to it. Testing the sound system with low voices, which build with confidence till they speak aloud and clear. They'll begin to relate and share. We begin to see the talk evolve into story telling. Some bring notebooks with poems or notes of things they didn't want to forget.

More will enter and approach the mic. We see gatherings around the open mic nights. People start shuffling in early, laying backpacks on tables, some get caught by accident, not understanding this isn't just some watering hole. No, it's a natural spring, and we drink because we're thirsty for the talk and the sound of our own unhurried voices.

The noise brings the rustlings in the streets thru the door. We catch ourselves having to look at our feet many times when a story is told on the hard footfalls that we hear under our own windows. No one knows whether to laugh or leave when a dwarf with nappy street hair and ruined shoes shuffles in, pointing at the on stage poet, yelling toothless, "Hey, shorty! Shut up! Shut up! Yeah, you, shorty." We catch ourselves believing for the first time that night. Yeah, we're scared. Those words are real. We live with them everyday,but never really see them up close — face to face.

Suddenly, without warning

the world's distance shrinks

to the lung size of a room.

(5/95)

SWEATING BULLETS

Dear *Next…*

Some thoughts on hosting my first reading:

Wednesday, 7:45 p.m. Living Planet. I've just read four pages of notes on how to "effectively" host a successful poetry reading, and I am more confused by them than a statistics text book. The usual host's notes are neat and concise, but they leave out more than they explain. At this point, if he had told me to "just act natural," I might have taken my clothes off!

8:00 p.m. All right. Get a grip on yourself. No, not there. Set up the candles, chairs, podium, sign-up book, sitting pillows. Turn down the lights, set out the free magazines and flyers. Where's the doorman? Where's the cash box? Why the hell does everybody ask me if they can go first, last, or have extra minutes? Yes, I realize you've driven an hour and a half. Yes, I know you have a set of important poems which will take a little longer than the allotted five minutes. Yes, I'm sorry some unthinking idiot has signed their name by your favorite number. Yes, yes, yes, and *NO, I CAN'T DO ANYTHING ABOUT IT!* I never realized what whiners we poets can be.

8:20 p.m. The doorman asks me if I'm ready to start. Of course I'm not ready, and no, I don't have time to grab you a cup of coffee. No wonder people take amphetamines.

8:25 p.m. I'm ready. All I have to do now is host the reading. No sweat, just get on stage and do your thing. HAH! Why the hell does the host blow on a conch shell to start the reading anyway? All I do is make a dying moose's mating call in B-flat, and the doorman laughs at me. I feel like saying, "Hi, I'm Brian and I write poetry…" There has got to be something seriously wrong with anyone who does this week after week… but I'm game.

Still, I'm grateful for the chance. For anyone interested, I say go for it. The worst that could happen can be treated in therapy. The best is, you might have as much fun as I did (and only need a few sessions).

Brian Howe, Long Beach

(6/95)

ON HOSTING

By John Gardiner

So... now it's my turn... I'm the Big Kahuna calling the shots every Thursday night at the Fahrenheit 451 reading in Laguna Beach. I'm the asshole who won't respond to your insistent finger on my shoulder at 9:45 in the middle of someone else's poem. It's my fault that you showed up near the end of the reading with a new prose piece that's "a little long, maybe ten minutes, but it's really good, and they gotta hear it." I'm the one who says, "three minutes max, and we're outta here." Or, "why not read it in three sections over the next three weeks?"

Fortunately, these things don't happen at this reading! I start at 8, take a ten-minute break AFTER the feature, motor through the second half of the list, announce that we have a 10 p.m. mandatory date at the Brewing Company ten doors down, after a 9:58 mandatory three puffs of boo in the underground parking lot around the corner! It's so simple! That last poet reading at 9:56 is the one under pressure, not me! He or she can hear the rumblings of "pot'n'beer" before that second poem is settled into. I have a "runner" who goes to the Brewing Company at 9:30 to insure that we have the best of the juke box between 10 and 11:30. Hey, I'm the host, and this is gonna be a smooth party. Just call me "Molasses" Gardiner...

I've heard *most* of you read at one place or another during the past ten years, some of you twenty years ago, and three or four of you thirty years ago when my guerrilla theater company disrupted your reading by doing very loud anti-war improv pieces. I want *all* of you at this reading because you're *good*, and deserve to be heard everywhere. It takes time. SoCal, please be patient! I need your phone numbers! I'm having fun. I want you to have fun! We've all been to readings that were worse than dental surgery, and hopefully this reading is, and will remain, a festive occasion. I'm looking for places where out-of-town poets can crash for the night, and walk on the beach the next day. I want poets to meet and fall in love at this reading! I want to meet a girl with sun in Pisces and moon in Scorpio...

Over half the readings in OC are in Laguna Beach. We have a responsibility to make and keep them strong. Perhaps we can branch out, and help start other readings, although it's hard to imagine a group calling themselves the Placentia Poets. Who knows?! Come down to Fahrenheit on a Thursday night and check it out. BYO...

(3/98)

Illustration by Walt Hopmans

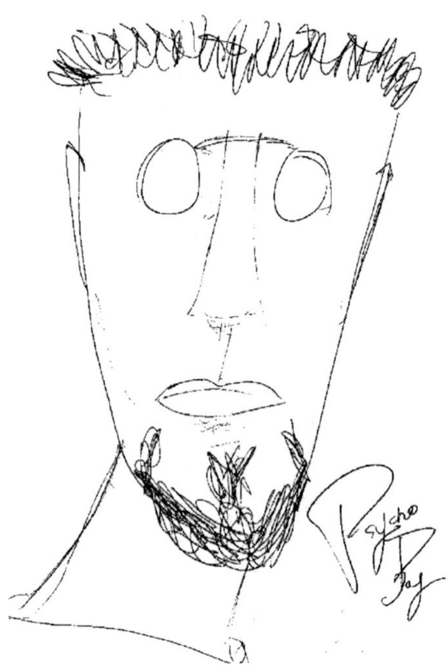

PSYCHO BOY SPEAKS

My good friend calls me up on the phone the other day and says he's starting a magazine that will focus solely on Performance Poetry. He goes on to ask me if I'll write a regular column for it, and assures me I can write anything as long as it has to do with performance poetry.

Now how could I pass up an opportunity like that, 'cause anyone who knows me will tell you I'm one opinionated bastard.

So anyway, here's what I'd like to say, and I think it's a perfect topic for this first column.

I think poets in general, and performance poets in particular, need to step back and look carefully at where it is we want to go as we head toward a new century.

And, ya know, it's not only a new century but a new age, a video interactive communications age, where anything and most everything can be learned, obtained, and processed in the privacy of our own homes.

And where does that leave poetry, an art that for the past thirty years has been slowly disappearing from the public forum anyway?

Why has it been disappearing? Because it carries the cement block of print around its neck. Those who decree these things have decided that poets make their reputation in print. And we, as poets, have bought it.

But, no one reads poetry anymore. Hell, no one *reads* anymore. Even I would rather watch *Moby Dick* than read it. Gregory Peck, standing on the deck, face to the foam, harpoon in hand. Those images are imprinted across hundreds of thousands of neural memory units. I mean, what I'm trying to say is that images and the spoken word are so much easier to digest.

So get with it. Stop burying your nose in a page at readings. Perform! Stop printing chapbooks. Make videos! Stop putting on *readings* in libraries and bookstores. Produce poetry shows in bars and concert halls.

Do we really want to continue performing our art for poets, whiners, suicidals, and college professors?

No. We as performance poets know better. The people who happen to stumble upon a performance by accident always comment on how surprised they were that they actually enjoyed poetry.

Get with it. Conform before we disappear.

(4/94)

LETTER FROM THOMAS RUSH

"O Lord, deliver me from the man of excellent intention and impure heart: for the heart is deceitful above all things, and desperately wicked."

— T.S. Eliot

Dear *Next...*

Just had to respond to "Psycho Boy Speaks." I find myself in total agreement that, as the new century approaches, we poets need to step back and take a hard look at where we want to go. It's just that the direction he seems to be suggesting is a turn in the road towards disaster, not only for poetry, but for American culture and art as a whole.

Print does matter. Writing matters. The act of writing poetry matters. Attempting to create *literature*, in and of itself, is one of the noblest ventures a human being can pursue. And though I feel performance is also

Illustration by Tom Foster

vital in not only building an audience for poetry, but also in expressing the essence of a poem, performance should never supersede the poem itself.

Don't get me wrong. I take pride in and work hard at my delivery, my performance. But God help me if I ever write a poem solely for performance. I am a poet first and foremost, a performer second (and let time and the echo decide if I am right or wrong). But what P-Boy is advocating, in my mind, turns all that around. And there is a great danger in this.

I mean, are we really willing to turn our backs on such brilliant local poets as Richard Nester or John C. Harrell because they don't blow the room up or cut themselves on stage? Are we going to allow ourselves and the ancient art of poetry to be degraded by some fool driving a nail through his scrotum and calling himself a poet? (Excuse me… A *performance* poet?) Do we really need MTV to validate what we are doing? Do we poets really want to dumb down with the rest of America? I certainly hope not. But if we are not careful, if we are too quick to chase the almighty dollar and some fleeting fifteen minutes of fame, then we will be judged, in the long run, as cheap hacks and fools, the instigators of poetry's demise.

True, one of the worst aspects of the current poetry scene is having to sit through "poets" who are not only boring but couldn't write a decent poem if their poor, sick mother's life depended on it. But equally appalling is the tendency of some people to get up in front of a crowd and perform some exhibitionistic act devoid of any merit in the name of art, poetry, performance, freedom of expression, etc., and then have the gall to claim to be a poet.

The best performance poets, people like Gary Tomlinson, Laurel Ann Bogen, Willie Sims, S.A. Griffin, Michael Zittel, and Frank Ortega, just to name a few of the many, can write well too. It would be a shame if their words were never printed on the page and were never read with some serious consideration. I suggest that Psycho Boy become an actor or start a musical group. I contend that *Next…*'s readers put down their video cameras and pick up a pen. Turn off the goddamn television! Put on some Mozart or Beethoven! Pick up a book! Read!

Thomas Rush, Anaheim

(5/94)

PRINT DEAD? BACK UP!

Some of Us Still Revel in Writing as a Sacred and Organic Process
By Christine Trzyna

Is there a place for print in 1994? Is everyone going to video, performance poetry — the big business of writing? Is writing only worthwhile if it results in paychecks and other prizes? Or perhaps is there value in the process itself?

I wake in the middle of the night. But it's ok. I'm in the mood to write. I keep stacks of recycled paper nearby. I delight in good pens, the kind that gracefully skate across those blank white pages, fulfilling them. My workshop, Writers Rendezvous, exists to burst through block (anyone can write about anything anytime and have fun doing it). But a writer in the mood doesn't need to break through any block. Suddenly, every muse you've ever conjured is there for you, whispering in both your ears. By morning you've manifested pages of original material.

Never mind that some day in the near future, you'll reread and edit down. You've written. You are a writer. How long did you write before you could admit that to yourself? The world? Doesn't it feel good? For me, writing is a sacred and organic process. It is a leap for me when I must neaten up and commit my work to the typewriter, where surely I will rewrite again. And again.

Typewriter? I don't own a computer yet. I have buyer's anxiety, which is better than buyer's remorse. When I got a manual, electric typewriters came in. Got an electric, electronic came in. Word processor? I'm sure I'll buy a computer that gets discontinued the next day. But more, as eye-appealing as upgraded print is, using a computer is just another step removed from the actual process of writing for me.

My attitude carries over to how I feel about readings. I think of the new poets I've heard, people who have been secretly writing for years. Their hands sweat as they lift dog-eared secret notebooks to their eyes and begin to speak. The romance of a reading would be blown for me if instead they plugged in their desk top computer and read from the screen.

Some of my best work is too personal for me to read from a stage. I can imagine the work in a chapbook however. It would please me greatly to happen upon someone reading my chapbook in the darkened corner of a coffee house. I have to work towards both revealing myself to the world and finishing the illustrations for my book.

Which brings me to my point. It's 1994 and the Southern California poetry scene is wide open. Superlative poets put on shows that are the talk of the town. There must be a place for the new poets to start out, free of criticism. For every poet who is marketing themselves big time, there's someone writing all alone in their room wondering if they could ever even let one other person read their work. For every investor of expensive desktop publishing systems, there's someone whose big purchase this week was a 99 pack of blue Bics. I like being part of a scene that has room for us all.

(6/94)

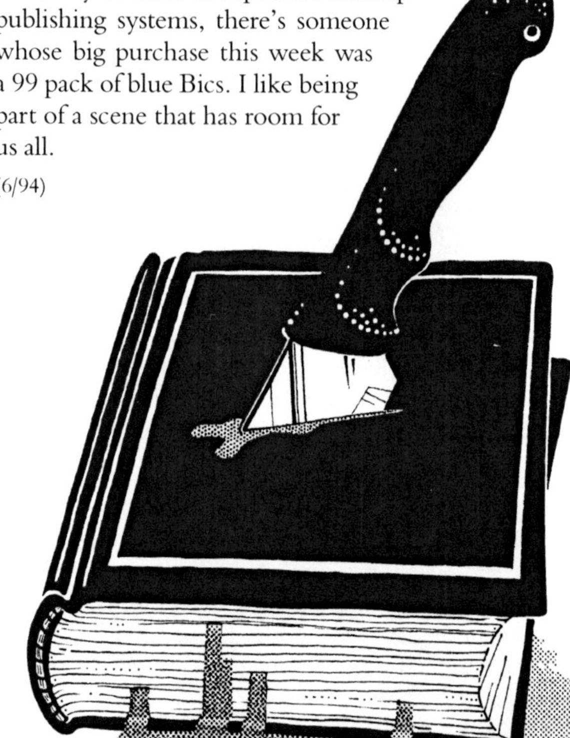

YOUR VOICE: THE ULTIMATE MEDIUM

By Lawrence Schulz

Look out! Poetry is about to perform the first carjacking on the information highway.

Kill your television set (who needs 500 channels anyway?). Burn any personal computer and smash the guy holding a video camera. Please laugh out loud at the next person who uses the word "interactive" in their vocabulary. Media is not cool. It is not hip. Media is nothing.

After all the talk of print being dead, videos taking the place of books, computers becoming electronic bulletin boards for people to communicate, something else will remain. It all comes down to this… one person talking to another person.

A voice and someone who listens.

People will be telling stories and creating poems long after the hype of what tomorrow will be is trash.

Don't believe in mass communication, computer-enhanced reality, or a global network linked together by computer that you can hold in your lap. You can either buy into that crap, blow your money and park your ass in front of a television big screen or a monitor for the rest of your breathing life, or you can start your own future.

The most dangerous person to this rosy future on the information highway is one who writes a poem or tells a story that will affect others. Beware of the person who can write a poem or repeat a story that other people will remember.

The oral tradition, this ability to write and perform what exists in the heart so that others will learn from it, is the one thing that will exist long after the talk that print is dead, television is dead, computers are dead and those who hailed them as "the next big thing" are dust.

If you want to be truly interactive write something down and express it to someone. If you believe in mass communication, do the same thing, to a group of people.

Illustration by Charles Ellik

Storytelling, reciting a poem, reading out loud, are forms of communication that will not die. At times they will be overshadowed by the glitz and jive of what some people think is hip or newsworthy. But don't worry, they will always be there. Those forms of communication exist each time you read to someone what you have written.

There is a dangerous person lurking on this information highway — the one who keeps the oral tradition alive.

The televisions are shut off and the computers are down.

There are people listening to a person speaking.

Poetry is alive once more.

(6/94)

THE ART OF LISTENING

By Lawrence Schulz

"If God has granted you the presence of a poet, then for God's sake listen…"
—*Robinson Jeffers*

Listening is a lost art… a lost art that is desperately trying to return again via poetry.

Country/bluegrass artist Bill Monroe once said that he did his best thinking while people were talking. Countless surveys by professional speakers show that an audience remembers very little of what is actually said during a speech. Most people are analyzing their own thoughts or preparing a rebuttal.

A poetry audience should be different. The audience should be part of the performance. They come to listen, hopefully for no other reason than to enjoy the poet's words.

Poetry has gone through many evolutions in the past five years. There are poetry videos, poetry slams, stand-up poetry, performance poetry, and who knows what else. It is an art form that can take many shapes while still maintaining its basic format. But it still comes down to the poet doing what he must to get the audience to listen.

Everyone has gone through the feeling of "are you listening to me?" For the poet this is not a casual question. The best way to think about getting someone to listen is to analyze how you listen. How do you sit when you are listening? Do you murmur to someone else while the poet is reading? What attracts your attention and what distracts you? This is the way a person begins to study the personal art of listening.

The hardest part about listening at a poetry reading is keeping still. This does not mean sitting still, but just being relaxed enough to concentrate on the poet's words.

When it comes to a poetry reading, rediscover your lost capacity to really listen. Most people are so bombarded by events that it becomes hard to focus out your own agenda and focus in on the poet-performer.

Don't worry about the bills, the girlfriend, the boyfriend, the spouse, the dog, the rent, the job… or that you are the next poet to speak. Focus in on the words from the person speaking now. You might learn something about this part of you that could help you way beyond a poetry reading. Listening is a talent too, and it takes time to develop.

Are you listening?

(7/94)

NO CONTACT = NO CONFLICT

Dear *Next…*

I have a few random thoughts on academic and performance poetry. I think there is no conflict between academic and performance poetry just as there is no conflict between the residents of San Clemente and the natives of Tijuana. There is no conflict because there is minimal contact.

The academic poets have prestigious employment. While some performance poets earn a livelihood from slinging words like Allen Ginsberg, Marc Smith of Chicago, Edward Haggard of Nashville, most work a variety of jobs to make ends meet.

The academic poets hold court in classrooms where the audience is attentive. Performance poets recite in bars or coffee houses where the audience may snap their fingers at you.

Poets invited to read in lecture halls are provided with an honorarium, and a guaranteed turn-out from English classes requested to attend. Performance poets booked for gigs travel at their own expense to uncertain venues and are often rewarded with the contents of a passed hat.

Academic writers are preceded by their achievements, awards, books, fellowships. Performance poets offer their verve and practice as they step up to the mic. Academic poets do not attend open mics; performance poets seldom attend academic functions because they are not invited or the schedule of events is not shared with the general public.

In short, the academic connection to performance poetry reminds me of how James Joyce describes Ireland's relationship to the Jews in *Ulysses*. "—Ireland, they say, has the honour of being the only country which never persecuted the Jews. And do you know why? —Why, sir? Stephen asked, beginning to smile. —Because she never let them in, Mr. Deasy said solemnly."

Joe Speer, Nashville, TN
(9/95)

WHAT IT IS, WHAT IT DOES

By Wayne Liebman

When I handed a chapbook of my poems to a colleague at work recently, he dutifully read it, and told me that while he liked the one about leaving the Andromeda Galaxy to Yale in my will (not my personal favorite), he was confused regarding what a poem was. The same confusion had been bothering me a long time, until I started writing poems in earnest a few years ago. Now that I am a poet I'm still confused; the confusion just bothers me less.

The most basic, "obvious" matters have always been difficult for me. I used to ask teachers what a poem was. None of the answers I ever got, when I got them at all, worked for me. They were like riddles. One teacher said, "Poetry is compressed, tightened prose." Not much help. One said, "A poem conveys in words something that's impossible to convey in words." Sounds good, but still not very useful. Another said, "Poetry is to prose as dancing is to walking." Well, sure. I knew that; sort of. But what was it that made dancing dancing? Grace? Rules? The expression of feeling? Didn't those things also apply to walking (prose) — wasn't there a right way to walk, and couldn't you walk with grace and feeling?

Like flowers and grass, poems seemed to grow everywhere. There ought to be a simple, graspable explanation of what one is. One of the problems was that I was really asking two questions. The first question was pure taxonomy: how do you recognize a poem when you see it? The second question concerned function: what does a poem do? Here's the way I've learned to approach the first question: A poem is a literary form, the oldest literary form. It's usually short (hardly anyone writes epic poetry anymore; poet Jack Grapes observes that the role of the epic poem — to underwrite the values of the tribe — has been appropriated by the movies). Poems should also give a feeling of satisfaction or pleasure. If there's none, move on to the next. That's what makes a horse race.

The last few hundred years, a sure way to produce pleasure in a poem was to rhyme. So much so that mostly all the poems we read in school rhymed, as well as the ones on Hallmark cards. As a result, some have the erroneous belief that if there's no rhyme, there's no poem. Au contraire. Dante rhymed. Shakespeare did and didn't. Virgil and Homer didn't. It's not easy to rhyme well in English now — "moon" and "June" are tired rhymes. They don't delight as they once did, and poets look for other, more subtle, ways of giving pleasure.

So how do you know it's a poem? By the line breaks. If the lines extend to the margin, as in a newspaper, it's prose. If the lines stop before the margin, it's a poem. It's that simple. The poet is indicating where to take a break. She's playing with breath and rhythm. She's adding pleasure. She might also play with meter and sound. The broken line — its immediate visual impact — is the essential clue that she's up to something. She's giving words a shape, using them as clay to make a form. She's writing a poem.

The poet Katha Pollitt suggests that one way to tell if the poet has been successful is to change the poem into prose by eliminating the line breaks – make it

into a paragraph. Does it feel any different? Is anything sacrificed, or might the poet just as well have written a paragraph in the first place? Good poems suffer a loss when translated to prose in this way.

All the above notes are about form. They answer the "what is it?" question. But there's also the "what does it do?" question: what does a poem do? This is the harder one; people have been trying to figure it out as long as they've been writing poems, and a lot of PhDs have been won and lost in the struggle. I think Margaret Atwood, the poet and novelist, has answered it as well as anyone. Writing about her childhood, she said:

On fine days we spent our time turning over rocks to see what was underneath. The most disappointing was nothing. Then, in ascending order, came worms, millipedes, spiders, beetles, ants' nests, toads, snakes, mice, newts, and salamanders. Newts and salamanders were the ultimate; they were extremely rare. Sometimes we just looked and meditated, and put the rock back. Sometimes we poked things with a stick to see what would happen. People often ask me, "What's the difference between writing poetry and writing fiction?"

And surely it is this: with a lyric poem, you look, meditate, and put the rock back. With fiction, you poke things with a stick to see what will happen.

So that's it. A poem is a quick, sharp observation, a moment laid open, illuminated, named. The poet has looked at (that is, experienced) something (a salamander?), seen or felt something (a salamander!), and it has turned out to be arresting, often, in a surprising way. This idea tells me not to worry so much what a poem "means" because the experiences people have don't always come with a meaning you can put your finger on, or care to. Moreover, it gives me a way into a poem. I can read it and ask, "Okay, what's the poet looking at, what's his experience? And what do I experience now?" The experience is the thing. And the poem is the report, wrapped up in paper and a bow.

Why the paper and bow? Because if the poet is really good, all that art and craft — the technique with words — comes to this: the poem will not only give me information about what the poet experienced, it will put me in his shoes and make that experience come alive for me. I'll have my own salamander. Moreover, it

Illustration by Brian Hagen

will be an interesting, delightful, surprising, or perhaps terrifying salamander, even if I didn't think much of salamanders before.

Is there a fit subject for a poem? You bet: anything goes. Anything you think about, feel about, wonder about, in your most public or private moments. Love and flowers? Sure. Doorknobs and zucchini? Why not? War and torture? Have you read the *Iliad* lately? Unspeakable, blasphemous, embarrassing things? Check out Anne Sexton's "Ballad of the Lonely Masturbator." Sometimes, the poet looks at words and sounds themselves — how they go together as artistic clay — without trying to make sense. It's all grist for the poetry mill. And because it's all grist, poems are the most basic, flexible, creative, exciting, challenging, enduring and universal of written forms. Freud said, "I never went anywhere that a poet hadn't already traveled." Poems move us over to another point of view. They break down barriers and taboos between people. A poem is a front row seat in someone else's psychic theater. A poem is an arrow aimed straight at you.

(11/97)

I WANT TO BE AN OPERA SINGER

Why the artist is open to criticism
By Carlye Archibeque, Reviews Editor

I want to be an opera singer. I have a little natural talent and most of my friends think I am very good. A few professionally trained opera singers think I should study the craft more before I start performing in front of people, but I feel the music when I sing and that is enough for me. I don't think I need to work on the craft at all. Most people would agree that this is a pretty ridiculous statement because no matter how well you sing in the shower, not all of us can be opera singers. Replace "opera singer" with "poet" and see how many people agree with the statement now.

Poetry, however, is a craft like any other, and once you go from the shower to the stage it is open to the interpretation and criticism (both good and bad) of others. It also has a rich and varied history that gives us guidelines for what is good and what is bad. Yes, there is good poetry and bad poetry. The problem with poetry is that, in most cases, the artist in question writes and performs their own work. This work usually consists of thoughts and feelings. The problem with the final product being critiqued is that it is hard for the poet to separate criticism of their work and criticism of their person. This problem also exists for the critic but in another direction.

The artist has a problem because they feel that if the thoughts and feelings that went into the work are valid, the work itself is also valid — a kind of reverse guilt by association. Critics have the burden or pleasure of looking at the work in a harsh light. There is no audience or personal relation with the artist that colors the critic's perception of the work. If the critic can't connect with the feeling of the work it is because the poet has not been able to convey it with their craft. The work stands alone when it is being reviewed. In some cases, such as with a small magazine like *Next...*, there is no way to find a reviewer who does not know an artist. In this case it is better to acknowledge the biases and preconceived notions in the review so that they don't come back to haunt you.

We all have artists, movies, music, etc. that we like despite our better sense. Something about the work appeals to us on a level that we can't quite figure out. Sometimes when we have a friend who is an artist we feel a compulsion to love their work as an extension of loving them. But while the former is a personal quirk, the latter is a great disservice to the artist. In both cases we end up defending work we realize is flawed for personal reasons. But in the history of all crafts some really horrible people are incredible artists (Hughes, Hitchcock, Michelangelo); and some of the best people are horrible artists or just plain mediocre (I won't encourage letter writing by naming names). Once an artist goes public with their work (and starts sending it to reviewers) they and their art should sleep in separate rooms. It is unhealthy to think that you are your work; ask Monroe, Cobain, Sexton, VanGogh, and on and on. It is, I realize, difficult (but not impossible) to separate yourself from your work. But if your art is craft, it has room for improvement; if it is too much a part of your ego, no good can come to your art or yourself. The goal of any artist should be to become the best painter, poet, or whatever they can. If your goal is to be loved, get a dog. If you want to be a good writer, prepare to be criticized; if you want to be a great writer, prepare to rewrite and make fun of your old work.

The knee-jerk response to criticism is to feel personally attacked and write a long letter (or have a friend do it) to the reviewer telling them that they just don't "get" your work or that they are too academic or politically correct, or whatever your argument is. The constructive response to criticism is to consider the comments made and the source of the comments. Did the critic have valid points or not? What can you take away from the review that will help you improve your craft? If there is nothing positive to take away, get over it, realize that not everyone will "get" your work and move on.

(6/98)

LETTER FROM SCOTT PRESTON

Dear *Next…*

I thought your readers might be amused by a bit of alternative canon information that I picked up from Baxter Black at the Cowboy Poetry Gathering in Elko two years back. Baxter is probably the most financially successful performer to use poetry as the bedrock of his act in American history. He plays upwards of two hundred gigs a year with a top-end fee of four grand, has certainly grossed well over a million dollars in sales of his self-published books alone (he sells cassettes and videos too), writes a column syndicated in rural papers throughout the West, does commentary on NPR and has a TV show with Colorado Public Television. He's also a certified Doctor of Veterinary Medicine, but found he could make more money on stage.

He is about as sharp a man as one is ever likely to be privileged to meet. So when Baxter tells me he commissioned a marketing study, I pay pretty damned close attention. What happened was, I had told Baxter I loved teasing my "other" poetry friends that he was the bestselling poet in the country. And he replied, quite modestly, "But I'm not."

Turned out that Baxter and his people at the Coyote Cowboy Company finally decided to see just how six-figure unit sales of $20 poetry books stacked up against everybody else's poetry book sales. The #1 bestselling poet in the United States, according to the study, is Shel Silverstein. #2 is Dr Seuss (and here Baxter hastened to add "I'm not sure you'll consider this poetry or not." I replied it sounded like poetry to me). #3 is T.S. Eliot, entirely on the basis of *Old Possum's Book of Practical Cats* — the rest of his life's work together wouldn't get him into the Top Twenty. The #4 slot belongs to Baxter Black.

Good for Jaimes Palacio for being able to sift a real poetry experience from any number of supposed ones despite every prejudice of opinion against it. His is the first informed assessment of Dr Seuss I've run into since that chat two years ago, and I was pleased to read it.

Scott Preston, Ketchum ID

(12/96)

DARE NOT CALL IT CENSORSHIP
By Bob Stane

(Bob Stane currently describes himself as a Coffee House Consultant. He was the owner of The Ice House Comedy Club, and considers it his business to make entertainers rich and famous.)

It's only practical. First decide what business you are in.

If you stand on a stage in front of people and talk, sing, or play you are in the entertainment business. Is this a surprise? Let's continue to separate fact from fantasy and self-deception from firm planning.

Would you like to be a successful poet? If so, that means playing to a large audience. If you want your thoughts to be recognized and seriously considered by a large group of people you have to be in a position to be seen, heard and read, often, by the biggest meaningful audience available. One of our great philosophers, Woody Allen, said "95% of success is just showing up." The trick is to be asked to show up, hope the Tooth Fairy is in the audience, and try not to shoot yourself in the foot. Almost all facets of the entertainment business play by the same rules. You have to be an *entertainer* and you have to be good enough to keep getting invited back. If you are good and if you are lucky, someone will see or hear you perform and give you that one big break.

This is where the shot in the foot comes in. Some people do it so often that they are a one-person "Gunfight at the O.K. Corral" of podiatry.

Poetry is the art of language. It is supposed to be done with skill, subtlety and gentle nuance. The larger part of the small mass appreciates poetry understated and clever. The thought in poetry should seep into the consciousness and fall upon the ear and mind in layered flavors. Grotesque gutter language found in boy's locker rooms in junior high school has no place in the portfolio of aspiring poets.

Are we talking about censorship? No, we are talking about practicality. We are striving for success and not the temporary and self-destructive achievement of verbal shock. Shock is not entertainment. Anyone can be shocking and go for the cheap reaction. It takes no skill or talent. Keep the language clean and visual. Play the dictionary as if it were a musical instrument.

Why is this practical? A bit of history: I owned The Ice House in Pasadena for seventeen years. It was designed to entertain audiences from 14 to 70. Entertainers were contracted to "play clean." No one was to be shocked or embarrassed. This kept the audience eclectic and forced the entertainers to stretch their minds and senses of humor for material that would appeal to the largest population. They had to be creative and not verbally foul. No cheap laughs. Entertainers wrote deeply, plumbing for real thoughts and emotions. They were not lazy and always had themselves ready for "the lucky break."

Because of this house policy we had a constant stream of bookers and producers from the motion picture and television industries dropping in to check out the budding performers and writers. Not once did any of those bookers have to think, "Yes, the act had talent. But he had a filthy mouth. I wonder if he cleaned up if he would still have good material?"

What they saw was what they got. Dozens of acts attained fame and fortune from the stage of The Ice House. The rule was, "If you can't say it on *The Tonight Show* you can't say it on the stage of The Ice House." Steve Martin, Jay Leno, David Letterman, Cheech & Chong, The Association, Craig T. Nelson, Gallagher, Robin Williams, and dozens of celebrities all sprang from The Ice House using material fit for middle-America television.

The stages of coffeehouses and small clubs are not the final destinations. They are the launching pads to books, publications, TV, and concerts. Keep your language surgically smart and clean. It is not censorship. It is your career. You never know who is in the audience. It could be the person who will pave your career path with gold. Don't give them an excuse not to hire you.

(11/94)

WHY CAN'T WE BE FRIENDS?

By Lynne Bronstein

Last Sunday I went to a publication party for *onTarget* magazine. Even if I had not been one of the contributors and therefore entitled to read, I would have enjoyed the event. Why? Because, in addition to the high quality of the work shared, there was an attitude I haven't often encountered at poetry events. It was a feeling of *friendliness*.

Everyone who came was welcomed personally by editor Anderson Stone. People settled into the rather crowded reading room of the Onyx and got to know each other quickly.

The reading took about two hours; nobody left in the middle (at least not that I noticed) and nobody read for more than five minutes. Everyone got their turn and nobody felt deprived. It was a wonderful afternoon. After it was over, I found myself wondering why it couldn't always be that way — and why it hasn't been that way for me at many events.

I've been "on the scene" for over twenty years. I used to go to readings at places that are extinct now—like Papa Bach's bookstore, Intellectuals and Liars, Déjà Vu. I've seen a lot of magazines come and go, too. And I'm sometimes amazed at my stick to-it-ness because the years have seen a lot of treatment of poets by other poets (who were also editors and entrepreneurs) that have caused me and others much pain.

I'm not talking about mere rejection of poetry here. I'm talking about the self-importance with which poets inflate their egos, trying to compensate for the way the mainstream culture ignores them. We're all pretty weirded out and we all have to find our way to deal with it. But seriously, I've seen this personal ego-need manifest itself in poets who hog reading time, poets who schedule themselves and their friends over and over again in reading series, editors who do not merely reject poets' work but tell them sarcastically that they are not and never will be, ahem, "ready" to be published. We've all met up with the inevitable cliques, and the people who make their personal taste in poetry the "law," not to mention the irresponsible types who don't return manuscripts even when there's an SASE attached.

There was even the time I went to another publication party for an anthology I was featured in, only to find the reading had been hijacked, if you will, by a small group of poets who wanted to hype their new anthology. I journeyed all the way to Long Beach from Santa Monica on this occasion, did not get to read, and found none of the people in charge cared at all that I had been left out.

Doubtless, I could ask people who read *Next…* to send in their horror stories and the magazine would be inundated with tales of neglect, misunderstanding, feuds, etc. I could start something that will never have an end! But I'm sounding off here because *Next…* is offering us a forum in which these problems can be addressed and discussed.

The *onTarget* party demonstrated to me that it doesn't cost anything for poets to try to be nice to each other. While opinions of poetry will vary, while not everyone will get immediate acceptance by the magazines or readings of their choice, while friendly rivalries and competitions are a healthy part of the scene, there is no reason for people to act like snobs. No reason, perhaps, except human nature. I'm saying that the sensitivity with which we credit ourselves could possibly be channeled into remembering each other's feelings—and knowing that none of us, no matter what our "credentials" and honors, has an absolute corner on the "truth" about poetry. In a time when our favorite art forms are very much threatened by, shall we say, he Newt-tralizing of America, we poets need more than ever to stick together.

(3/95)

THE KID AT THE MICROPHONE

By Victor D. Infante

True story: I'm back by the poetry section of the bookstore I work at, and I come across a kid,

Illustration by Walt Hopmans

about fourteen, reading through *Bleach*, a Temporary Vandalism poetry collection. The kid's mother comes by, sees this, and says "Why don't I get you a real book?" I interject (disguising my annoyance) by saying, "Actually, that collection's pretty good." The mother smiles and rolls her eyes, nods, and walks on. I slip the kid a *Next…*, wondering if I should hide it in a paper bag.

I'm constantly forced to wonder where people get these weird ideas about poetry, local or otherwise. I mean, let's face it, it's kind of odd. A *lot* of people seem to think poetry ended with Robert Frost, and should be nice and safe. (Rumor has it Frost chased his family around the house with an axe, so go figure.) I would think parents would be overjoyed to have their kids reading anything. Or writing, or expressing themselves in any way. I do not understand the poetry stigma I regularly encounter.

What I do understand is that I see a whole bunch of high school-age poets at readings on a regular basis, some of them really good. I'm all for this. As an adult poet (he says at the ripe old, fresh-out-of-college age of 23) I firmly believe young people should be encouraged to pursue poetry, even if it is only a phase for them. Most of them, when they stop reading and either write privately or give it up all together, will remember their experience pleasantly. They will not grow into the rather demented mother mentioned in the anecdote above. Even if they don't all go on to MTV Spoken Word Tours and have books published by Black Sparrow, they will continue to provide an audience for poetry, and encourage others to do so. Besides, those few that do turn into stars need to be nurtured and encouraged to continue.

Maybe I'm a bit of a do-gooder, but I honestly believe that, if poetry is to continue as a viable art-form, poets need to actively protect their future: teenagers. This is the kid in black at the microphone reading "Oh dark, terrible, miserable day." Let him read, you'll get your five minutes, and besides, his very presence there is probably sticking it to the above-mentioned mother, and I couldn't be happier about it.

(11/95)

WHEN POETS LIE
By David Madgalene

I believe that poets have an artistic obligation to tell the truth. Note I did not say "moral obligation." I know better than to attempt to appeal to the "morals," if any, of poets. Nor do I speak of Big Truth with Capital Letters. I speak of little everyday truth, the truth with a little "t," the truth I transgress when I say one thing and do another.

Have you ever had a poet lie to you? Tell you one thing and do another? We are the poets. We're the ones who are supposed to respect the language by telling the little "t" truth. Words are our currency. Every time a poet lies, he or she devalues language, and thus, he or she devalues poetry since poetry is composed of words.

A friend told me that the current chaos in Russia is a direct result of a language breakdown. Vis a vis an Orwellian scenario, the Soviets so abused the language that words have no meaning anymore. If words have no meaning, then nothing that is said or written can have meaning, and society has no recourse but to break down until if and when words acquire value again.

We in America are on the verge of this collapse of the meaning of language, if we are not already there. A deadbeat dad like Newt Gingrich touts "family values." Rush Limbaugh equates feminists with Nazis. General Electric is "helping people" by building atomic bombs. But I'm pointing my finger at the alleged standard-bearers of the language, the keepers of the Word, we poets.

I know of a guy who was a pariah in his local performance poetry community. You know why? He told the truth. True, he could be a little brusque about it and he alienated the grapevine, so they told lies about him! The irony being that this guy was the only guy you could trust! He was your only friend — because he told the truth. If your presentation on a given night was good, he said so, and, if your presentation was lousy, he said so. Don't we go to the readings for feedback? Isn't it better to know that when we score, we score, and, when we miss, we miss? Better this than to have poets lie to us, pat us on the back, and, invariably say, "Good reading, babe!"

We're poets, by God! We should be able to speak the truth and do so with tact! If we can't do that, than who are we, and what is poetry if not truth with tact? What kind of poet am I if the best feedback I can give my brother or sister is, "You suck and so does your poetry?" Even if this were a semi-accurate assessment, aren't we poets supposed to be concerned with saying something as specifically as possible? The poet in full possession of their faculties would neither say "You suck" or "Good reading, babe," if the truth were, "Well, kid, you're gonna have to give up the convenient rhymes and the mother goose metrics if you want to make it with this crowd."

I heard of a fellow who liked to shoot videos of the readings. His camera work was atrocious, never in focus; his product was a disservice to the poetic community. Everyone laughed at him behind his back. One man told him to his face that his videos were so amateurish that they actually hurt the poets. That one man, out of an entire community of poets, told the truth.

There's another fellow who thinks he's unique but you find him or one of his cousins anywhere you go. He resembles, in spirit, if not always in person, a fat, ugly, loutish, drunken brute. He rambles on and on way past his five minutes reciting a seemingly endless litany of personal problems with the planet and certain of its denizens. He staggers out into the audience as he spews – spitting upon them, blowing smoke into their faces, spilling mass quantities of beer upon them, pawing them, clawing them! He even yanks the pony-tails of little girls! People get up and leave the readings never to return. He's gotten the poets kicked out of more than one venue! This is the same one who hassles (i.e. worse than heckles) everyone else when they read — the same one starting fights at the bar and trying to cop a feel out in the parking lot. Yet they pat him on the back and they peg him as the next Bukowski!?! My man had just one friend and this one friend told him the truth, "Put a plug in the jug, babe. Give up the juice!"

I'm not even going to address the issue of what I call the "promoter consciousness" in performance poetry. But this business of putting a "positive, commercial" spin on everything is deadly to this little thing of ours. Hype is the antithesis of poetry or should I say poetry is the antithesis of hype? Yet how many poets do we know of, big names at the academy, as well as our own honky-tonk heroes, whom, truth be told, are hype, whole hype, and nothing but hype?

As poets, we are in the business of reclaiming the language from the Machiavellian politicians and the televangelists, the Rod McKuens and the MTV rappers, the movies and the big corporations, the "poets" of Madison Avenue and the solipsistic professors, the computer nerds and the Reagan babies, the Neo-Nazis and talk show infotainment etc. ad infinitum, who have willingly in their own self-interests manipulated language to the point of emotional, spiritual, and psychological bankruptcy.

As poets, we have an artistic obligation to tell the truth. If we, the poets, do not honor language, who will? And, when and if the whole damn things collapses (don't kid yourself — it's held together with a rubber band), are we going to go down knowing that we did our damndest to keep and respect the Word, or, do we go down knowing that we sold out the Muse for a mess of pottage?

(3/96)

POETRY AS A MEANS FOR SOCIAL CHANGE
By G. Murray Thomas

I was at an open reading the other day, one which shall remain anonymous. "Poet" after "poet" got up and delivered political diatribes. Some of them contained poetic use of language and interesting images, a few even rhymed, but I hesitate to call any of them poems. Still, I don't begrudge their using the stage for this purpose.

I have long felt that one of the greatest strengths and greatest weaknesses of the current poetry scene is the number of people involved for whom the fact of expression is more important than the form of expression.

The weakness is obvious to anyone who has sat through more than an occasional open reading (and no doubt to those who couldn't manage to sit through even one). Political diatribes are just one example of such poems, there are also all those works of tormented teen angst, anti-man/woman/white/ black/brown/alien (legal, illegal, or extraterrestrial) or just plain everybody rants, religious (and anti-religious) preaching, and the vast majority of love poems. All are cases of somebody who has something to say and no art or subtlety in how they say it. They drive audiences away and/or mad, and make the rest of us grateful for time limits.

So why do I think this is also great? Despite talk shows, gangsta rap, the Internet, and free speech movements, too much still goes unsaid in our society. What is primarily missing is the expression of honest and personal feelings. People think they're expressing themselves when they repeat a line created by some corporate adman. The very act of writing poetry, even bad poetry, forces the writer to confront his or her true inner feelings. Often writing poetry is an act of discovery of how one truly feels. Even bad poetry ends up containing those feelings. More, good poetry can often express complex emotions and other "inexpressible" thoughts.

Secondly, a poetry reading is a rare situation where (at least some) people actually listen. A good audience listens and considers the poetry presented. A good audience is receptive to the words, images and ideas of the poetry.

This combination of speaking honestly and truly listening is the basis of something we call communication. We will never be able to solve today's intractable problems without communication. And communication is sorely lacking in today's world.

Here lies poetry's power as a medium for change — communication, the exchange of ideas and perspectives, the opening of one's mind to alternate viewpoints. A poem will never end poverty, stop war, clean up the environment, cure cancer or otherwise solve the world's problems. But it just might alter someone's thinking, so they can come up with, or participate in, the solution.

I'm not just talking about political diatribes here, either. In fact, in their didacticness, they are sometimes the least effective in changing people's minds. Every poem has the power to alter one's thoughts. A single line or image may provide a new perspective, open new possibilities in the listener's mind. And once new ideas are started, who can tell where they might end up?

(6/97)

A CONTRACT BETWEEN FRIENDS

By Robert Arroyo, Jr.

Among the many things poetry is, it is a dedication to the minutiae of language with regards to communication. This may seem a no-brainer, but how many times have you read a poem and have taken from it absolutely nothing because you couldn't figure out what the poet was talking about? Meaning is explored and revealed through the subtle selection and placement of words on the page, but not so subtly done that the verse becomes too enigmatic or a poet's personal code. While most often the poem is a personal dialogue, no matter if it is written in first, second, or third person, its ultimate aim is to disseminate information. Remember, when we write we descend into our most private areas where implication and meaning are revealed in fragments that we then attempt to translate into images. While these images may not be part of the public domain, they must be recognizable when sketched out with words (recognizable not in the sense of "common," but of "clarity").

Generally, when we read a poem, we don't know anything about the poet's life and so we perceive him through his skill in communicating ideas. And it's not even so important that we perceive the person behind the words, but that we are subsumed into the vision the poet creates. A former teacher once told me that to truly love poetry, you have to give yourself over to the poem you're reading. You have to turn off the inner critic and immerse yourself not only in the language, but the world each poem attempts to create. To do that, the reader has to assume there's an unspoken contract between him and the poet: "I, the poet, will utilize symbols the reader can comprehend and therefore be able to interpret or extrapolate meaning from the vision I have put to paper. I, the reader, will trust the poet knows what he is doing, and so will not impose my own world view upon the poem, in order to fully experience the vision."

Setting your ego aside is not an easy thing to do.

In a way, every poem asks for a suspension of disbelief: the reader is asked to set aside his vision of reality for the poet's vision. It's not that the version of reality any particular poet presents is so different from

182

that of a reader, it's just that the vision is slightly blurred through the poet's perception, and then clarified through his skill in rendering it in verse.

I keep coming back to this point about skill, and it's an issue of respect. Respect the artform you work in enough to research it, learn about it. Respect the reader by knowing and understanding your art form. Sure, you can flail around in the darkness of your creative light until something good happens, but so much more can be accomplished if you are familiar with the groundwork your artistic forbears have laid. The artistic community is more than just the poets you hang out with, but all the poets that have gone before you. Even a cursory knowledge of the history of poetry can help you find yourself in the tradition. Trust me, nothing anyone is doing now is absolutely original. All have their roots in the past, and clueing into that past can only help them move their work forward.

So much contemporary poetry suffers from the stance that a poet's word is inviolate because it is representative of how he interprets the world. That would be fine if poetry was solely about the poet's ability to interpret what he envisions, but the act of interpretation is twofold: first, the poet interprets his vision, and then the reader interprets the poet's representation of that vision. For a poet to think he operates in a vacuum is not only the pinnacle of arrogance, but the cellar of common sense. Poetry is a customer service business as well as a self-serving business. No matter what anybody says, we all want a certain validation that can only be achieved through acceptance by our peers, but it is also a noble goal to be accepted by those who do not write poetry.

To have your work loved and appreciated only by other poets is a low aim. I believe the real quest is to reach those who do not write poetry, but go to readings to be moved and/or to be entertained, to get in touch with our common humanness. More than likely, these people have read poetry before and so have standards that might be even higher than other poets. If poetry is to not only survive, but thrive, these are the people we have to befriend. Let's welcome them into our cloistered world. Offer them a cup of coffee.

Tell them how we feel.

(9/98)

New Write Bloody Books for 2012

Strange Light
The *New York Times* says, "There's something that happens when you read Derrick Brown, a rekindling of faith in the weird, hilarious, shocking, beautiful power of words." This is the final collection from Derrick Brown, one of America's top-selling and touring poets. Everything hilarious and stirring is illuminated. The power of *Strange Light* is waiting.

Who Farted Wrong? Illustrated Weight Loss For the Mind
Syd Butler (of the sweet band, Les Savvy Fav) creates sketchy morsels to whet your appetite for wrong, and it will be delicious. There is no need to read between the lines of this new style of flash thinking speed illustration in this hilarious new book. Why? There are not that many lines.

New Shoes on a Dead Horse
The Romans believed that an artist's inspiration came from a spirit, called a genius, that lived in the walls of the artist's home. This character appears throughout Sierra DeMulder's book, providing charming commentary and biting insight on the young author's creative process and emotional path.

Good Grief
Elegantly-wrought misadventures as a freshly-graduated Michigan transplant, Stevie Edwards stumbles over foal legs through Chicago and kneels down to confront the wreckage of her skinned knees.

After the Witch Hunt
Megan Falley showcases her fresh, lucid poetry with a refreshing lack of jaded undertones. Armed with both humor and a brazen darkness, each poem in this book is another swing of the pick axe in this young woman's tunnel, insistent upon light.

I Love Science!
Humorous and thought provoking, Shanney Jean Maney's book effortlessly combines subjects that have previously been thought too diverse to have anything in common. Science, poetry and Jeff Goldblum form covalent bonds that put the poetic fire underneath our bunsen burners. A Lab Tech of words, Maney turns language into curious, knowledge-hungry poetry.
Foreword by Lynda Barry.

Time Bomb Snooze Alarm
Bucky Sinister, a veteran poet of the working class, layers his gritty truths with street punk humor. A menagerie of strange people and stranger moments that linger in the dark hallway of Sinister's life. Foreword by Randy Blythe of "Lamb of God".

News Clips and Ego Trips
A collection of helpful articles from *Next...* magazine, which gave birth to the Southern California and national poetry scene in the mid-'90s. It covers the growth of spoken word, page poetry and slam, with interviews and profiles of many poets and literary giants like Patricia Smith, Henry Rollins and Miranda July. Edited by G. Murray Thomas.

Slow Dance With Sasquatch
Jeremy Radin invites you into his private ballroom for a waltz through the forest at the center of life, where loneliness and longing seamlessly shift into imagination and humor.

The Smell of Good Mud
Queer parenting in conservative Oklahoma, Lauren Zuniga finds humor and beauty in this collection of new poems. This explores the grit and splendor of collective living, and other radical choices. It is a field guide to blisters and curtsies.

OTHER WRITE BLOODY BOOKS (2003 - 2011)

Great Balls of Flowers (2009)
Steve Abee's poetry is accessible, insightful, hilarious, compelling,
upsetting, and inspiring. TNB Book of the Year.

Everything Is Everything (2010)
The latest collection from poet Cristin O'Keefe Aptowicz,
filled with crack squirrels, fat presidents, and el Chupacabra.

Working Class Represent (2011)
A young poet humorously balances an office job with the life
of a touring performance poet in Cristin O'Keefe Aptowicz's third book of poetry

Oh, Terrible Youth (2011)
Cristin O'Keefe Aptowicz's plump collection commiserates and celebrates
all the wonder, terror, banality and comedy that is the long journey to adulthood.

Hot Teen Slut (2011)
Cristin O'Keefe Aptowicz's second book recounts stories of
a virgin poet who spent a year writing for the porn business.

Dear Future Boyfriend (2011)
Cristin O'Keefe Aptowicz's debut collection of poetry tackles
love and heartbreak with no-nonsense honesty and wit.

38 Bar Blues (2011)
C. R. Avery's second book, loaded with bar-stool musicality and brass-knuckle poetry.

Catacomb Confetti (2010)
Inspired by nameless Parisian skulls in the catacombs of France,
Catacomb Confetti assures Joshua Boyd's poetic immortality.

Born in the Year of the Butterfly Knife (2004)
The Derrick Brown poetry collection that birthed Write Bloody Publishing.
Sincere, twisted, and violently romantic.

I Love You Is Back (2006)
A poetry collection by Derrick Brown.
"One moment tender, funny, or romantic, the next, visceral, ironic,
and revelatory—Here is the full chaos of life." (Janet Fitch, *White Oleander*)

Scandalabra (2009)
Former paratrooper Derrick Brown releases a stunning collection of poems written
at sea and in Nashville, TN. About.com's book of the year for poetry.

Workin' Mime to Five (2011)
Dick Richards is a fired cruise ship pantomimist. You too can learn
his secret, creative pantomime moves. Humor by Derrick Brown.

Don't Smell the Floss (2009)
Award-winning writer Matty Byloos' first book of bizarre, absurd, and deliciously
perverse short stories puts your drunk uncle to shame.

Reasons to Leave the Slaughter (2011)
Ben Clark's book of poetry revels in youthful discovery from the heartland
and the balance between beauty and brutality.

Birthday Girl with Possum (2011)
Brendan Constantine's second book of poetry examines the invisible lines
between wonder & disappointment, ecstasy & crime, savagery & innocence.

The Bones Below (2010)
National Slam Champion Sierra DeMulder performs and teaches
with the release of her first book of hard-hitting, haunting poetry.

The Constant Velocity of Trains (2008)
The brain's left and right hemispheres collide in Lea Deschenes' Pushcart-Nominated book of
poetry about physics, relationships, and life's balancing acts.

Heavy Lead Birdsong (2008)
Award-winning academic poet Ryler Dustin releases his most
definitive collection of surreal love poetry.

Uncontrolled Experiments in Freedom (2008)
Boston underground art scene fixture Brian Ellis
becomes one of America's foremost narrative poetry performers.

Yesterday Won't Goodbye (2011)
Boston gutter punk Brian Ellis releases his second book of poetry,
filled with unbridled energy and vitality.

Write About an Empty Birdcage (2011)
Debut collection of poetry from Elaina M. Ellis that flirts with loss,
reveres appetite, and unzips identity.

Ceremony for the Choking Ghost (2010)
Slam legend Karen Finneyfrock's second book of poems ventures
into the humor and madness that surrounds familial loss.

Pole Dancing to Gospel Hymns (2008)
Andrea Gibson, a queer, award-winning poet who tours with Ani DiFranco,
releases a book of haunting, bold, nothing-but-the-truth ma'am poetry.

These Are the Breaks (2011)
Essays from one of hip-hops deftest public intellectuals, Idris Goodwin

Bring Down the Chandeliers (2011)
Tara Hardy, a working-class queer survivor of incest, turns sex,
trauma and forgiveness inside out in this collection of new poems.

City of Insomnia (2008)
Victor D. Infante's noir-like exploration of unsentimental truth and poetic exorcism.

The Last Time as We Are (2009)
A new collection of poems from Taylor Mali, the author
of "What Teachers Make," the most forwarded poem in the world.

In Search of Midnight: the Mike Mcgee Handbook of Awesome (2009)
Slam's geek champion/class clown Mike McGee on his search for midnight
through hilarious prose, poetry, anecdotes, and how-to lists.

1,000 Black Umbrellas (2011)
Daniel McGinn's first internationally released collection from 'everyone's favorite unknown
author' sings from the guts with the old school power of poetry.

Over the Anvil We Stretch (2008)
2-time poetry slam champ Anis Mojgani's first collection: a Pushcart-Nominated
batch of backwood poetics, Southern myth, and rich imagery.

The Feather Room (2011)
Anis Mojgani's second collection of poetry explores storytelling and
poetic form while traveling farther down the path of magic realism.

Animal Ballistics (2009)
Trading addiction and grief for empowerment and humor with her poetry,
Sarah Morgan does it best.

Rise of the Trust Fall (2010)
Award-winning feminist poet Mindy Nettifee
releases her second book of funny, daring, gorgeous, accessible poems.

Love in a Time of Robot Apocalypse (2011)
Latino-American poet David Perez releases his first book
of incisive, arresting, and end-of-the-world-as-we-know-it poetry.

No More Poems About the Moon (2008)
A pixilated, poetic and joyful view of a hyper-sexualized,
wholeheartedly confused, weird, and wild America with Michael Roberts.

The New Clean (2011)
Jon Sands' poetry redefines what it means to laugh, cry, mop it up and start again.

Miles of Hallelujah (2010)
Slam poet/pop-culture enthusiast Rob "Ratpack Slim" Sturma
shows first collection of quirky, fantastic, romantic poetry.

Sunset at the Temple of Olives (2011)
Paul Suntup's unforgettable voice merges subversive surrealism
and vivid grief in this debut collection of poetry.

Spiking the Sucker Punch (2009)
Nerd heartthrob, award-winning artist and performance poet,
Robbie Q. Telfer stabs your sensitive parts with his wit-dagger.

Racing Hummingbirds (2010)
Poet/performer Jeanann Verlee releases an award-winning book
of expertly crafted, startlingly honest, skin-kicking poems.

Live for a Living (2007)
Acclaimed performance poet Buddy Wakefield releases his second collection
about healing and charging into life face first.

Gentleman Practice (2011)
Righteous Babe Records artist and 3-time International Poetry Champ
Buddy Wakefield spins a nonfiction tale of a relay race to the light.

How to Seduce a White Boy in Ten Easy Steps (2011)
Debut collection for feminist, biracial poet Laura Yes Yes
dazzles with its explorations into the politics and metaphysics of identity.

CPSIA information can be obtained at www.ICGtesting.com
Printed in the USA
LVOW030850150312

273210LV00001B/2/P